Windows Server 2012 Unified Remote Access Planning and Deployment

Discover how to seamlessly plan and deploy remote access with Windows Server 2012's successor to DirectAccess

Erez Ben-Ari

Bala Natarajan

BIRMINGHAM - MUMBAI

Windows Server 2012 Unified Remote Access Planning and Deployment

First published: December 2012

Production Reference: 1141212

Published by Packt Publishing Ltd.
Livery Place
35 Livery Street
Birmingham B3 2PB, UK.

ISBN 978-1-84968-828-4

www.packtpub.com

Cover Image by Artie Ng (artherng@yahoo.com.au)

Credits

About the Authors

Erez Ben-Ari is an experienced Technologist and Journalist, and has worked in the Information Technology industry since 1991. During his career, Erez has provided security consulting and analysis services for some of the leading companies and organizations in the world, including Intel, IBM, Amdocs, CA, HP, NDS, Sun Microsystems, Oracle, and many others. His work has gained national fame in Israel, and he has featured in the press regularly. Having joined Microsoft in 2000, Erez has worked for many years in Microsoft's Development Center in Israel, where Microsoft's ISA Server was developed. Being a part of the release of ISA 2000, ISA 2004, and ISA 2006, Erez held several roles in different departments, including Operation engineering, Software testing, Web-based software design, and testing automation designs. Now living in the United States, Erez still works for Microsoft, currently as a Senior Support Escalation Engineer for Forefront Edge technologies, which include Forefront UAG and TMG.

As a writer, Erez has been a journalist since 1995, and has written for some of the leading publications in Israel and in the United States. He has been a member of the Israeli National Press Office since 2001, and his personal blogs are read by thousands of visitors every month. Erez has also written, produced, and edited content for TV and radio, working for Israel's TV Channel 2, Ana-Ney Communications, Radio Haifa, and other venues.

Erez has also authored four other titles, including *Microsoft Forefront UAG 2010 Administrator's Handbook*, *Packt Publishing* and *Mastering Microsoft Forefront UAG 2010 Customization*, *Packt Publishing*. His publications have been critically acclaimed, earning 5-star reviews from all readers and have been a monumental success. They have paved the way for many customers to deploy these solutions in some of the largest organizations in the world.

> To my dear colleagues Mohit Saxena, Billy Price, and Tarun Sachdeva, and to my co-author Bala, for supporting me and helping me in my quest to master this technology and bring it to light.

Bala Natarajan has an engineering degree in Electronics & Instrumentation from India. He graduated in 1987 and started his career as a System Support Engineer for Unix, Novell NetWare, and MSDOS. From 1994 onwards, he specialized in Computer Networking to provide large enterprises in India with design and support for LAN and WAN networking using Cisco and Nortel networking gears.

He moved to the US and worked in a large telecom company as a dedicated Support Engineer to connect over 300 school districts in the state of Washington. He joined Microsoft in 1998 as a Support Engineer in the Platforms Networking team and the Enterprise Security team. He worked as a pre-release product Support Engineer for TMG 2010, UAGDA.

In 2011, he moved to the Windows Core networking team as a Program Manager for DirectAccess.

About the Reviewers

Jordan Krause is a Microsoft MVP for the Forefront network security technologies, and specializes in DirectAccess, which is a part of Forefront Unified Access Gateway (UAG) 2010 and the new Unified Remote Access (URA) in Windows Server 2012. As a Senior Engineer and Security Specialist for IVO Networks, he spends the majority of each workday planning, designing, and implementing DirectAccess using IVO's DirectAccess Concentrator security appliances for companies of all shapes and sizes.

Committed to continuous learning, Jordan holds Microsoft certifications as an MCP, MCTS, MCSA, and MCITP Enterprise Administrator. He regularly writes tech notes and articles about some of the fun and exciting ways that DirectAccess can be used, here: `http://www.ivonetworks.com/news/`.

> Thank you to Ben and Bala for putting together this great resource. Bala, I appreciate your time answering my questions the last time I was in Redmond. Ben, what can I say? Thank you for your friendship. I would also like to thank the crew at IVO, without whom I would have missed out on many amazing opportunities.

Jochen Nickel is an Identity and Access Management Consultant working for Inovit GmbH in Switzerland, and tries everyday to understand new business needs of his customers, to provide a better, more comfortable, and flexible workstyle through Microsoft Remote Access technologies.

He has been working in a lot of projects, proofs of concepts, and workshops with Direct Access and Forefront Unified Access Gateway since they were added to the Microsoft Remote Access technologies.

Jochen is very focused on DirectAccess, Forefront Unified Access Gateway, Active Directory Federation Services, and Forefront Identity Manager.

Newly added to his interests is Dynamic Access Control in Windows Server 2012.

Furthermore, he developed and wrote a lot of workshops and articles about these topics.

His greatest passion is to spend as much time as possible with his family to get back the energy to handle such nice and interesting technologies.

He regularly blogs at www.inovit.ch/blog.idam.ch.

> I would like to thank Ben for giving me the chance and the opportunity to be a small helper in this project by serving as a technical reviewer.

John Redding has worked as a Technical Support Engineer on various Internet server products such as the first generation Netscape SuiteSpot and the second generation iPlanet server suite since the mid 90s. In 2003, John joined Whale Communications, where he worked as a Senior Support Engineer for the e-Gap and IAG SSL VPN products, which ultimately led to product support for UAG.

John Redding is currently a Senior Consultant in the Identity and Access Management group at Certified Security Solutions, where he regularly does DirectAccess deployments.

www.PacktPub.com

Support files, eBooks, discount offers and more

You might want to visit www.PacktPub.com for support files and downloads related to your book.

Did you know that Packt offers eBook versions of every book published, with PDF and ePub files available? You can upgrade to the eBook version at www.PacktPub.com and as a print book customer, you are entitled to a discount on the eBook copy. Get in touch with us at service@packtpub.com for more details.

At www.PacktPub.com, you can also read a collection of free technical articles, sign up for a range of free newsletters and receive exclusive discounts and offers on Packt books and eBooks.

http://PacktLib.PacktPub.com

Do you need instant solutions to your IT questions? PacktLib is Packt's online digital book library. Here, you can access, read and search across Packt's entire library of books.

Why Subscribe?

- Fully searchable across every book published by Packt
- Copy and paste, print and bookmark content
- On demand and accessible via web browser

Free Access for Packt account holders

If you have an account with Packt at www.PacktPub.com, you can use this to access PacktLib today and view nine entirely free books. Simply use your login credentials for immediate access.

Instant Updates on New Packt Books

Get notified! Find out when new books are published by following @PacktEnterprise on Twitter, or the *Packt Enterprise* Facebook page.

Table of Contents

Preface

It's 5:45 p.m., and in just a few sweet moments, you can finally finish the day's work and run out home. Suddenly, the phone rings, sending a shudder through your spine. You recognize the number immediately. It's Mr. McClueless from the downtown office, again. "Sorry, buddy," he whines, "my kids screwed up my computer again." Yeah, right! His "kids". Your stomach turns in protest, realizing you can kiss that planned steak dinner goodbye, as you're about to spend the next 2 hours walking the guy through setting up the VPN for the sixth time this month. If you only had direct access, you would probably be stuffing some serious sirloin into your mouth instead.

Well, it's probably too late to save this dinner, but direct access is so easy to set up now, that you can actually promise your boss (and by that we mean your wife, of course) that starting tomorrow, dinner will be served on time!

Hello Unified Remote Access!

Customer support can be funny, but remote access is serious business. Ever since the Internet came into our homes several decades ago, people have been using various solutions and technologies to connect to the corporate network, and work remotely. Many technologies came our way over the years; analog modem dialup initially, then ISDN, and most recently DSL, Cable, LTE, and WiMAX. Whatever connection type your users are using, virtually all solutions involve one thing in common: when the user needs to connect, he has to launch some kind of program to establish that connection. This inherent design has always been a burden, as users find various ways to mess up the connection (and let's face it...sometimes...rarely...it's not even their fault).

A few years ago, Microsoft came up with the concept that became known as **DirectAccess**, and integrated it into Windows Server 2008 R2. The big deal was that finally, the connection configuration was configured automatically via Group Policy, so the IT department didn't have to set up each computer separately. Secondly, the DirectAccess (often referred to unofficially as **DA**) connection was designed to automatically establish itself as soon as the computer leaves the corporate network and connect to the public Internet. With DirectAccess, the entire thing was as seamless as a cellular service. The user goes home, opens his laptop and he is virtually on the corporate network. No software to configure and re-configure, and no buttons to push.

Initially, DirectAccess was easy for users, but not so much for us administrators. To set up DirectAccess, you would have to configure many complex settings in Group Policy and a lot of good and smart administrators found themselves giving up on it after weeks of fiddling. Then, in January 2010 Microsoft came out with **Forefront Unified Access Gateway (UAG)**.

UAG, which is Microsoft's enterprise-class application publishing and remote access server, includes a special interface designed to allow the configuration and deployment of DirectAccess in a way that's a lot friendlier than before, such as support for IPv4-only networks via NAT64 and DNS64, and support for array-deployment. The product was a tremendous success, and was adopted by some of the largest companies in the world, as well as governments and military organizations. The following is a screenshot of the UAG console:

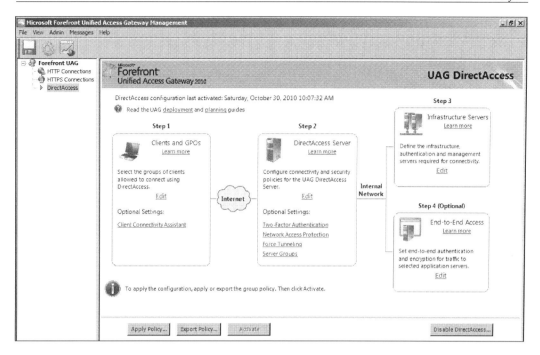

This great success led to a decision to enhance DirectAccess, and with the release of Windows Server 2012, a new interface was built, that no longer required UAG to be in the picture. The technology was also renamed to **Unified Remote Access**, and with Windows Server 2012, you could configure it straight out of the box as a *role*, without purchasing or installing any additional software. In addition, several aspects of it have been simplified, making it even more approachable and usable than before.

A child could do it! (well...almost)

When designing Unified Remote Access, Microsoft realized that not all organizations can meet the complex requirements that DirectAccess imposed. For example, with DirectAccess, you had to assign two consecutive public IP addresses to the server, and these IPs could not be NAT addresses. You also needed to set up a digital certificate infrastructure and assign certificates to all computers that would use DirectAccess. These imposed a steep learning curve that deterred many administrators from even looking into this technology, let alone successfully implementing it. Windows Server 2012 Unified Remote Access makes things a lot simpler by allowing you to host the server behind a NAT firewall, and using a component called **KerbProxy** to provide tight security even without certificates.

Other changes to the technology are about making life easier for everyone. Before Windows Server 2012, client computers needed to be brought onto the corporate network to receive the Group Policy update which configured them for the connection. Now, that is no longer needed and the computer can be configured wherever it is. Another enhancement to the user experience is the integration of a special piece of software called the **Network Connectivity Assistant (NCA)** into Windows 8. The NCA provides the user with the information about the connection, making things easier to handle if there's a problem. The NCA is similar to the **DirectAccess Connectivity Assistant (DCA)** that was used with earlier incarnations of DirectAccess. The DCA was a separate optional install, but NCA comes with Windows 8, making things easier for everyone:

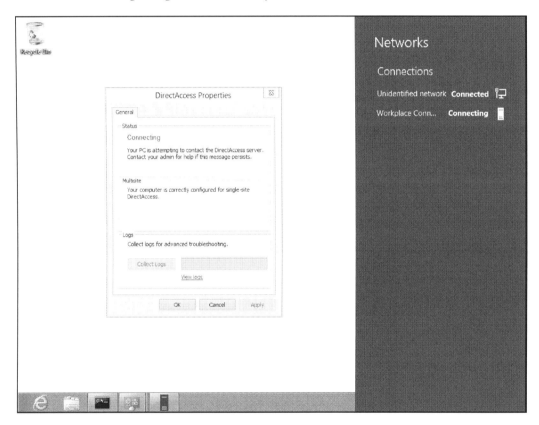

Take charge, anywhere

Managing DirectAccess may have been challenging, but managing Unified Remote Access is easy as pie. A new Remote Access **management console** allows you to manage the server from anywhere, and also manage multiple servers from a single place, including your own desktop. Since the Unified Remote Access role also includes traditional VPN functionality (which you might be familiar with as RRAS), you can also manage VPN through the Unified Remote Access console. It also provides you with many monitoring options, including the health status of Remote Access components, connection statistics of all types of Remote Access clients including DirectAccess and VPN, detailed reports and real-time information gathering. If you're not a big fan of the mouse, you can use **PowerShell** scripting to configure, manage, monitor, and troubleshoot your server and clients. PowerShell also lets you create automation to handle many tasks and free up some of your precious time for Angry Birds.

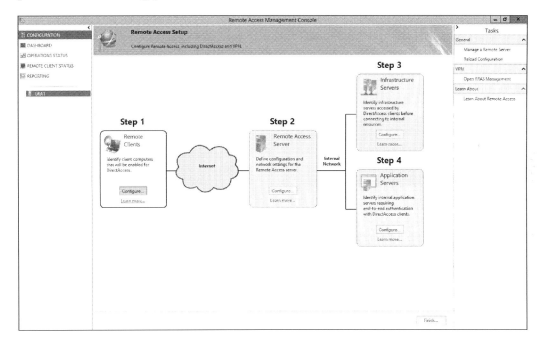

One of the most important enhancements built into Unified Remote Access is support for multiple geographic locations. You can deploy Unified Remote Access servers all over the globe to provide users with the ability to connect to a server that is closer to them in terms of roundtrip time for the packets, and you can also use regular load balancing to distribute users evenly across multiple servers in a single location. The service does not provide for full session failover, but since the connection does get re-established automatically, the user experience is seamless even in the event of a server going offline. For load balancing, you can use a third-party load balancer, or Windows' own integrated **NLB**.

Faster is better

Another improvement that Unified Remote Access offers is in the performance department. Unified Remote Access, when installed as a Hyper-V guest VM in a Hyper-V host running Windows Server 2012, can utilize **Single Root I/O Virtualization (SR-IOV)**, which allows it to perform better when the server is virtualized. SR-IOV is a specification that allows a **PCIe** device to appear to be multiple separate physical PCIe devices, and when properly implemented within the BIOS and operating system, it can improve data transfer performance significantly.

In addition, Unified Remote Access provides improved performance of both the transition technology protocols **Teredo** and the **IP-HTTPS** connection option. IP-HTTPS is one of several possible client connectivity options, and with the IP-HTTPS in DirectAccess with Windows Server 2008 R2 and UAG, data would be encrypted both with IPsec and SSL. This double-encryption was overkill that consumed significant CPU resources, and now in Windows Server 2012, the IP-HTTPS uses SSL without encryption (the technical term is **null-encryption**), which reduces the CPU usage and thereby improves data transfer rates. In Windows Server 2012, the underlying IP stack has also improved a lot. One of the improvements is providing **Receive Side Scaling (RSS)** for UDP traffic as well. This allows the Teredo traffic (which is based on UDP traffic on port 3544) to utilize all cores of the CPU, and thereby uniformly spread the load across all of the cores. This allows more client density per server, allowing higher scale deployments.

The built-in PowerShell **cmdlets** allow the Unified Remote Access role to be installed on a Windows Server in **Server Core**. Server Core mode is a server that is installed with a reduced set of services and options, allowing tighter security and improved performance, as less resources are used by the operating system, freeing them up for use to service users accessing remotely.

Lastly, Unified Remote Access provides the ability to *offload* the IPSec encryption to specialized hardware. By using dedicated hardware, the system's CPU is free to handle other tasks, improving the capabilities of the server beyond what additional CPUs and memory can provide.

How does it work?

If you haven't used DirectAccess before, the entire thing may seem mysterious. How does it compare to more traditional VPN solutions? What does it do under the hood? How the heck does it work without any additional software?

The concept of Virtual Private Networking is built around the idea of sending your confidential data over an open medium (the public Internet) and protecting it with encryption. Over the years, various encryption protocols and methods have been in use, such as PPTP, L2TP, and SSL. VPN connections work with some kind of client software which does all the work. The client software establishes a connection to the target VPN server, and authenticates the user to the server. Then, the software creates a virtual network card, which makes the whole thing transparent to the user and his applications. When an application sends out data, the virtual NIC intercepts it, encrypts it, and sends it out to the VPN server. The VPN server decrypts it, and sends it out onto the corporate network.

Unified Remote Access is no exception to that concept. The security piece (encryption) is done using IPsec, which is a very advanced security protocol that was designed for the twenty-first century. As in the previous versions of DirectAccess (with Windows Server 2008 R2 and Unified Access Gateway 2010), the advanced setup of Unified Remote Access 2012 uses the two IPsec tunnels mechanism. This mechanism uses two stages that complement each other. The first tunnel is an intermediate step, because all it can do is provide the means for the client to perform the next step of the authentication. Then, the second tunnel is established, with the first tunnel providing the path to perform the authentication for it.

In the first tunnel, the Windows Firewall uses two levels of authentication. The first authentication uses computer certificates (this is why the Certificate infrastructure was required to distribute the machine certificates to all client machines and the DirectAccess server). The second authentication in the first tunnel uses the NTLM credentials of the computer account in the domain (this is why DirectAccess requires that all clients be domain members). The two levels of authentication make it highly secure. Because the computer account is used in the first tunnel authentication, the tunnel can be established even before the user logs on to the machine. This allows the domain administrator to connect to the client securely for the purpose of remote-management, even before the user is logged on to the machine. For this reason, this first tunnel is also called the **machine tunnel** or the **management tunnel**.

The second tunnel also uses two levels of authentication, but this time, the computer uses certificates for the first authentication and Kerberos for the second. Since it uses the user's Kerberos tickets for the IPsec encryption, it is also called the **user tunnel**. This tunnel is used to reach the entire corporate network (as opposed to just the domain controllers, which the first tunnel allowed the client to reach). You might be wondering why we need all this trouble and don't just use Kerberos authentication for the first tunnel to begin with. Well, to perform Kerberos authentication, the client has to talk *directly* to the domain controller. At the stage where the client starts connecting to DirectAccess, it can *only* connect to the DirectAccess server and cannot connect to the domain controllers (because they are inside the network). However, NTLM authentication does not require the client to talk to the domain controllers directly, and the DirectAccess server verifies the credentials against the domain controller for the client. Once the credentials have been verified, the tunnel is established and the client can now talk to the domain controllers directly, paving the way for the Kerberos authentication to go through.

You can think of this like going into an apartment building; you need the front-door key to get into the building, and then your apartment key to get into your apartment. Your front-door key only lets you see the apartment doors and not into the apartments themselves, and by gaining access into the building, you have the means to approach and unlock the apartment itself.

The first tunnel can actually have a scope that's a bit wider. The administrator can define it to allow access to other servers, such as a WSUS, NAP, and SCCM servers, if he chooses to. If so, the tunnel can also allow the client to check for security updates or perform other secondary security checks before proceeding with setting up the second tunnel. We will talk about how to set up the health policies to control access in the later chapters.

Before URA with Windows Server 2012, many customers faced challenges with deploying computer certificates, which made deploying DirectAccess difficult. In Unified Remote Access 2012, Microsoft addressed this by adding an option for a simpler setup. This setup allows the Kerberos authentication to take place via the first tunnel (the machine tunnel) using a special service on the URA server. This service, known as **Kerberos Proxy** or **Kerbproxy**, removes the obstacle by being the middle-man, and proxying the Kerberos authentication process.

One limitation of the Kerberos Proxy is that it requires all client machines to be Windows 8 Clients. The Kerberos Proxy option makes everything very secure, but also easy to set up without having to redesign your network.

As opposed to most VPN solutions, you do not have to install any software on your client for URA. It's not that such software is not needed... it is, but it comes built-in to the operating system. The magical seamless connection is conjured up by the Windows Firewall. The original purpose of the Windows Firewall is to block malicious traffic, but the **Windows Filtering Platform (WFP)** also has the ability to create, manage, and establish the virtual network that we need.

The configuration for the firewall is provided to the client using Group Policy, which is the key to the easy manageability of the solution. Instead of providing users with complex instructions on setting up the connection, or spending hours on the phone walking through wizards, the administrator uses the Unified Remote Access console or PowerShell scripts to create the Windows Firewall connection security rules. Then, when the client applies the Group Policy updates, the client computer is automatically configured with these settings.

With almost all other VPN solutions, the user needs to launch the connection to the VPN server, but with URA, this is done automatically, and here's how. The DirectAccess configuration becomes effective depending on whether the machine is inside the corpnet or outside the corpnet. The key pieces of the URA architecture are the name resolution and location awareness that helps the client to decide whether to apply the URA connection or not; that is, when the user turns on his computer, or resumes it from being suspended, the operating system detects whether it is able to establish corporate connectivity. The location detection happens through its ability to connect to a specific server, which we refer to as the **Network Location Server (NLS)**. This server is installed within your internal network as part of the URA setup, and it stands there like a virtual lighthouse. The URA client attempts to make a secure connection to the URL of the NLS server whenever it becomes aware of a new network connection. The URL of the NLS server is defined as part of the URA server setup, and stored as part of the client GPO. This way the client automatically knows which server it has to connect to in order to determine whether the client is on the corporate network or not.

If the client gets an HTTP response code 200, that means the client can resolve the name of the NLS server and make a secure HTTP connection to it. This confirms that the client is physically inside the corporate network, and therefore, there is no need to establish the URA connection. If, however, the NLS does not respond (and we have to make sure the NLS won't respond to clients on the outside... we will talk more about that later), the client deduces that it's outside the corporate network, and the Windows Firewall springs into action, and starts establishing the IPSec tunnel for the connection. This happens almost instantly, and once the tunnel is up, the user's experience is identical to being physically connected to the corporate network. We will talk more about the NLS server configuration in the planning chapter later. The users can access any internal server, using any port and protocol, and even if there's some kind of network interruption, the client will automatically re-establish the tunnel seamlessly as soon as the network is back. All the connection security rules are already configured in the client GPO and when the client GPO applies to the machine there is no further manual configuration needed by anyone. That is why URA clients don't need to have additional software installed or any additional user action.

From an administrator's perspective, the deployment consists of installing a Windows 2012 server and configuring the various settings for the Unified Remote Access role. Once the server is ready, the settings are deployed to clients using Group Policy, so there's little to do. You define to which computers and groups the policy will apply, and once users who have been defined in that scope leave the office and connect to the public Internet, their computers will automatically establish the connection. You also have the option of joining clients to the domain and applying the Unified Remote Access policies to them remotely, so even if your users are spread across the country, you can still provision them to connect easily.

Still apprehensive about IPv6?

If you heard that DirectAccess or Unified Remote Access uses IPv6, then that is correct. However, even if you know nothing about IPv6, don't fret. Unified Remote Access does indeed use IPv6, but it also has several transition technologies, which means that you do not have to change anything on your network. Unified Remote Access works seamlessly with virtually any resource, whether it is fully IPv6 capable or IPv4-only. In addition, you do not have to learn a lot about this new technology to deploy, use, or support Unified Remote Access. We would still encourage you to learn the basics of IPv6, and we will discuss this in the first chapter of this book, but strictly speaking, you can get by fine without this.

In case you're wondering, the reason for going with IPv6 is not just to be cool. One of the goals of Unified Remote Access is to allow remote clients to be managed by the administrator as long as they are powered on (even with the user not logged on to the system). This should be possible with the clients in a variety of public and private networks, and behind different firewalls. IPv6 addressing gives the administrator the ability to reach to those clients no matter where they are, and without the user initiating any connection. This allows the administrator to reach to those remote clients and keep them updated with corporate policies, and ensure the clients stay healthy. Another advantage of this technology is that it takes care of the age-old problem where a user's home network uses the same IP subnet as the corporate network. With IPv6, this situation no longer causes problems with the remote connection.

Love UAG?

If you're one of the lucky people who have deployed DirectAccess with UAG, and you're looking into upgrading to Unified Remote Access, you're in luck, as this book is written by two of the leading experts on UAG DirectAccess.

There are some similarities between the configuration console you used with UAG and the one used for Unified Remote Access, and most of the concepts and technologies you have learned while working with UAG still apply. If you have good understanding of DirectAccess, then following the procedures in this book will be a breeze. Unfortunately, though, there is no direct upgrade path to convert your UAG Servers to become a Unified Remote Access server. You will have to install a new Windows 2012 server, and configure the Unified Remote Access role from scratch, though you will be able to copy many of the settings directly. The best news, though, is that since deployment of Unified Remote Access can be a lot simpler, it should come as quite an easy task, especially if you are one of the poor souls who had to burn hours on the phone with one of us to get UAG DirectAccess to work in the first place. It also allows a parallel install of a Windows Server 2012 based deployment and moves users to the new deployment gradually from UAG.

Access to everyone

As with most operating systems, Windows 8 is available to the public in several editions. However, to use Unified Remote Access, you will require the *Enterprise* edition of Windows 8. There is also backward compatibility with Windows 7. We will discuss the supported Client and Server versions in later chapters.

If you do intend to provide access to Unified Remote Access to Windows 7 or Windows Server 2008 R2 clients, it's important to know that you will be required to configure a certificate infrastructure (also known as a **PKI**, or **Public Key Infrastructure**). A PKI will also be required if you intend to use two-factor authentication for your users.

We hope that this brief glance has you psyched already. The road ahead is wide and may be long for some, but once done, the ease of use for your users will be spectacular, and you are sure to feel the reduction in support volume once you finish ironing out the kinks. Get ready for some exciting times!

What this book covers

This book covers the following topics:

Chapter 1, Understanding IPv6 and IPv4-IPv6 Interoperability, will discuss the classic IPv4 technology versus the newer IPv6 and how they affect your planning and deployment.

Chapter 2, Planning a Unified Remote Access Deployment, will examine the various components of your deployment and how to plan for various scenarios.

Chapter 3, Preparing a Group Policy and Certificate Infrastructure, explores Group Policy and PKI and shows how Unified Remote Access relies on them.

Chapter 4, Installing and Configuring the Unified Remote Access Role, will see how to install the URA role and the basic configuration options.

Chapter 5, Multisite Deployment, will cover the advanced scenarios related to multiple geographic locations for URA servers.

Chapter 6, Cross-premise Connectivity, will teach you some of the new options URA offers for cloud-based deployments.

Chapter 7, Unified Remote Access Client Access, will discover how URA works with different clients and how it affects your deployment.

Chapter 8, Enhanced Configurations for Infrastructure Servers, will delve into tweaks and options you can configure for some advanced scenarios.

Chapter 9, Deploying NAP and OTP, deals with Network Access Protection and One-Time Password options that can improve the security of your URA deployment.

Chapter 10, Monitoring and Troubleshooting Unified Remote Access, will help you gain knowledge of how to keep track of your server's and clients' status, and how to resolve problems that you might encounter.

What you need for this book

To deploy Unified Remote Access, you will require a functional Windows Domain using Windows 2003 and onward, as well as at least one computer running Windows Server 2012. You will need to be running an IPv4 or IPv6 network on your servers as well, and you will require administrative privileges on your domain too. For your clients, you will require at least one client running Windows 7 or Windows 8, though we strongly recommend starting your deployment with a Windows 8 client. As mentioned earlier, URA requires that your Windows 8 clients run the Enterprise edition of Windows 8, and that if you have Windows 7 client, that they run the Enterprise or Ultimate edition of that operating system.

Who this book is for

This book is intended for the IT administrator with a strong knowledge of networking and deployment of the Microsoft family of operating systems and software. You should have a sound understanding of TCP/IP, as well as deploying and supporting Windows Server and Client operating systems. Understanding of common Remote Access and VPN terms will serve you well throughout the book, though we will be explaining these terms as we go along.

Conventions

In this book, you will find a number of styles of text that distinguish between different kinds of information. Here are some examples of these styles, and an explanation of their meaning.

Code words in text are shown as follows: "The way this works is by Windows creating a virtual network card named `isatap`, and assigning itself an IPv6 address that's based on the computer's IPv4 address."

New terms and **important words** are shown in bold. Words that you see on the screen, in menus or dialog boxes for example, appear in the text like this: "When a client has been configured with URA, it will show up as a **Workplace Connection** item when the user clicks on the network notification icon on his/her system tray."

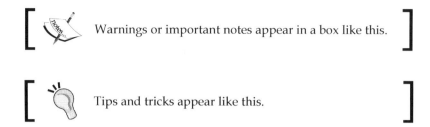

Warnings or important notes appear in a box like this.

Tips and tricks appear like this.

Reader feedback

Feedback from our readers is always welcome. Let us know what you think about this book—what you liked or may have disliked. Reader feedback is important for us to develop titles that you really get the most out of.

To send us general feedback, simply send an e-mail to feedback@packtpub.com, and mention the book title via the subject of your message.

If there is a book that you need and would like to see us publish, please send us a note in the **SUGGEST A TITLE** form on www.packtpub.com or e-mail suggest@packtpub.com.

If there is a topic that you have expertise in and you are interested in either writing or contributing to a book, see our author guide on www.packtpub.com/authors.

Customer support

Now that you are the proud owner of a Packt book, we have a number of things to help you to get the most from your purchase.

Downloading the example code

You can download the example code files for all Packt books you have purchased from your account at http://www.PacktPub.com. If you purchased this book elsewhere, you can visit http://www.PacktPub.com/support and register to have the files e-mailed directly to you.

Errata

Although we have taken every care to ensure the accuracy of our content, mistakes do happen. If you find a mistake in one of our books—maybe a mistake in the text or the code—we would be grateful if you would report this to us. By doing so, you can save other readers from frustration and help us improve subsequent versions of this book. If you find any errata, please report them by visiting http://www.packtpub.com/support, selecting your book, clicking on the **errata submission form** link, and entering the details of your errata. Once your errata are verified, your submission will be accepted and the errata will be uploaded on our website, or added to any list of existing errata, under the Errata section of that title. Any existing errata can be viewed by selecting your title from http://www.packtpub.com/support.

Piracy

Piracy of copyright material on the Internet is an ongoing problem across all media. At Packt, we take the protection of our copyright and licenses very seriously. If you come across any illegal copies of our works, in any form, on the Internet, please provide us with the location address or website name immediately so that we can pursue a remedy.

Please contact us at copyright@packtpub.com with a link to the suspected pirated material.

We appreciate your help in protecting our authors, and our ability to bring you valuable content.

Questions

You can contact us at questions@packtpub.com if you are having a problem with any aspect of the book, and we will do our best to address it.

1
Understanding IPv6 and IPv4-IPv6 Interoperability

At the beginning of this book, we promised that you wouldn't have to learn IPv6 to partake in the wonderful Unified Remote Access technology, and that was true. Nevertheless, understanding IPv6 and the transition technologies is not only a chance to prepare for the inevitable day when IPv6 becomes the common standard, it may also come in handy if you have to troubleshoot advanced problems with Unified Remote Access. In addition, if you are required to plan complex environments that integrate Unified Remote Access and other networking solutions, you might find the following information more than useful.

The topics we will cover in this chapter are as follows:

- My network's fine, so if it ain't broken, why fix it?
- The IPv6 addressing schemes
- IPv6 address assignment
- IPv6 and name resolution
- A little more about DNS
- Multiple stacks
- Operating system compatibility
- Protocol transition technologies
- ISATAP
- DNS64 and NAT64
- 6to4
- Teredo

- IP-HTTPS
- Practical considerations for IPv6 and IPv4
- Unified Remote Access and Group Policy
- Public Key Infrastructure (PKI)

My network's fine, so if it ain't broken, why fix it?

When the good folks at ARPA developed the protocols that our networks rely upon, they designed the 32-bit IP number system, which back then provided an IP to every single living man, woman, and child on the planet, with almost a billion addresses to spare. One thing they didn't count on was that the definition of a computer and a network would expand so much. Besides the fact that the world population has doubled since then, we all have a computer at home, one at work, a smart phone, and often some tablet stashed around the house somewhere too. It's not unusual to see a home network using 10 or more IP addresses. As a result, the entire range of 4,294,967,296 addresses has long since been allocated years ago, and since then, obtaining a public IP has been relatively hard and expensive.

An interim solution in the form of **NAT (Network Address Translation)** has been developed, and has been a viable workaround for pretty much everyone, but NAT has its own disadvantages. For one thing, NATing an address changes the headers in packets, and that causes problems with highly secure protocols such as IPsec. It also presents problems to certain application-level protocols such as FTP. Another challenge is performance, as the packet's header changes take time and resources. Ultimately, millions of businesses world wide are using NAT successfully, but one might consider it more of a workaround than a real solution.

IPv6 offers a solution to everything, as well as a design that is thought-out ahead significantly. For one, it allocates 128 bits for addressing, which provides us with an immense number of addresses. The actual number is 3.4×10^{38}, which gives every human being billions of IPs of his own. In fact, it would be virtually impossible to run out, as we would run out of space on the planet before we run out of addresses.

There are, of course, many other advantages to IPv6 over IPv4, such as built-in IPsec security, built-in address auto-configuration, improved performance for mobile routing, improved performance for routers, and more. We won't go into full details here, but we're sure that if you wanted to know all that, you'll have already found your way into any one of the lovely 600-page books dedicated to IPv6.

The IPv6 addressing schemes

You've probably seen various network cards with IPv6 addresses, and after many years of sticking to simple four octet IP addresses, it may be a little intimidating seeing all those zeros and colons. "How the heck am I expected to remember my own IP address, let alone my entire network?",you must be thinking. Well, you probably won't remember as much, but after a few weeks of actually looking at the numbers, you'll start to see patterns, and things will make more sense. Here's an example:

```
C:\>ipconfig /all

Windows IP Configuration

   Host Name . . . . . . . . . . . . :
   Primary Dns Suffix  . . . . . . . :
   Node Type . . . . . . . . . . . . : Hybrid
   IP Routing Enabled. . . . . . . . : No
   WINS Proxy Enabled. . . . . . . . : No
   DNS Suffix Search List. . . . . . : hsd1.wa.comcast.net.
   System Quarantine State . . . . . : Not Restricted

Ethernet adapter Onboard Nic:

   Media State . . . . . . . . . . . : Media disconnected
   Connection-specific DNS Suffix  . :
   Description . . . . . . . . . . . : Intel(R) 82567LM-3 Gigabit Network Connection
   Physical Address. . . . . . . . . : 00-22-19-34-F2-0E
   DHCP Enabled. . . . . . . . . . . : Yes
   Autoconfiguration Enabled . . . . : Yes

Tunnel adapter isatap.{F64B9BA8-7490-4577-99C4-91F31D3C624F}:

   Media State . . . . . . . . . . . : Media disconnected
   Connection-specific DNS Suffix  . :
   Description . . . . . . . . . . . : Microsoft ISATAP Adapter
   Physical Address. . . . . . . . . : 00-00-00-00-00-00-00-E0
   DHCP Enabled. . . . . . . . . . . : No
   Autoconfiguration Enabled . . . . : Yes

Tunnel adapter Teredo Tunneling Pseudo-Interface:

   Connection-specific DNS Suffix  . :
   Description . . . . . . . . . . . : Teredo Tunneling Pseudo-Interface
   Physical Address. . . . . . . . . : 00-00-00-00-00-00-00-E0
   DHCP Enabled. . . . . . . . . . . : No
   Autoconfiguration Enabled . . . . : Yes
   IPv6 Address. . . . . . . . . . . : 2001:0:4137:9e76:3494:b4:e7ee:3d10(Preferred)
   Link-local IPv6 Address . . . . . : fe80::3494:b4:e7ee:3d10%12(Preferred)
   Default Gateway . . . . . . . . . :
   NetBIOS over Tcpip. . . . . . . . : Disabled

Tunnel adapter isatap.hsd1.wa.comcast.net.:

   Media State . . . . . . . . . . . : Media disconnected
   Connection-specific DNS Suffix  . : hsd1.wa.comcast.net.
   Description . . . . . . . . . . . : Microsoft ISATAP Adapter #2
   Physical Address. . . . . . . . . : 00-00-00-00-00-00-00-E0
   DHCP Enabled. . . . . . . . . . . : No
   Autoconfiguration Enabled . . . . : Yes

C:\>
```

The preceding screenshot is from a simple home client, and even though it should come as no surprise to you if you've been in the IT business for the past few years, the sheer amount of NICs on this computer may throw quite a curve ball. In reality, just the first interface is real, and the other three are virtual network interfaces. These NICs are there specifically to be a part of Unified Remote Access, and soon, you'll learn to love them!

Because the address space for IPv6 is so large, some measures were taken to make the addresses as readable to humans as possible. Had we used the regular 10-digit decimal system, an address would be comprised of 40 digits, which would have been quite crazy. Instead, the **IETF (Internet Engineering Task Force)** decided to employ the 16-digit hexadecimal system, which uses the letters A to F in addition to the digits 0 to 9. Hexadecimal notation is common with programming, and is also used in the MAC addresses. You don't really have to understand it, but do know that using it makes us able to write an IPv6 IP address with only 32 characters, so that's a 20 percent savings right there. For example, an IPv6 address could be `2002:1010:00F0:FFFF:F0C0:99AA:1000:AB00`.

The colon symbol is used simply as a visual separator, just like we use commas when writing long decimal numbers (such as 1,000,000).

To make things even easier, something else that we can do is to cut out some of the zeros. This makes the numbers hard to grasp at first, but when the time comes to type or write the number somewhere, you'll start to appreciate this measure.

The first rule of IPv6 shorthand is that you can omit any leading zeros in a group. This means that if you need to write this:

`2002:0010:FF00:0CB0`

You can remove the first two zeros in `0010`, and the first zero in `0CB0`. Naturally, this is not a real address, being half the size, but for our explanation, it will do. The resulting number is:

`2002:10:FF00:CB0`

There, we saved ourselves writing three digits. If we want to apply this to a group of four consecutive zeros, we can, but we still have to leave one zero, so the number:

`2002:0000:FF00:0CB0`

Will be cut to:

`2002:0:FF00:CB0`

The second rule is that if the number has a large group of consecutive zeros, they can all be cut and replaced with a double colon. For example, the number:

```
2002:1000:0000:0000:0000:FF00:A101:1800
```

Can be shortened to:

```
2002:1000::FF00:A101:1800
```

As you can see, we didn't cut out the three zeros in the second group. Those have to stay because they are part of the number `1000` (just like when writing regular decimal numbers, you can cut 010 to 10, but not to 1). Also, if the number has two separate groups of consecutive zeros, only one of them can be cut. In that case, the zeros that you can't completely cut out can still be shortened according to the previous rule. So the number:

```
2002:0000:FF00:0000:0000:0000:1001:0011
```

Can be cut to:

```
2002:0:FF00::1001:11
```

It's actually easier to expand shortened numbers than compress them. Let's look at the number from the previous screenshot. As you can see, Windows shows them with lower-case, and that's perfectly fine:

```
2001:0:4137:9e76:3494:b4:e7ee:3d10
```

 Here, two of the groups were abbreviated; so what would be the full number? (Answer at the end of the chapter!)

In addition to the number itself, you will often see a `%` sign on the tail of the address, followed by a number. For example:

```
Tunnel adapter Teredo Tunneling Pseudo-Interface:

   Connection-specific DNS Suffix  . :
   Description . . . . . . . . . . . : Teredo Tunneling Pseudo-Interface
   Physical Address. . . . . . . . . : 00-00-00-00-00-00-00-E0
   DHCP Enabled. . . . . . . . . . . : No
   Autoconfiguration Enabled . . . . : Yes
   IPv6 Address. . . . . . . . . . . : 2001:0:4137:9e76:3494:b4:e7ee:3d10(Preferred)
   Link-local IPv6 Address . . . . . : fe80::3494:b4:e7ee:3d10%12(Preferred)
   Default Gateway . . . . . . . . . :
   NetBIOS over Tcpip. . . . . . . . : Disabled
```

This is referred to as **interface index**. You will see these interface indices on addresses that are link-local addresses, which are addresses that are automatically assigned to each active network interface. These link-local addresses have the same network prefix starting with FE80, so to make routing possible they get assigned that extra number representing the interface identifier that the operating system assigns to each NIC.

Another thing that's important to know about IPv6 addresses is that each address is split in the middle, with the left part being the **network ID** and the right part being the **host ID**. This may come as some relief, as you no longer have to try to figure out which part of the address is the network ID and which is the host ID by using the subnet mask as you often do with IPv4.

Some organizations would still need to split their network into subnets, of course. In such a situation, the network ID (the left half of the address) may be split up further as needed (for example, three out of the four groups being the routing prefix and the fourth being the subnet ID), but that's more relevant to those who are actually upgrading their network to IPv6 and as such is beyond the scope of this book.

IPv6 address assignment

With IPv4, one would assign addresess in one of the three following ways:

- Via **DHCP (Dynamic Host Configuration Protocol)**
- By manually assigning the addresses
- Using **APIPA (Automatic Private IP Assignment)**

With IPv6, these three ways are still available, although we refer to the third as **stateless address autoconfiguration** or **SLAAC** (which also makes this one of the best acronyms in computer history alongside FAQ and SCSI). SLAAC is used when the system assigns itself the link-local address (the one starting with FE80) that we discussed earlier.

The reality is that most administrators deploying **Unified Remote Access (URA)** will want to know as little about IPv6 as possible, and would rather not have to even think about messing around with DHCP scopes or subnetting. As luck would have it, you don't really have to, because the fantastic ISATAP mechanism will help you work things out. **ISATAP (Intra-Site Automatic Tunnel Addressing Protocol)** is a protocol transition mechanism, which provides a way for computers to communicate, using IPv6 over an IPv4 network, and part of that is an automatic generation of an IPv6 address. The way this works is by Windows creating a virtual network card named `isatap`, and assigning itself an IPv6 address that's based on the computer's IPv4 address. This would happen on all your modern desktops and servers (Windows XP, Windows Vista, Windows 7, Windows Mobile, Windows Phone 7, Linux, and even some versions of Cisco IOS). A computer or network device on your network will be designated as an ISATAP Router (more about that later) and your hosts will learn of its existence by querying your DNS server.

As you can see in the following screenshot, this computer assigned itself the ISATAP address of `2002:2f6b:1:1:0:5efe:10.0.0.3`. Did you see those dots at the end? Yes! This shows us that the address was generated from the computer's IPv4 address of `10.0.0.3`. Easy as pie!

```
Administrator: Command Prompt                                          _ □ x

Tunnel adapter isatap:

    Connection-specific DNS Suffix  . :
    Description . . . . . . . . . . . : Microsoft ISATAP Adapter
    Physical Address. . . . . . . . . : 00-00-00-00-00-00-00-E0
    DHCP Enabled. . . . . . . . . . . : No
    Autoconfiguration Enabled . . . . : Yes
    IPv6 Address. . . . . . . . . . . : 2002:2f6b:1:1:0:5efe:10.0.0.3(Preferred)

    Link-local IPv6 Address . . . . . : fe80::5efe:10.0.0.3%16(Preferred)
    Default Gateway . . . . . . . . . :
    DNS Servers . . . . . . . . . . . : 10.0.0.1
    NetBIOS over Tcpip. . . . . . . . : Disabled

C:\>
```

If you prefer, you can ask your ISP to assign you an IPv6 subnet, and then create a DHCP scope from it to assign real addresses, and you could even assign those addresses manually to hosts. You can also work with your ISP to devise an IPv6 address allocation plan, if your network is complex.

We'll say this again, though you don't have to do any of this for the purpose of implementing URA. The reason for this is even though URA clients do use IPv6, the URA server will actually route that traffic and encapsulate it as IPv4 to the hosts on the corporate network. We will discuss this in more detail shortly.

IPv6 and name resolution

Just like IPv4, IPv6 networking requires name resolution, and luckily, the Windows DNS service has been IPv6 ready for many years. IPv6-ready DNS can store name records for IPv6 resources, which is referred to as **AAAA** records, or **Quad-A** records. Modern Windows computers register both their regular addresses and their IPv6 addresses in DNS automatically, and when another computer attempts to resolve it, DNS will default to resolving the IPv6 address. The following screenshot shows the Windows Server 2012 DNS Manager, with several computers registered with both IPv4 and IPv6 addresses.

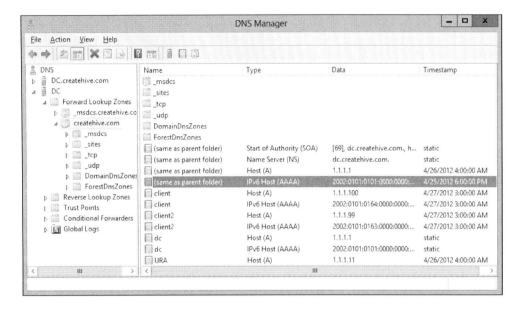

Since URA clients will be using IPv6 addresses, an IPv6-capable DNS is good to have around, so that when your corporate network computers try to connect to URA clients, DNS will help to resolve the addresses properly. One situation where things are a little more challenging is when an internal server is only capable of IPv4 traffic. This would include older operating systems, such as Windows 95, and certain devices running proprietary operating system or network stacks that haven't been updated.

To address such a situation, where the URA clients need to access an IPv4-only internal resource, the URA server role includes a function referred to as **DNS64** (pronounced DNS Six-to-four) as well as another function referred to as **NAT64** (pronounced NAT Six-to-four). However, it's important to know that this help can go only in one direction. This means that the IPv4-only internal server won't be able to initiate a connection to the URA client unless it is upgraded to fully support IPv6. The real-world impact of this is typically remote management. If one of your goals is remote management of remote clients, you will have to make sure that you have IPv6 capable servers for this task. Shouldn't be too hard to make this happen, right?

A little more about DNS

We discussed the special DNS records used for IPv6, and that brings up the question of which DNS server to use. Most organizations that deploy URA would typically all be using Microsoft DNS servers, and the good news is that Microsoft's DNS started supporting IPv6 way back in 2003. This means that even if your domain is a bit older, you're still good to go and don't need to upgrade the DNS. If your environment is using UNIX or Linux, you're going to have to make sure your DNS servers are running BIND version 9 at least, though we're sure you've gone there a long time ago, following the numerous security vulnerabilities discovered in the older versions of BIND.

Another aspect of DNS with regards to URA is the matter of *internal vs. external name resolution*. Your URA clients will have to be able to correctly resolve the public hostname of your URA server or your server array. While connected to the corporate network, the clients will have to be able to resolve the names of internal servers they need to contact.

If your organization is using the same DNS domain structure on the internal network and on the public internet, referred to as **split-brains DNS**, it can be tricky because you need to decide if you want URA users to access the published resources externally or internally. In such a case, you need to make sure that as clients move from using the internal DNS server on the corporate network to using the public DNS server that their ISP is hosting, they are still able to resolve all the appropriate URLs, and do so correctly. A problem could happen, for example, if there is a resource that is supposed to be accessible from both the internal network and the public one. Perhaps your SharePoint server is set up this way, or the company's public website may be. In such a situation, you have two options. One is to make a choice and have that resource available either internally or externally (only to the URA users!). The other option is to configure the resource with an alternative internal name.

A very important part of the DNS resolution mechanism for URA clients is the **Name Resolution Policy Table** (**NRPT**). This is a piece of the name resolution mechanism on a URA client that is in charge of controlling how the client resolves internal and external hostnames. This table comes into play when the client is outside of the corporate network, and is used to manage the way name resolution is done on the client. When URA is on, the client needs to be able to resolve internal corporate network names, but still resolve public hostnames on the internet. The public DNS server that the client is configured with is still around, doing its job, and the URA server will be in charge of helping resolve internal hostnames. The NRPT simply tells the client for which network resources it should contact the URA server, and for which it should not. For example, the NRPT might say "For any hostname that ends with `Createhive.com`, perform name resolution through the URA server, and for anything else, use the public DNS server you have configured". You will be configuring this later as part of the URA role setup, so we'll examine this with more detail later on, but keep this concept in mind as it's very important.

Multiple stacks

Pretty much every operating system released in over a decade supports IPv6 and we refer to this as **dual stack**—both an IPv4 TCP/IP stack and IPv6 TCP/IP stack. You would have probably noticed this in your network interface configuration page:

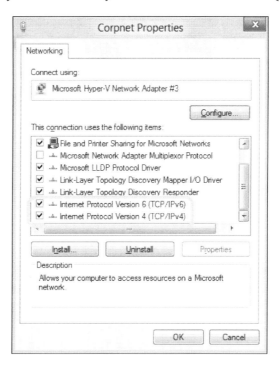

The reality is that a lot of administrators aren't sure why they need this and disable the IPv6 option on all their computers. This might be some misguided attempt to optimize the network, such as disabling NetBIOS, but in reality, it would be a pretty bad idea. By disabling IPv6, you're limiting the computer's options and so Microsoft recommends keeping this enabled. If you've been doing this for a while, it's time to start thinking how to undo it. The easiest way would probably be by running a script on all hosts via your domain login script. The article available at `http://support.microsoft.com/kb/929852` can help you make this happen (though it applies to Windows 2008 servers and onward only).

This is even more important on the URA server itself. If you've implemented disabling IPv6 automatically in any way, make sure your URA server is excluded from this. Without IPv6, the URA server cannot perform its role.

Operating system compatibility

Even though few companies in the United States have switched to IPv6, other countries have been faster to adopt it. The leaders are Japan, China, South Korea, and Australia. To make things easier, Microsoft developed IPv6 support many years ago, and starting with Windows Vista, it was enabled by default.

On older operating systems, IPv6 was available as an extra add-on. In Windows XP, for example, all you have to do to add it is open a command prompt on the client and run the command `netshint ipv6 install`. On Windows 2000 computers, you can add IPv6 by installing an add-on pack from `http://www.microsoft.com/en-us/download/details.aspx?id=21676`.

On other operating systems such as MacOS, Linux, and others, IPv6 is supported as well. Macintosh computers have had IPv6 support since Mac OS v10.3 (also known as Panther, released in late 2003). Linux kernels have supported IPv6 since the year 2000, with some code implemented in version 2.1.8 of the kernel, and any distribution using version 2.6 or later should support it fully.

To be clear, the preceding paragraph doesn't mean that these systems can become URA clients; we are only talking about the ability of the operating system to use IPv6, which impacts how it will integrate into the network.

Protocol transition technologies

Ultimately, not many organizations are ready for IPv6, and even those that are can't always go ahead full steam, as the costs can be significant. Many models of network hardware such as switches and routers can be upgraded to support it, but quite a few still don't, not to mention various embedded OS devices like vending machines, cash registers, entry control systems, and others. To make things easier, several transition technologies have been developed. We've already mentioned a couple of them, and now is the time to go into more detail and understand a bit about all of them and how they affect your network and deployment plans.

ISATAP

As we said before, ISATAP is a mechanism designed to allow IPv6 capable hosts to communicate over an IPv4 network. This would be useful if your network infrastructure (not referring to the cables, but to routers and the like) is older hardware.

ISATAP has some conceptual similarities to the connection mechanisms used by URA clients, but it is only used on the internal network and has a different purpose. It is designed to allow your URA clients to access IPv6-capable hosts (such as application servers or other computers on the internal network) even though your infrastructure is an IPv4 network. With ISATAP, the IPv6 data is encapsulated inside an IPv4 packet header, so the network infrastructure just passes it along, not knowing what's really inside. Hosts that are able to use ISATAP have a dual stack, meaning that they are configured with both an IPv4 IP address and an IPv6 IP address that is based on the IPv4 address. That IP starts with a standard prefix followed by five address groupings and then the IPv4 address.

To facilitate ISATAP, your network needs an ISATAP Router. This is not a physical router, but a software component that the URA server provides (you can also configure other servers to host this functionality). When you configure the URA role, you have the option of setting up the server as an ISATAP router. You can also configure any Windows server to be one, so you can have your URA server perform this function or configure it on another server.

When ISATAP capable hosts boot up, they will also need to know whether to use ISATAP or not, and for that, they will query the DNS server. In an environment that uses ISATAP, the DNS server would have an entry that will resolve the hostname ISATAP to the IP of the ISATAP router. Clients that are successfully able to resolve this will contact the IP provided, and will get their ISATAP configuration from the ISATAP router.

As an administrator, you have the option of either using ISATAP or not. Like any technology, ISATAP has advantages and disadvantages, and Microsoft does not recommend deploying it, except as a temporary means of enabling IPv6, while the organization prepares for full IPv6 implementation. In *Chapter 8, Enhanced Configurations for Infrastructure Servers*, we will discuss the advantages and some of the challenges of ISATAP, as well as how to enable this feature or move it to another server. If you want to enable ISATAP right now, follow these steps:

1. Open your domain's DNS server management tool.

2. Create an A record named `isatap` under the forward lookup zone of your domain name.

3. Populate it with the IP of the URA server (if the URA has both an external and internal NIC, use the IP of the internal NIC).

4. Open **Registry Editor** on the DNS server.

5. Navigate your way to `HKEY_LOCAL_MACHINE\SYSTEM\CurrentControlSet\Services\DNS\Parameters`.

6. Double-click on the **GlobalQueryBlockList** value.

7. Remove the name **isatap** from the list (it's perfectly normal for it to contain nothing else, but it would probably have **wpad** as well, which you should leave alone).

8. Click on **OK** and exit **Registry Editor**.

9. Restart the DNS service or reboot the DNS server.

10. Repeat steps 4 to 9 on all your DNS Servers.

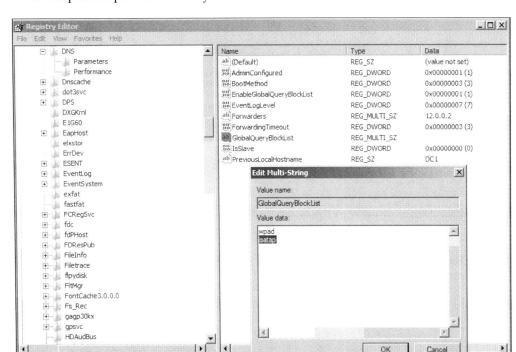

Well, we have ISATAP to take care of IPv6-capable hosts, but what if we want to access hosts that can't use ISATAP? Older operating systems, such as Windows 2000 and older are not able to use ISATAP—the component is not included in the operating system. This also pertains to many non-Microsoft platforms that you might be running. For them, URA includes two additional services—DNS64 and NAT64, which are discussed in our next topic.

DNS64 and NAT64

URA clients communicate using IPv6, and so for things to work correctly, any resource they need to communicate to must resolve to an IPv6 IP address. The DNS64 service helps take care of that. DNS64 (pronounced DNS six-to-four), as its name suggests, is in charge of resolving the IP addresses for the URA clients. When a URA client needs to communicate with an internal hostname, the DNS64 component provides an IPv6 address that represents the IPv4-only host.

NAT64 (pronounced NAT six-to-four) performs an action that somewhat resembles what traditional NAT does, but specifically for IPv6 transition. The acronym is the same—Network Address Translation—but where traditional NAT "translates" traffic from public IPs to private IPs and vice-versa, NAT64 translates traffic from IPv6 hosts to IPv4 hosts and vice versa.

> It's important to keep in mind that these two are almost completely transparent to both you and your users. The URA wizard will turn those on, and that's it.

6to4

As opposed to the mechanisms we described earlier, 6to4 is more of a client-side mechanism. It's designed to allow IPv6-capable hosts, such as your URA clients, to communicate with your URA server over the Internet, significant parts of which are still only IPv4 capable.

6to4 is a component of the operating system, which takes the form of a virtual network adapter. You can even see it in the computer's device manager:

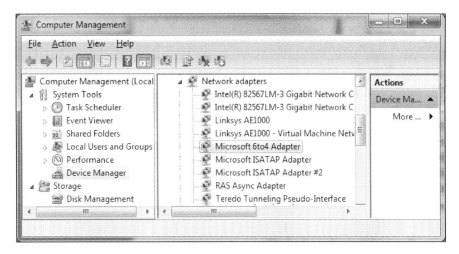

For 6to4 to work, the operating system assigns itself an IPv6 address which is based on its IPv4 address. Then, when the computer needs to communicate with another IPv6 host, such as your URA server, the 6to4 component embeds the IPv6 packets in the payload portion of an IPv4 packet with protocol type 41. These IPv4 packets are then sent to the IPv4 address of the URA server, which extracts the IPv6 packet back, and passes it along to the IPv6 stack.

One challenge with 6to4 is the fact that protocol 41 is blocked by default on many networks. If either the client's ISP or the ISP that your corporate network uses blocks this protocol, 6to4 communications won't work. Another potential pain in the neck is that 6to4 cannot work behind a NAT network, because a 6to4 address is generated only when the client has a public IPv4 address (as opposed to ones that are behind a router and have a NAT address). Since home routers, which perform NAT translation, are very common these days, this effectively blocks the 6to4 mechanism. Thankfully, there are additional mechanisms like IP-HTTPS and Teredo, which we'll discuss in the next sections.

The bottom line of this, as far as you are concerned, is that you have little control over this option. When you configure your clients to use URA, some of them will establish their connection using 6to4, but only those that have a public IPv4 address. This means, of course, that only a small portion of your clients will do so. Those which cannot use it will automatically fall back to one of the other mechanisms, which we will discuss next.

Teredo

For URA clients connecting from the Internet, Teredo is another client-side transition technology, which is the fallback when 6to4 cannot be used. When a URA host is unable to use 6to4, usually because the protocol 41 is blocked, Teredo springs into action. With URA, Teredo is yet another virtual network card (as opposed to the pesky Teredo Navalis clam!), and this is how it looks:

```
Tunnel adapter Teredo Tunneling Pseudo-Interface:

   Connection-specific DNS Suffix  . :
   Description . . . . . . . . . . . : Teredo Tunneling Pseudo-Interface
   Physical Address. . . . . . . . . : 00-00-00-00-00-00-00-E0
   DHCP Enabled. . . . . . . . . . . : No
   Autoconfiguration Enabled . . . . : Yes
   IPv6 Address. . . . . . . . . . . : 2001:0:4137:9e76:3494:b4:e7ee:3d10(Preferred)
   Link-local IPv6 Address . . . . . : fe80::3494:b4:e7ee:3d10%12(Preferred)
   Default Gateway . . . . . . . . . :
   NetBIOS over Tcpip. . . . . . . . : Disabled
```

You can also see it in the preceding screenshot, at the bottom of the screen. The Teredo adapter is included with modern Windows computers.

Teredo also encapsulates the IPv6 packets within IPv4, but it uses UDP packets on port 3544 instead of protocol 41. With UDP being more ubiquitous than protocol 41, it's less likely to be blocked by the network infrastructure, and therefore more likely to go through in most networking environments. In addition, Teredo has a special mechanism that allows it to transcend through NAT networking, so it can work even if the client is behind a home router.

On a Teredo client, such as your URA clients, the operating system assigns itself a unique IPv6 address, which is also based on its IPv4 address. The address begins with the prefix 2001:0000, followed by the IP of the Teredo server (4137:9e76 in the preceding screenshot). The address also has the UDP port mapped on the NAT device (b4 in the preceding screenshot) and finally, the public IPv4 address of the host (e7ee:3d10 in the preceding screenshot). This IP is not the IP of the host itself, but the public address that the NAT device uses.

Some of these numbers are obfuscated with a binary inversion of the bits. For example, the externally mapped UDP port is b4 as shown in the preceding screenshot, but that's actually FF4B (65355). To calculate the number, if you care to go that deep, launch your **Calculator** and switch it to the Programmer mode. Then, perform b4 xor ffff and you will arrive at this result:

The IP of the host is obfuscated similarly.

 Do you know what IP it actually represents? (Answer at the end of the chapter!)

Once Teredo comes into play, the server performs a discovery process to determine the type of NAT that the client is behind, which helps it determine how to communicate with it reliably. Once this process concludes, the IPv6 traffic is encapsulated and the communication process can continue.

The practical considerations for using Teredo are few, as you have little to do. Just like 6to4 that we mentioned earlier, the user or you have little control over which mechanism is used—it depends on the network infrastructure. If the network blocks protocol 41, 6to4 cannot be used, and the client will automatically fallback to Teredo, and there's nothing you can really do about that (other than, of course, to tell the user to connect to the internet somewhere else, where protocol 41 is not blocked).

There are actually several types of NAT connections. These are:

- One-to-one NAT, also known as Full-cone NAT
- Address-restricted cone NAT
- Port-restricted cone NAT
- Symmetric NAT

Occasionally, Teredo may run into a situation where even it is unusable. This could happen in certain networks where the type of NAT cannot support Teredo, or when UDP port 3544 is blocked by the network infrastructure or ISP. It's pretty rare, but not unheard-of, and in such situations, an affected client will automatically fall back to yet another mechanism, which we will discuss shortly. One thing you can do is manually disable the Teredo interface, and that's something you might need to do as part of troubleshooting. We will discuss troubleshooting URA in *Chapter 10, Monitoring and Troubleshooting Unified Remote Access* of the book.

IP-HTTPS

IP-HTTPS is the third IPv6 transition mechanism used by URA clients and is the last fallback mechanism in case both 6to4 and Teredo fail to connect. With IP-HTTPS, IPv6 packets are encapsulated inside the HTTPS traffic, which is sent over the TCP/IP port 443. From the three client-side transition mechanisms, IP-HTTPS is the most reliable, because almost no network blocks HTTPS traffic, and so it's virtually impossible for this mechanism not to work (beyond specific misconfiguration or other technical malfunction, of course).

With the previous incarnation of Unified Remote Access (that is, DirectAccess), IP-HTTPS was considered to be a less desirable option, because the addition of the SSL encryption that HTTPS uses was somewhat of an over-kill, as the connection already uses IPsec. Double Encryption is not only redundant, but also costly, as it forces the client and server to work harder to encrypt or decrypt each packet twice. However, with URA, the SSL traffic actually does not encrypt the data (we refer to this as null-encryption), so there's less work for the client and server to do, and this results in better performance. In other words, if you have implemented DirectAccess in the past, and are used to thinking badly of IP-HTTPS, forget about it, as it's no longer an issue. In the following screenshot, you can see the IP-HTTPS virtual NIC in a Windows 7 computer's device manager:

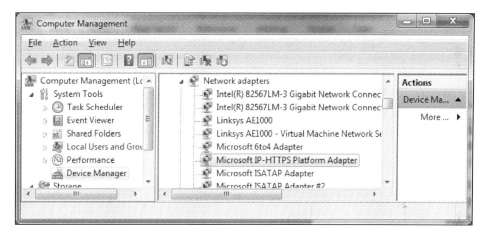

On a client, IP-HTTPS is automatic, and there's nothing for you to configure. On the URA server, you will be required to get a digital certificate, which will be used by the server to prove its own identity to clients. This requires some planning and may be a bit of an effort to get. Also, it can prove costly, if you get it from the more expensive certificate providers. We will discuss this process later, when we will see how to configure the server.

Practical considerations for IPv6 and IPv4

As we've said quite a few times already, you can fully deploy URA with little to no knowledge of IPv6, because all the above technologies are designed to be almost completely automatic. By default, modern operating systems are ready for IPv6, as well as the transition mechanisms, so you don't have to configure anything. When you configure the URA role, the server will install and configure all the transition technology components, and the only thing you need to do is set the DNS record, as we described earlier. On your clients, there's little to do either, as a standard Windows client contains all the components you need. This isn't to say that deploying URA will be easy—you have quite a way ahead of you, but once you configure that and deploy to clients by using Group Policy, you will have virtually nothing else to worry about.

Many people prefer to learn just the bare minimum they need to survive and deploy something, and if you're one of them, you might prefer to put all this new terminology aside. However, it is important to keep in mind that these technologies are here to help you. By being there, in all their complexity, they provide your users with the kind of automation and redundancy that will let you and your support personnel sleep better at night.

As we mentioned earlier, one challenge that you might be looking at is working with resources on your network that are limited to IPv4 only. This applies to the following:

- Internal resources limited to IPv4 connectivity
- Software that cannot use IPv6

For internal resources that cannot use IPv6, we mentioned DNS64 and NAT64, which will allow your URA clients to access them anyway, by translating this traffic. However, the reverse is not possible, and if you want some remote management server to connect to your URA clients and perform some action on them, it will have to fully support IPv6. If it does not, your only option is to upgrade the server.

A more common situation is one where the URA clients use some kind of software that isn't IPv6 compatible. One common example is Lync 2010, which cannot be used over a URA connection. The current Lync 2013 works over IPv6, but in order for voice and video calls to work, the round trip time between Lync 2013 client and server should be less than 50 ms. The limitation is because of the way **SIP (Session Initiation Protocol)** works for voice communications, and at the time of writing, affects virtually any **voice over Internet Protocol (VoIP)** software on the market.

This doesn't mean that you cannot use Lync 2010 or other VoIP on a URA client, just that the traffic cannot be configured to go through the URA tunnel. Instead, you will have to publish your VoIP server on the public Internet, just like you would do if you didn't have URA. Then, configure the Lync application on client computers to use the public server to establish the voice sessions, and things should work out well.

 A piece of software called App46 by IVO networks aims to allow IPv4-only applications running on URA clients (as well as Windows 2008 R2 DA clients and UAG DA clients) to communicate with servers on the corporate network (though it doesn't alleviate the Lync VoIP situation). If you have identified IPv4-only software that you need URA clients to use, contact IVO networks to see if it is a suitable solution for you.

Unified Remote Access and Group Policy

If you have a modern Windows network, the concept of Group Policy is probably not new to you. For Unified Remote Access, this mechanism is very important, as it's the main delivery mechanism for URA configuration. While many commercial VPN technologies require you to configure the VPN settings on the client manually (at least to some degree), with URA, all this is taken care of by Group Policy.

To this end, the URA server creates a set of policies in your domain and these are defined for the scope of a special security group (or groups) that you choose. Once members of these groups connect to the domain, they receive an update to their Group Policy, which includes the various settings they require in order to connect. This is an extremely convenient mechanism, as the unpleasant experience of having each user configure his connection is no longer going to be part of your life. It also means that your users won't be able to simply erase their configuration or damage it. In fact, to do so, they will have to work mighty-hard! This is not to say that URA deployment is always problem-free, but at least that part is taken care of.

We will learn how to configure and deploy the policies in *Chapter 3, Preparing Group Policy and Certificate Infrastructure*. However, if you have never used Group Policy, now would be a good time to pull out those MCITP books (or MCSE, if you're nostalgic) and brush up on that topic. The article available at `http://technet.microsoft.com/en-us/library/cc725828(v=WS.10).aspx` may also be helpful.

Public Key Infrastructure (PKI)

The role of **PKI (Public Key Infrastructure)** in URA is important to understand. With Windows 2008 R2, it was required to deploy certificates to every computer that needed to be a DirectAccess client, but this is no longer a mandatory requirement today, thanks to a component that proxies Kerberos authentication instead of using a certificate for the IPSec authentication. It's important to note, though, that this component can be used only if all your URA clients are Windows 8 clients. If you will be deploying this to the Windows 7 clients, you will still require this infrastructure, and we will discuss this in more details in the next chapter.

Even if you choose to deploy URA without issuing certificates to clients, there are other certificate requirements. Earlier, we mentioned that one of the IPv4-IPv6 transition technologies is IP-HTTPS. This requires the URA server and client to communicate with SSL, and for that, you will require a certificate. This can be achieved with a self-signed certificate, produced by the URA server as part of the setup, and it even publishes the root certificate through Active Directory so that your clients can trust it with no need for manual intervention.

The certificate used for this purpose is a server certificate and will be presented to the URA client by the URA server as a means of proving its authenticity. If you prefer, you can use a regular certificate, which can be purchased from any of the many commercial certificate providers such as Verisign, Thawte, and Geotrust. Using a public certificate provider for this situation has costs, of course. Another option is to use the Windows Certificate Authority role that's built into every Windows Server product and create a regular certificate at no cost. The challenge with using an "internal" certificate provider like that is the fact that all your URA clients will have to trust it, which means that if it's not integrated into your domain, you will have to find some way to deploy its root certificate to all clients. Another challenge is that a certificate generated by a certificate authority contains a **CRL (Certificate Revocation List)**, which needs to be accessible to the client as part of the connection process. For this to work, you will need to publish the CRL to some publicly accessible website, and that may be somewhat challenging. We will discuss this topic in more details later on, but you can prepare for this by reading up on managing a Windows certificate authority through the article available at `http://technet.microsoft.com/en-us/library/cc738069(v=ws.10).aspx`.

Summary

This chapter introduces quite a bit of jargon and may be a little hard to swallow at first. It should not, however, prevent you from going forward and start dealing with the next steps of deploying URA. In the next chapter, we will discuss planning your deployment, and go through various considerations and scenarios. If you don't feel 100 percent comfortable with all the terms and technologies introduced here, don't worry—you can always come back to it, and after having played with the actual interface of URA a bit, things will make a lot more sense!

- Answer to question 1:

  `2001:0000:4137:9e76:3494:00b4:e7ee:3d10`

- Answer to question 2:

  The obfuscated IP `e7ee:3d10 is 1110011111101110:0011110100010000` in binary. Inverted, it is `1100000010001:1100001011101111` or `1811:C2EF` `in hex`. Now, convert each two hex digits to decimal, to arrive at the IP `24.17.194.239`.

2

Planning a Unified Remote Access Deployment

Unified Remote Access comes in many shapes and forms, allowing you to configure it to fit your organization's needs and abilities perfectly. Smaller organizations may prefer a simplified deployment that requires less moving parts, while larger organizations may need to deploy multiple clusters of servers that span the globe. Organizations with very stringent security policies may need additional components to come into play, such as **Network Access Protection (NAP)** or **Two Factor Authentication (2FA)**. To accommodate your needs perfectly, your first task will be to plan the deployment and get acquainted with the various deployment scenarios. In this chapter, we will discuss:

- Server requirements and placement
- Basic scenarios
- PKI
- GPO
- Client platforms (and unsupported clients)
- Cloud scenarios
- Advanced scenarios (NAP, OTP, Arrays, Multi-geographic, and Forced tunneling)
- How much can my server handle?

Let's start our planning by getting to know the pre-requisites for deployment of this role.

Server requirements and placement

The URA server role poses very few requirements, technically. To be compatible with the operating system itself, you need a 64-bit CPU running at 1.4 GHz or faster and at least 512 MB of memory. 32 GB of disk space are also required, and if your server meets this, you're off to a solid start. It's kind of a "duh", but we'll say it anyway; you need a network card. Beyond that, keep in mind that the server is going to have to do a lot of work accepting connections, encrypting and decrypting traffic, dealing with authentication, and more. Unless this is just a trial-run or lab environment, don't skimp on the hardware. It's not easy calculating the capacity requirements of URA, but in the following sections you can find some more information about capacity planning.

Something that may be of far bigger importance is the placement of the server. We already said you need a network card, and you need to make sure traffic from the Internet can come into the server. You also need to allow traffic from the server to the internal network. Most organizations will prefer to put the server inside their DMZ, with some kind of firewall in front of it. An extra firewall is not a requirement, because Windows Server 2012 contains an enterprise-class firewall that has proven itself well since its introduction in Windows Server 2008. If, however, you place the URA server behind additional firewalls or routers, make sure that the appropriate ports and protocols are not filtered. The URA server needs you to provision access to the following:

- Protocol 41
- UDP port 3544
- TCP port 443
- ICMPv6 Echo

Each of these needs bi-directional access. Protocol 41 is required for the 6to4 client connections, UDP 3544 is required for Teredo client access, and TCP 443 is required for IP-HTTPS client access. The ICMPv6 Echo traffic is used by the system to test and qualify the network connections. If you are exceptionally apprehensive about incoming traffic, URA can still function without the first two, which would force all clients to connect by using IP-HTTPS.

As for traffic coming from the URA server into your network, it's really simple—you should allow any and all traffic in both directions. We treat URA connected clients as being part of the internal network, and so you need them and their applications to have access to any resources that they would normally have access to while inside the office. Allowing all traffic gives them the ability to work at full capacity, even while working remotely.

Capacity planning for URA

If you are planning to deploy URA for a large user base, proper capacity planning is of critical importance, allowing you to choose the appropriate hardware to service your intended audience and provide an acceptable service level.

Key facts to keep in mind about capacity planning for this sort of technology are that resource utilization is rarely fixed and client distribution has some random elements to it. This means that in a real-world environment, it's hard to predict how many clients will be using 6to4, how many will use Teredo, and how many will use IP-HTTPS. Also, you might have a large number of concurrent connections, but some users will be idle and send only small amounts of traffic, while others may be moving tons of data around constantly (for example, if they RDP into computers on the internal network). This also means that there's no specific finite number of concurrent users that a certain combination of hardware supports, and that there's no mathematic formula that will tell you exactly what hardware you need for a specific number of users. If you are asking your server to handle a number of users that exceeds its capacity, the server won't turn itself off like an overloaded fusebox, but as it struggles to handle the work, service level will degrade and you might find yourself getting calls from people complaining that their connection takes a long time to establish, or that it takes forever to open sites or documents.

As a general rule, the most important resource for a URA server is network bandwidth. If your server needs to service 1,000 users, and your WAN connection to the Internet is a fourth level T-carrier line running at 274 Mbps (this is in bits, which is equivalent to 34.272 Megabytes per second), it can provide an average transfer rate of only 274 Kbps (34 Kilobyte per second) per user. It's commonly agreed that a transfer rate of less than 500 Kbps is considered to be "slow", though yours or your organization's concept of what is an acceptable speed may vary.

The second important resource is CPU, as the URA server needs to do a lot of math when it encrypts and decrypts the data for the IPsec tunnels, as well as the certificate-related work. The server memory is of lower importance. If your server is hosted as a virtual machine, make sure you plan for **Single Root I/O Virtualization (SR-IOV)** hardware, as it allows the virtual machine to use all the cores of the host CPU.

Another consideration is the **Receive Side Scaling (RSS)** configuration of the network card. RSS is a technology that enables packet receive processing to scale with the number of available computer cores. Different network cards support a different number of RSS queues, and if that number is lower than the actual number of CPU cores your server has, the CPU will be under-utilized, and cores are a terrible thing to waste. In such a situation, you can reduce the waste by using more network cards and teaming them together. Windows Server 2012 supports a new teaming feature called **Load Balancing and Failover (LBFO)**. To use this feature, you have to specify the BaseRssProcessor and NumRssProcessors settings for each of the teamed NICs. This can be done in the advanced properties of the adapter in Device Manager. If you have 16 available cores and are teaming two adapters, one would use eight cores starting at CPU 0 and the other would use another eight cores starting at CPU 8. For more information about this and to learn how to configure this with PowerShell, refer to the article available at `http://technet.microsoft.com/en-us/library/jj574168.aspx`.

Another thing you need to configure to make the best of the **network interface card (NIC)** teaming is to configure it for switch-dependent teaming mode. This mode depends on the network switch that the NICs are connected to distribute incoming data across all the NICs. To configure this, you can use the `LbfoAdmin` utility, which is part of the operating system.

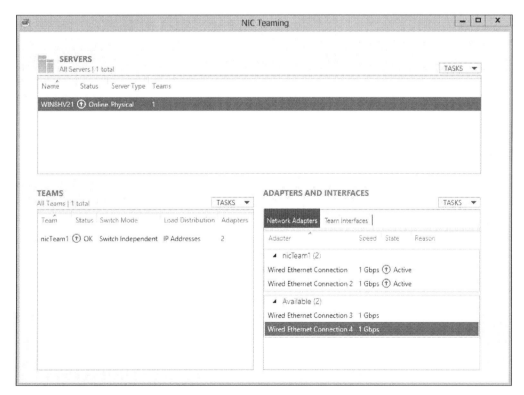

You can also use the `New-NetLbfoTeam` PowerShell cmdlet. For more information about the `New-NetLbfoTeam` cmdlet , visit `http://technet.microsoft.com/en-us/library/jj130847.aspx`.

If you are planning to service a large amount of users, you might consider using a load-balanced array. This is something that we recommend whole-heartedly, as it also helps in case of a server crash. In case you plan for using multiple servers, a second server can double your capacity, but keep in mind what we said earlier about network bandwidth, as having more servers doesn't make your network any faster.

Another thing to keep in mind about load balancing is that it obeys the law of diminishing returns—with more servers, the servers have to work harder to keep track of each other, and so at some point, the benefit gained from adding another server may not be worth its cost.

One last thing to keep in mind is that even though URA doesn't use a lot of memory, do keep an eye on it and don't skimp too much. The reason for this being important is that if memory utilization increases, the system might need to do more paging (where chunks of memory are written to the hard drive to free up memory), which can put a load on the CPU itself.

Finally, here are some test results that we have obtained in the test lab. The tests were performed with RSS enabled and with an RSS queue size set to 8. During the tests, test clients were distributed to have 30 percent Teredo clients and 70 percent IP-HTTPS clients.

Low-end server

The server was running a 4 Core Intel Processor from the Westermere family and 4 GB of memory. One set of tests included 750 clients and another 1000 clients, both with a throughput of about 80 to 85 Mbps. With both tests, the CPU usage was around 50 percent and memory utilization was around 25 percent.

High-end server

The high-end server was running an 8 Core Processor, also from the Westermere family, but this time with 8 GB of memory. We tested 1500 clients with a throughput of about 150 Mbps, resulting in a comparable CPU and memory usage of around 50 percent and 25 percent respectively.

Server requirements – considerations

Before proceeding into any further scenarios, here are the things that you should be jotting down as part of your planning:

- Does your intended server meet the memory and CPU requirements of the operating system?

- Does the server have a fast enough CPU to service the targeted number of clients and what is the type of work they will be doing while connected?

- Are you planning on connecting the server with one leg on the Internet and one on the corporate network, or some other topology? If so, do you require any routing configuration or changes to be performed?

- Do the network infrastructure and ISP connection have sufficient bandwidth to support the requirements while providing a reasonable user experience? If you have an existing VPN solution in place, it could help you get an idea about how much traffic is going on.

- Will your organizational security policy allow you to open the required ports? Will it require some kind of change management procedure?

- Will you be using split tunneling or forced tunneling?

Basic scenarios

The simplest scenario allows you to deploy Unified Remote Access with minimal planning and preparation. In this scenario, almost everything is covered by the URA server itself, as opposed to other scenarios, where you might need additional servers or infrastructure. This kind of deployment is ideal for organizations that prefer to invest the minimal amount of time and resources.

As part of this deployment, you will use the following functions and roles:

- Windows Domain
- Group Policy
- Location Server
- URA Server
- Self-signed certificate
- Kerberos Proxy
- Permission requirements

The basic requirement for any and all URA scenarios is that your computers, as well as the URA server itself, are all members of a domain. The domain will serve as the infrastructure for authentication and for configuring the clients to connect. Unlike traditional VPN, with URA you do not create the configuration manually on the client computers, and all the required settings are applied to the client as part of Group Policy. The Group Policy mechanism identifies mobile computers automatically, and when these computers get the Group Policy applied these settings are applied, and the client is ready to use URA the next time it connects to the public Internet. You can also choose to have this policy applied to other computers by creating a specially designated group for that purpose in Active Directory, and assigning specific clients or other groups to it.

 To identify mobile computers, URA uses a WMI filter. To learn more about this process, read the article available at `http://technet.microsoft.com/en-us/library/dd261948.aspx`.

This method of configuring client settings via Group Policy is convenient as it does away with the crude process of manually installing and configuring each client with the VPN client and/or settings. It would probably be a relief for your tech support people knowing that the clients can't simply delete or uninstall this; so once a client has been configured, it would be rare for them to need any additional setup or support.

If your domain structure is more complex than a simple domain, keep in mind that clients from other domains in the forest that hosts the URA server's domain can participate (or, in other words, you can set up just a single URA server to service the entire forest). If you want the URA server to service clients in other domains that are not in the same forest, you can set up a two-way trust between these domains or forests in order to accomplish that.

Network Location Server

Network Location Server (NLS) is a server, which will be used by URA clients to detect when they are inside your corporate network. This is a very important function, because unlike traditional VPN, the user can't simply turn their URA connection on or off. When the computer is connected to the corporate network, it should behave like any regular client, and we would want the connection to be off so that the computer can communicate with the corpnet resources directly. This is not only to avoid wasting resources by going out-and-around, but also in case something is wrong with the connection and we want to apply new settings to it via Group Policy.

The URA clients have a component referred to as **Network Location Awareness (NLA)**, which detects their location by trying to contact the location server routinely. If they fail in getting a response or are unable to resolve the name of the NLS, they deduce that they are on the public Internet and turn on the URA connection. If they succeed, the URA connection stays off.

The communication process is a simple HTTPS connection. The location server runs a secure website to which the client connects. If the connection succeeds (the HTTP connection succeeds and gets a `200 OK` response code), the client determines that it's inside the network and acts accordingly. With a basic URA scenario, the web service role is automatically configured by the URA wizard and the URA server serves as the location server, so the NLS doesn't require additional manual configuration.

One thing that is important to understand with regards to the location server is that it's more than a key component to URA. Since its very existence is what allows the clients to know they are inside the network, any malfunction in that functionality is a major negative impact on your network. If the URA server is offline, your clients won't be able to connect from home, but if the server is completely down (taking with it the location service), your mobile clients will think they are outside the corporate network even when they are inside. This would cause them to attempt to start the URA connection, which would fail, of course, and none of these clients will be able to connect to any resource on the internal network. This is a grim situation to say the least. For this reason, you might want to consider separating this role from the URA server even if your deployment is relatively small and configure at least two servers in a redundant setup.

URA certificates

Another piece of the setup is certificates. **Certificates** are used for two purposes with URA:

- The Network Location Server uses a certificate to prove its identity to connecting clients
- The URA server uses a certificate to prove its identity to clients which use IP-HTTPS to connect

These two certificates can be generated by the URA server itself (a self-signed certificate), and that's usually the easiest option. You can also elect to use your own certificates. If you use your own location server, you will need to generate the certificate for it on your own. We will discuss this later in this chapter.

An important part of the basic setup of URA in general is the authentication. The standard authentication scheme for Windows Domains is **Kerberos**. Kerberos authentication is not simple, but in a situation where the connecting client (a URA client in our situation) is coming from the Internet, it makes things a little more complicated than the way it works when authentication is done from inside the network. To make things as easy as possible, URA installs a service called **Kerberos Proxy** (and sometimes also referred to as **KerbProxy** or **KDC Proxy**). This service allows the connecting client to perform Kerberos authentication against the domain seamlessly and without the cumbersome **PKI (Public Key Infrastructure)**. Before this service came along, every organization that wanted to use DirectAccess had no choice but to configure a complex setup of a certificate authority and certificate distribution, and it was the most common cause of problems with the DirectAccess deployments.

Technically, the URA client creates a secure connection, using TLS, to the Kerberos Proxy service running on the URA server. The service sends the request to the domain's domain controller (which is a Kerberos **Key Distribution Center** or **KDC** for short), fetches a Kerberos ticket for the client, and forwards it to the client. Once a ticket has been obtained, it can be used for subsequent connections to domain resources.

Basic scenario considerations

The things you need to consider and decide upon for this scenario include the following:

- Do you want your server to connect to the Internet with a public IP or host it behind a NAT device?

- Do you have your computers and users organized into groups in Active Directory, which would allow you to assign them the URA Group Policy?

- Does your domain have a compatible DNS server or do you need to upgrade your DNS infrastructure? (You must be running DNS on Windows 2003, Windows 2008 SP2, Windows 2008 R2, Windows Server 2012, or a version of Bind that supports dynamic updates and AAAA registration.)

- Does your intended URA server meet the hardware requirements for the Windows Server 2012 operating system and this role?

- Do you want to set up your own location server?

- Do you want to defer to the self-signed certificates generated by the URA server or create your own?

Having made these decisions, you are almost ready to start the installation procedure for Unified Remote Access, which we will discuss in *Chapter 4, Installing and Configuring the Unified Remote Access Role*. However, if you are planning to use some of the more advanced scenarios, such as offering support for Windows 7 clients or multisite, you should read on and get a better understanding of some of the additional concepts.

PKI

As we said earlier, URA can work fine without deploying your own certificate infrastructure by using the Kerberos Proxy. There are, however, circumstances where you will not be able to use it. Such a situation is when you need to have Windows 7 clients use URA. The code that runs the connection on Windows 7 computers cannot work with the Kerberos Proxy, and so these clients will require their own certificates in order to launch the IPsec tunnel, and this means that you will have to configure a full PKI infrastructure to support these clients.

Another situation is one with organizations that already have a PKI deployed and would rather use it instead of the self-signed certificates generated by the URA role, or instead of the Kerberos Proxy role. This does complicate things quite a bit, but may serve some organizations better. One reason is control; by having your own PKI infrastructure, you can control exactly which certificates are being created and affect what they can and cannot do. For example, you can revoke a certificate as a means of blocking a specific client's access to URA.

Another situation where this might be required is if you want to use **Two Factor Authentications (2FA)**, which requires its own PKI. In addition, a multisite configuration also requires that you deploy a full PKI. We will discuss these two scenarios with more detail later.

If you chose to use your own PKI, chances are that you know fairly well about the technology and how to use it, so we won't delve into it too deeply. However, you must understand that this affects four things:

- IP-HTTPS
- URA client certificates
- Location server identity verification
- Certificate for the URA server

IP-HTTPS, which we discussed briefly in *Chapter 1, Understanding IPv6 and IPv4-IPv6 Interoperability*, is a connectivity method from URA clients to the URA server, with which the IPv6 traffic is encapsulated within IPv4 packets. These packets are HTTPS packets, and even though the connection does not really encrypt the data as normal HTTPS traffic does, we still need the IP-HTTPS server (which is the URA server) to prove it's really who it says it is by presenting a valid certificate. For all intents and purposes, this is a simple server certificate that is set for the public hostname your URA server will be responding to. Creating a server certificate is a simple process, which you are probably very familiar with. However, it does have two aspects that are sometimes missed.

First, since the certificate will be presented by the URA server to clients, the clients will have to be set up to trust the CA that issued the certificate. This means you have to make sure all URA clients have the CA's root certificate installed in the trusted root certification authorities' container, as shown in the following screenshot:

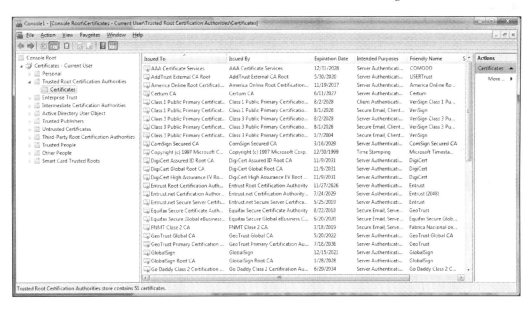

Second, a certificate has a very important field called the **CDP (CRL Distribution Point)**. The CDP is a pointer to a URL, which stores the **CRL (Certificate Revocation List)**. A CA server publishes the CRL to specific locations defined by the administrator, and a part of the certificate validation procedure is checking that the certificate has not been revoked. If a client reads a certificate, but is unable to read the CRL, it may, if it was programmed to do so, deduce the certificate to be invalid (hey, what happened to innocent until proven guilty!). This may seem to be a no-brainer, but in reality, many organizations forget that the CA server is internal and its CDPs are also internal. The URA client, being external, cannot read those and fails the connection.

To work through this, one thing you can do is configure some form of publishing for the CDP. You can probably configure your corporate firewall to publish the URL on the CA server to the Internet. You could also reconfigure the CA server to push the CRL automatically to some web server that you are already publishing. Another option you might prefer is to configure the CA server to not include a CDP in the certificate at all. This defeats the purpose to some degree (if you don't care much about the security that CRL provides, you might be simply better off using a self-signed certificate to begin with), but that's your decision, of course. The preferable option for pretty much everyone is to buy a certificate from a commercial certificate provider. Public providers publish their CDPs, so that takes that burden off you and your organization.

For the process of the IPSec tunnel creation, if you're not using the Kerberos Proxy service, each URA client will require its own certificate, and that requires a tad more planning. If you choose to use your own PKI, you will need to provision computer certificates, using client and server authentication certificates. The ideal tool for this is the Certificate Authority role in Windows, because it integrates with Active Directory and allows you to configure autoenrollment. Using **autoenrollment** gives a certificate to every computer on your domain (unless you limit the scope, of course), so you don't have to manually do this. It also automatically renews the certificates for clients, rather than having you or your support group work with every user reactively when their certificates expire. If you have a PKI that uses a non-Microsoft CA, this is perfectly fine, as long as the properties of the certificate match the basic requirements for IPSec authentication, which are as follows:

- The certificate is stored in the computer store (machine store)
- The certificate contains an RSA public key that has a corresponding private key that can be used for RSA signatures
- The root certificate authority that issues the certificates is trusted by all parties

Do not confuse RSA public and private keys, mentioned in the preceding list, with commercial solutions offered by the company named RSA. The preceding section refers to the RSA algorithm used to create the asymmetric public/private key pair used for encryption.

If you prefer using manual enrollment, which can work fine as long as you figure out a routine to maintain the certificates so that your users don't find themselves stranded in the research station in Antarctica with an expired certificate.

The location server certificate is the easiest one to work out, because the server is located inside the organizational network. You still have to make sure the CA that issues the certificate for it is trusted by all clients, but at least you don't have to worry about the CRL issue, because, unless you really try to make your network complicated, it should be accessible to all clients without any (or at least not a lot of) configuration.

PKI considerations

The things you need to consider and figure out regarding PKI are:

- Do you want to use an internal CA to deploy an IP-HTTPS certificate or a commercial provider?
- If you plan on using an internal CA for IP-HTTPS, do you need to arrange for the CRL to be published to the Internet?
- Do you intend to deploy URA to Windows 7 clients, requiring you to use your own PKI?
- Do you intend to use multisite deployment, requiring you to use your own PKI?
- Do you intend to use two-factor authentication, requiring you to use your own PKI?
- Do you prefer to use an internal CA to deploy client certificates instead of using Kerberos Proxy?
- If using an internal CA, do you want to use autoenrollment or manual enrollment?
- If using an internal CA, do you want to use an enterprise CA or stand-alone CA?
- If using an internal CA, do you need to deploy root or intermediate certificates to all clients?
- If using an internal CA, is your infrastructure ready, or does it require the addition of templates, or some other configuration changes to kick into action?

Group Policy

Group Policy is one thing that you cannot really get around with when deploying Unified Remote Access, even with the simplest of configuration scenarios. Group Policy is the key mechanism for storing and passing configuration options for URA, and as such requires a better understanding than average, and you stand to gain a lot from it by working properly. In the following screenshot, you can see a piece of the Group Policy that is configured on a domain as part of URA setup:

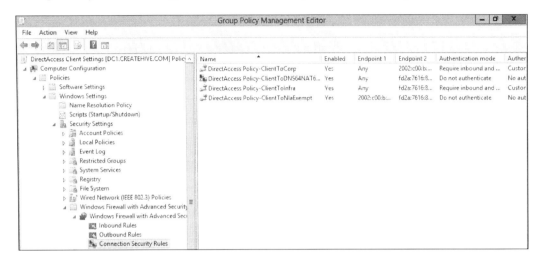

The good news is that you don't have to do a lot on your own. In fact, if your domain is in order, you may not need to do anything. After all, Group Policy is a built-in feature of Windows Domains and even though it sometimes needs care, it's pretty rare.

The core functionality of URA is based on an IPsec tunnel between the URA clients and server, on which the traffic is encrypted using IPsec. The system component that establishes the tunnels and performs the required authentication is the Windows Firewall, which has been an important part of the Windows family of operating systems for almost 10 years now. To do its job, the firewall needs to know various parameters that are used to establish the tunnels, and those parameters are stored in Group Policy and passed along to clients with it. When you configure the URA role, the wizard automatically creates the various settings into two sets of policies and sets the scope for them. One set of policies is applied to the URA server itself (as well as other URA servers, in case you're setting up a cluster) and the other is applied to all designated URA clients. To make things easier, the URA express setup wizard creates a WMI filter to apply the client policy to all mobile computers in the domain. You might prefer to designate specific groups to which you want the policy applied in addition or instead of the WMI filter. This might be useful if you want certain desktop computers to connect to URA or if the mobile computer WMI filter misses certain computers.

WMI (Windows Management Infrastructure) has built-in mechanisms that can interact with the computer's hardware directly. It integrates with Group Policy in the form of filters, which can determine if the computer is a mobile computer or another type. To do so, Group Policy on the client queries `Win32_ComputerSystem`, and if `PCSystemType` is `2`, it is determined that this is a mobile computer and applies the URA policy to it.

When you configure the URA role on your server, you will need to define certain parameters and settings, and the URA role wizard will translate these into the appropriate settings in Group Policy. This process concludes with the creation of the policies in Active Directory and setting their scope. The wizard can create the new policies for you, and for this, it will have to run with the context of a user with the appropriate level of permissions to create new group policies. You can also ask the wizard to use existing policies and simply add the appropriate settings into these existing policies. This can be beneficial to some organizations, because unlike the policies that are automatically generated, the wizard does not alter the existing security settings on pre-defined GPOs.

Another, not uncommon, situation is one where the person configuring the URA role (presumably you, fearless reader) is an administrator of the URA server, but their account does not have full permissions to do everything on the domain, such as creating or updating Group Policy. In such a situation, the URA wizard also allows you to save the policy as a PowerShell script (a `.PS1` file). In this situation, you take the file and give it to someone else within the company who does have the permissions to use it. It's a bit cumbersome, but sometimes that's the only way to go. This is more common in larger companies who like to spread responsibility among different people, either for political reasons or as a means of implementing checks-and-balances.

A situation some organizations might run into when deploying URA (earlier we've seen this with deployment of DirectAccess 2008R2 and UAG DA as well) is one where the scope definition for the policies is incorrectly set and includes too many computers. Most often, this happens because the administrator wants everyone to enjoy URA, without realizing that applying the policy to everyone actually includes computers that are really better off being left out. For example, the location server needs to be off this benefit, and so do the URA servers themselves. They do have their own policy, as we said, but if they try to apply the client policy to themselves, the results would be not only tragic, but somewhat embarrassing too (remember the last time you saw a guy sporting a shiner and claiming that he "ran into a door"?).

Last thing to keep in mind is that Group Policy can, sometimes, become problematic. If you have never used Group Policy for anything, it's possible that your domain schema has collected some virtual dust over the years, and may not work properly when the time comes to deploy. One such situation is that the policy replication is corrupt and won't apply to clients properly, or at all, after you configure it. Another situation we have seen is one where the default domain policy contains a configuration which is not in accord with what you need, but it goes unnoticed until you deploy URA, and suddenly you start getting calls from users about some change in behavior that you didn't see coming. To prevent any mishaps, we suggest implementing a dry run of Group Policy with some simple settings before starting to deploy URA. This way, you can be sure it's all ticking nicely before coming up to your deployment deadlines. The flip side of this is the URA Group Policy changing some settings that you have used thus far and catching you off-guard with some major function having been changed or turned off. We cannot specify all the URA options here, but if your domain has a policy that is very complex or large or one that has a lot of security and/or firewall settings, it might be a good idea to deploy URA in a limited fashion (a pilot group or a closed lab environment) and inspect the resulting policies carefully.

So, here are the considerations regarding Group Policy:

- Is your domain set up for Group Policy?
- Will the WMI mobile computer filter include all the relevant computers, or would you need to manually add clients?
- Will the WMI mobile computer filter apply to clients you don't want on URA yet, or at all?
- If you plan to expand the scope beyond the filter, do you have a clear definition of which computers to include and a group for them to be part of?
- Does your account have the permissions to create the group policies in the domain?
- If not, do you have a designated partner to help deploy the policies?
- Do you plan to let URA create its own policies, or have it populate your existing ones?
- Are you confident enough in your domain to deploy URA straightaway, or do you prefer to experiment in a lab or with a pilot group of some kind?

Client platforms (and unsupported clients)

You might be used to VPN solutions which give you some client installer and allow you to deploy it on any client. Unfortunately, the kind of remote access we are talking about here does not provide such limitless freedom. DirectAccess is an enterprise-class solution, and as such, only supports the higher-end **SKUs** (**Stock-Keeping Units**).

As you probably know, Windows 8 is available to the public in four editions:

- Windows 8
- Windows 8 RT
- Windows 8 Pro
- Windows 8 Enterprise

The first one in the preceding list is comparable to the Home editions that Windows 7 and Vista had, while the Pro edition is comparable, of course, to the Pro editions of the previous incarnations of Windows as far back as Windows 2000. RT is the code name for the edition of Windows 8 that will be compiled for ARM processors and run on tablet computers such as Microsoft's Surface RT tablet.

The Enterprise SKU offers several other features over the Pro one, including the ability to use URA, which matters the most in the context of this book. The Enterprise edition is the only edition that supports URA, and that's important to keep in mind. Another thing that is important in this context is that this edition is only available to organizations and cannot be bought in stores directly (even if you say pretty-please... it just isn't produced as a boxed product). Support for URA is available in both the 32-bit and 64-bit versions of the operating system.

You can read more about the features of the various editions of Windows 8 in the articles available at:

- http://windowsteamblog.com/windows/b/ bloggingwindows/archive/2012/04/16/announcing- the-windows-8-editions.aspx
- http://windowsteamblog.com/windows/b/business/ archive/2012/04/18/introducing-windows-8- enterprise-and-enhanced-software-assurance-for- today-s-modern-workforce.aspx

URA also offers backward compatibility for Windows 7 clients, which means that if you were running DirectAccess until now, you can safely upgrade and keep the same level of service. The available editions of Windows 7 are a bit more complex than those of Windows 8. The available editions are as follows:

- Windows 7 Starter
- Windows 7 Home Basic
- Windows 7 Home Premium
- Windows 7 Pro
- Windows 7 Enterprise
- Windows 7 Ultimate

URA (as well as DirectAccess) is only supported on the two higher-end editions Enterprise and Ultimate, and like Windows 8, both 32-bit and 64-bit versions are supported.

As we explained earlier when discussing PKI, there are some differences in the way DirectAccess and URA are implemented with Windows 7. Windows 7 computers cannot use the Kerberos Proxy, and so if you intend to use them, you need to deploy your own PKI.

Technically, there's not much to do in order to prepare clients for URA. All clients have to be domain members and be set to apply Group Policy. If your corporate image that is installed on clients has some features turned off by default, it might require some changes. One is the IPv6 network stack, which needs to be enabled. Another is the Windows Firewall, which needs to be on as well. If your image has these disabled, you might need to come up with an efficient way of enabling it back for all prospective clients. Depending on what you did, it may be addressed with Group Policy itself or possibly with a script.

Another thing worth looking into is third-party networking and security software. Sometimes, networking software, such as software that controls the WIFI NIC, or security software, such as an antivirus scanner, can interfere with the operating system and cause issues. The realm of third-party solutions is infinite, and it's hard to predict how a certain product or combination of products will work together, but it's definitely something to keep an eye out for.

We discussed the three available client connectivity methods earlier (6to4, Teredo, and IP-HTTPS), and if you recall, we mentioned that they depend on the connectivity the client has. Clients that have home networks or connect from a controlled network such as a hotel will typically connect with Teredo, while clients in a more restricted network may fall back to IP-HTTPS. Your control of this is typically limited, but one thing to note about this is that cellular and MIFI-based connections are by far the most challenging. If your employees are using company-provided cellular or MIFI connection, it would be a good idea to at least run some tests with this connection to make sure it does not hinder anything.

Additional client considerations

When talking about clients, we also need to consider the person using the machine. Preparing your users for URA is also important. Some users will accept the new thing at face value and will be simply happy that they can connect to corporate servers from anywhere. Others will be surprised that they no longer have to run any specific software or perform an action to get connected. A topic that often comes up with new users is the matter of boundaries. "If I'm connected all the time, what happens if I browse a website for personal reasons? Will the company be able to see my credit card information? Will the company keep track of what I do? What if I'm an animal lover and like movies about cats and beavers?" These are some of the questions we've heard over the years from users new to this.

The answers, of course, depends on the company policy and intentions. Even when users are connected to URA, traffic to Internet servers goes out directly (unless you have configured forced tunneling, which we will discuss a bit later in this chapter), so you can't track users without installing special software for that. However, your URA users are probably using company laptops, so the company has the right to dictate certain guidelines regarding what can and cannot be done on company-owned assets. These guidelines probably applied even before URA, but sometimes, people are oblivious to that train of thought until something like this comes along. Perhaps this is a good chance to educate fellow workers about their boundaries or perhaps it's time to reconsider them and maybe change them a bit, to make life a bit easier. Watching animal kingdom may be universally objectionable, but you can't expect employees to travel with two laptops, and switch between them anytime they want to check their Hotmail account, right?

Here are the things you should look into and consider with regards to client support:

- Are your intended URA clients running supported versions of Windows 7 and Windows 8?

- If not, do you have an upgrade plan for them?

- If you will be supporting Windows 7 clients, are you ready for the added complexity in implementing the server?

- Is there any network or security software or hardware that may conflict with URA?

- Is your corporate image configured in a way that may interfere with the URA settings, such as IPv6 or the Windows Firewall being turned off?

- Are a large group of your users using a potentially problematic network that might require further investigation or a pilot group?

- Are you or your support personnel ready to clearly answer users' questions about URA and how it affects their work?

- Does your company have a policy affecting the usage of company laptops in a way that may trigger a sociological challenge?

Cloud scenarios

In the past few years, "cloud" has been receiving a lot of attention, both from companies such as Microsoft, Amazon, and Apple, and from the press. Companies all over the globe have adopted various cloud-based solutions, and satisfaction levels are high. In fact, for some organizations, using the cloud has become the top priority and so the topic of using Unified Remote Access with cloud-based solutions has also been the focus for many.

Naturally, cloud means a lot of things, and so you might be asking yourself what is it, really, to use URA in the cloud? The answer is far from simple, but the crux of this is site-to-site VPN. With URA and the cloud, you place a URA server in your corporate network. Then, servers hosted in the cloud establish a URA connection to your server (you can think of these hosted server as clients, if it makes it easier to understand) and thereby joining the networks together. This can be a simple setup between your internal network and the cloud (through your Internet Service Provider), and it can be a more complex setup with redundancies. For example, you could set up your URA server to connect to two different ISPs (via two network cards on the URA server), thereby protecting your business continuity against the failure of the ISP connection or the NIC itself.

Of course, protecting business continuity can be done without URA, but that would typically be done using a load balancer that controls the connection and switches over the connection if it detects one is dead. Load balancers such as this can be quite expensive, so using URA may save a lot of money.

Using URA can also help you with a connection to cloud-based platforms, such as Azure. In this situation, you set up a URA connection between the Azure data center and your on-premise URA server, and this provides you with a secure always-on connectivity between the two.

These two options are not dissimilar in concept than other site-to-site VPN solutions, but doing this with URA provides for better security, thanks to the robustness of IPsec, and also better reliability, thanks to URA's automatic establishment and re-establishment of the connection.

From a design perspective, there is not a lot to plan. Naturally, your cloud servers will have to be Windows 2012 servers, and you'll need to make sure your Internet service provider or providers, are ok with the whole setup. You wouldn't want them to block your access because of the unusual traffic patterns, and you'd want to make sure they can and will support you if there's a problem. You will also need to consider the bandwidth use incurred by this, to make sure a bottleneck is not created on one hand, and to control the line costs on the other. You do not have to set up a special URA server just for this function, though you will have to consider and configure the routing to make sure traffic flows correctly and doesn't go round-and-round inside your network unintentionally.

Advanced scenarios

In addition to all the things that we discussed thus far, URA offers several other advanced scenarios and features which we will discuss now. These are as follows:

- **NAP (Network Access Protection)**: This is a mechanism that inspects client machines and allows them access to the network only if they meet certain criteria dictated by the organization's security policy

- **OTP (One Time Password)**: This is an option to extend the authentication mechanism to have **Two-Factor Authentication (2FA)**

- **Arrays**: This is the option of configuring multiple URA servers to work in a cluster and provide fault tolerance and load balancing

- **Multi-geographic distribution**: This is the ability to build multiple URA servers and place them at distinct geographical locations to provide protection against disaster, or to improve the service level by reducing network latency

- **Forced tunneling**: This is the ability to force all traffic on the client to go through the URA tunnel and the corporate network, which provides a higher level of security

NAP

Network Access Protection (**NAP**) is a technology that is not unique to Unified Remote Access. First introduced with Windows Server 2008 (as a server) and Windows Vista (as a client), NAP provides an infrastructure to allow you to protect your network from clients that pose a threat to it.

VPN servers are access points from the public Internet into an organization's network and are therefore a good place to implement NAP. A VPN server would be a NAP enforcement point, and URA servers are, for that matter, VPN servers. To implement NAP in your network, you need to deploy an entire infrastructure, which includes NAP enforcement points—**Health Registration Authorities** (**HRAs**), **Health Policy Servers** (**HPSs**), and **Health Requirement Servers** (**HRSs**). Modern Windows operating systems have a NAP client built into them, so at least that part is taken care of.

It is beyond the scope of this book to document everything about NAP, but if you don't use it and are interested in learning more read the guide available at `http://technet.microsoft.com/en-us/network/bb545879.aspx`.

If you choose to integrate NAP into URA, your URA server will take on the additional role of a NAP enforcement point and you will need to configure that role in a similar fashion as with any other enforcement point. The article available at `http://technet.microsoft.com/en-us/library/dd296899(v=ws.10).aspx` discusses NAP enforcement points with all the versions of Windows Server.

This link also discusses requirements for a NAP enforcement point, but to save you some time, we can tell you they are not hard to meet. Pretty much any server that meets the Windows Server 2012 requirements would be good to go, and one additional requirement is for some disk space. 10 GB is the minimum and 100 GB is recommended.

One thing to remember about NAP is that installing the servers is the easy part. The difficult part comes from the fact that some of your clients will not actually meet the NAP requirements, and therefore, may not successfully connect. This invariably leads to various levels of frustration with users, which might include senior executives who want to connect **NOW**, and don't care if you have to spend all week cleaning up a virus that mysteriously and coincidentally appeared on the network around the time they came back from a vacation in Hackistan.

Naturally, there is much more to learn about NAP and we will discuss it in more details in *Chapter 9, Deploying NAP and OTP*.

OTP

One-time password (OTP) is a generic term for a variety of products that provide added security by requiring a second authentication factor from connecting users. A common type of OTP is RSA SecurID, which is either a physical device (which typically looks like a keychain) or a piece of software that generates a unique numerical key every single minute, without which the user cannot connect. The software could run on another computer, on a mobile phone, or even from a dedicated website. Other variations of OTP include a server, which sends the user a unique key via an SMS message to their phone.

Integrating OTP with URA is very attractive, because the very nature of URA scares many security people. Many think that since URA is always on, if a laptop is stolen, the thief may find it easy to breach the network. In reality, of course, this is not true. Certainly, a stolen computer poses a threat, but a computer that uses URA is no more of a threat than any other computer. In fact, one might say that it's safer, because even though a classic VPN dialler does require the user to enter a password, many users store that password on the computer itself.

The way OTP works with URA is based on short-lived certificates. When a user logs in to URA, he is required to provide the OTP, and after it's verified, a specially designated certificate server inside the network issues a certificate to the client. This certificate is used for the purpose of the authentication (**Kerberos authentication**). If the client disconnects his session and wants to reconnect, he cannot re-use the same certificate because it's intentionally short-lived, and so the OTP process is triggered again and a new certificate is issued. The lifetime of the certificate would typically be around four hours.

For the most part, a URA deployment with OTP is very similar to a regular one. The most significant difference is that you require a certificate authority to deploy the certificates to OTP clients. This scenario also requires that you use your own PKI for generating certificates for IPsec authentication, though you can use the same CA server for both the IPsec PKI and the OTP PKI. The CA server itself needs to be running at least Windows 2003 Server, and if you like, you can even use the same server you are running URA on for this purpose.

Many organizations need to have some users *exempted* from the need to use OTP when connecting, and that is one of the options. As you can imagine, an Active Directory *security group* would be used for this, and so you should create such a group prior to setting this up and populate it with users that are eligible to be exempted.

The actual process of feeding in the one-time password upon establishing the URA connection is handled by the **Network Connectivity Assistant** (**NCA**), which we mentioned earlier as part of the preface to the book. The NCA is a part of the Windows operating system on Windows 8 computers. However, Windows 7 computers do not have it built-in, so if you plan on supporting these, you will need to download and deploy it to all clients. For Windows 7 computers, this software is called the **DirectAccess Connectivity Assistant** (**DCA**). The DCA has multiple purposes, OTP being only one of them, so it might be a good idea to deploy them to your clients anyway. You can download it from `http://www.microsoft.com/en-us/download/details.aspx?id=29039`.

As for the OTP solution itself, the market offers many, and not all are supported. The requirements of the OTP solution are that it is based on **RADIUS (Remote Access Dial-In User Service)** and that it uses **PAP (Password Authentication Protocol)** over RADIUS. Microsoft does not maintain or publish a list of supported solutions, so if you're not sure, it would be best to contact your OTP provider and ask if they have tested their solution with Microsoft URA or DirectAccess. Asking this would be good not only for the purpose of making sure it would work, but also to figure out the level of support you might expect in case something doesn't work out. Generally speaking, you could expect the bigger providers to have performed more extensive testing and to have more experience with new and emerging solutions such as URA. One feature of OTP that is not supported with any provider is the ability to set a new PIN via the URA client or the ability to use next tokencode mode.

Next tokencode mode is a mode that's used if a user enters the correct PIN, but an incorrect tokencode. Typically, after the tokencode is typed in incorrectly for three times, next tokencode mode is engaged, and then the user must wait for a new tokencode to be generated to proceed.

One more thing to keep in mind is that setting up OTP is considered to be an advanced task, and could therefore be challenging to people new to this technology. It is recommended to start with a regular setup of URA, and only when everything is working correctly, enable OTP. This way, if things don't work out, it's easier to narrow down the possible causes and work them out. This step-by-step approach is popular with most people.

Things you should consider when planning an OTP deployment are as follows:

- Do you have an OTP infrastructure already, or not? If not, it's best to make sure if it will support URA officially by the provider, to reduce the risk of finding out later that it cannot be done.

- If you do have an OTP infrastructure, does it support PAP over RADIUS?

- Is your intended CA server strong enough to handle the rapid generation of certificates to all URA users (some of which may require many certificates every day)?

- Do you have a list of users who will be exempted from OTP?

- Do you intend to deploy this to Windows 7 clients? If so, you need to plan on deploying the DCA to them.

- Is your project's schedule ready to accommodate the additional configuration and testing of OTP on top of the URA deployment?

Arrays

A URA server **array** is a group of two or more URA servers that work in tandem to provide fault tolerance and load balancing. With an array (also referred to as a cluster), the servers share the same configuration and are constantly aware of each other's status. If one of the servers stops responding for some reason (such as a computer crash, a power outage, a NIC failure, a hard drive or other hardware failure, and other problems we have learned to recognize and appreciate as IT administrators), the other cluster member or members re-converge and redistribute the load amongst themselves automatically.

In addition, a server cluster is usually designed to perform load balancing—automatically distributing incoming connections amongst the array members. This is a cost-effective way of increasing your service scope without expending money on very high-end hardware or expanding it beyond what a single server can handle.

To build a URA array, you can install the URA role on multiple servers and then set up load balancing between them. Because the URA settings are deployed via Group Policy, there is no need to configure everything on all members. The settings required to have the additional servers accept incoming connections are transferred to them as part of them is inheriting Group Policy when they are joined to the domain. The load balancing can be performed by either the **Network Load Balancing** (**NLB**) service, which is built-in to Windows Server 2012, or using a third-party load balancing solution, such as those offered by F5, Citrix, Cisco, Riverbed, and many others.

How arrays work with load balancing

When the Windows Network Load Balancing service is deployed, each of the servers in the array is assigned a virtual MAC address and they are all assigned the same virtual IP address. Because the connection attempt coming from the clients is targeted by IP, all functional array members receive the request simultaneously. All servers inspect it, and perform a special calculation to decide if they are the array members which should handle the request. Depending on certain parameters of the client, such as its IP address, one of the array members will conclude the calculation with a *yes* and process the request, while all other members conclude that they are not the ones who should and drop the request.

The array members are in constant communication amongst themselves, and if one of them becomes unresponsive for any reason, they re-converge and update with regards to the server which is no longer dancing in this party. This change affects the calculation, and so the connections that would have been handled by the dead server are now spread across the members.

Array challenges

One challenge with arrays using Windows NLB comes from the fact that you need to carefully plan your IP assignment and routing. In an array, every server has its own **dedicated IP address (DIP)**, but there is also a **virtual IP address (VIP)** that is shared among the members. The virtual IP is what clients will be connecting to when they initiate a request, and so the DNS name that you choose for your server needs to resolve to the virtual IP, and not to the dedicated IPs. If you have a router or firewall in front of the servers, you only need to set it up with a single public IP for the purpose of URA, and that IP needs to have a clear route to the URA server's VIP.

Another often-problematic aspect of this is datalink layer routing. When you enable Windows NLB, the NIC on every server is assigned a MAC address that is different than the physical one it had originally. While this is automatic and the address choice and assignment shouldn't concern you, it might upset your network hardware. Most of us use network switches all around, and a switch has smart circuitry that moves Ethernet packets around based on the MAC address. When one of its ports receives a datagram, it looks at the source and destination MAC address in order to forward it only to the switch port or ports that are relevant. For this reason, it may not like the fact that the MAC address has changed with no apparent reason (to the switch, that is). In such a situation, the switch may discard the traffic or forward it to the wrong port, which could mean that one or more of your URA servers will not be able to send or receive traffic properly.

Addressing this potential problem depends on the switch itself. Some switches will require you to log in to their management interface and reset the MAC address table, or explicitly unblock the spoofed MAC address. Other switches do not have a management interface, and the only thing you can do is reset the switch (which could make you unpopular with owners of other servers or services in the organization who depend on it) or simply wait for it to realize that the network has changed (which would usually happen within a few hours). We recommend reading through the user manual of your network device to see if there are any specific suggestions or information about this issue.

A similar situation may happen with server virtualization. Virtualization platforms set up virtual network switches and virtual network cards, and they also do not always appreciate it when someone else jumps in and changes stuff. The result could be a communication failure between the array members. Usually, this would be addressable by configuring everything correctly, and some virtualization vendors have even gone to the trouble of offering specific guides to setting up their infrastructure for Microsoft's NLB. A guide from VMWare is available at `http://www.vmware.com/files/pdf/implmenting_ms_network_load_balancing.pdf`.

Microsoft's own Hyper-V platform has a special setting for this as well. If your URA server is hosted as a virtual machine, enable the option **Enable spoofing of MAC addresses**. Naturally, this setting is available only when the VM is turned off:

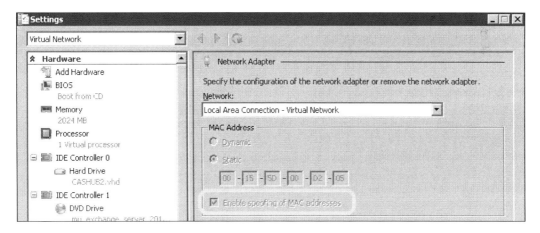

One thing to keep in mind is that URA doesn't offer *session failover*, even when using an array. If one server goes down, the clients will treat this as any *regular* disconnect and will try to reconnect. Their connection attempt will go to the *new* server, which has been assigned to them and the connection will establish pretty fast. However, one must keep in mind that a URA connection, as fast as it might be, is not instant. Also, if your server was hosting 200 connections and suddenly your second server has to handle those 200 being moved to it, it might slow down things a bit. It's very likely that most of your users will not feel anything, but for some, the short disruption might be noticed. For example, if they were in the middle of downloading some file, the download might break in the middle.

You need to consider all of the above when planning your array. If your primary objective is to service a large customer base, and therefore load balancing is of the highest priority, it's pretty clear that you need to set up multiple servers. If, however, you are more concerned about a server crash, perhaps all you need to do is set up your URA server as a virtual machine, and then keep a cold copy of it on some other server (possibly even in a different data center). This is not as effective as an array which responds to a crash instantly, but it will save you a significant amount of money, both in licenses and in maintenance costs. Of course, when we are talking about maintenance costs, it's not just electricity and hardware maintenance—it's also the time and effort it takes to keep a server up. Even if the additional servers take only a few hours a month to maintain, update, and back up, these extra hours might serve the organization better by being dedicated to developing and testing solutions to other problems.

If you go ahead with setting up an array and plan on using a third-party load balancing solution, it's very important to keep in mind that some solutions were not designed for a scenario such as this. Many load balancing appliances are designed for publishing simple websites, and their default configuration might mishandle the connection to the URA server. One reason this may happen is if the load balancer doesn't keep affinity (a.k.a. persistence) properly, and sends traffic from one client to multiple array members. A URA session is set up between one server and one client, so if packets destined to one server reach another, it will not know what to do with them. Setting up affinity correctly is critical for a successful and reliable connection. Usually, setting up the affinity based on source IP address will be just fine, but do consult the user manual of your load balancing solution for any tips and gotchas related to VPN load balancing. If you're lucky, they might even have specific data related to URA.

A second issue affecting many load balancers is their tendency to try and optimize the network by controlling connections. Many load balancers monitor various connection parameters and might decide some connection is stale or hung, and close it. This sort of thing would typically be handled by the URA client's automatic re-establishment of the connection, so the client may not even notice, but on a large scale deployment, it could lead to a higher load on the server (because it has to re-establish connections more often) and lowered reliability of the connections in general. To prevent this, we suggest, as usual, reading through the documentation of the load balancer, especially if you receive reports of problems from many users.

As we said in the beginning of this section, with an array, you need to manually install the URA role on all members. Once the role is installed, Group Policy will take care of setting up the server to accept incoming connections for you, but it's still up to you to set up the certificates. If you have elected to use autoenrollment, the IPsec certificate is taken care of, but you will need to manually install the server certificate used for IP-HTTPS. Since both servers will be answering to the same public hostname, the certificate needs to be configured similarly. To reduce costs, most organizations will simply want to install the same certificate on both computers. To do so, you can simply *export* the certificate from one server and then import it into the same container on the other server or servers. When performing the export, keep in mind that you must also export the private key of the certificate. The export and import procedures are detailed in the articles available at `http://technet.microsoft.com/en-us/library/cc731386(v=ws.10).aspx`.

Note that some certificates may not allow you to export them with the private key, and if so, you'll have to obtain the certificate separately from your provider for each of the servers. Also, even if an export is possible, your provider may still dictate (via their license terms) that you only use it on one computer and pay extra for any additional copies in use.

One aspect of load balancing and arrays that is particularly hard to do is to calculate exactly how many servers you would need to handle all your clients. We have provided some capacity planning information earlier in this chapter, but ultimately, the best way to really know how many connections your own server can handle is to deploy one server for a pilot group and monitor the server's responses with a performance monitoring tool.

One option many organizations are looking for is hosting your servers at different physical locations, and we will discuss this topic in the following section. Until then, here are the things that you need to take into account when planning to use an array of servers:

- How many servers do you need to support my clients?
- Do you need a live array, or is a cold clone enough?

- Do you need to use windows NLB or a third-party load balancer?

- If using a third-party load balancer, are you sure it's fully capable of managing session-sensitive data such as a VPN connection?

- If using NLB, is your network equipment ready to handle the MAC address spoofing used by NLB?

- Does your certificate provider allow you to export the certificate from one computer and import into another?

- Do you need to go through a certain procedure to procure the IPs needed for the servers or adjust the routing?

- Do your switches and routers support multicast or unicast for intra array traffic?

Multi-geographic distribution

Having multiple servers can help you achieve a certain level of fault tolerance, but as any security professional knows, good fault tolerance requires that the fault tolerant servers are placed in different geographical locations. This is helpful in protecting against a catastrophic event such as fire, flood, act of terrorism, or other events that affect large regions. Another advantage of doing this is in allowing users located in different regions to connect to the server that is closest to them, thereby reducing network latency and reducing the load on inter-site links. For example, if your organization has branches in the US and in the UK, having the UK-based users connect to a URA server in the US is a double waste. It's wasteful because sending every packet across the globe to the US wastes a lot of time, and also because these users will typically be using mostly servers in the UK branch, and so the WAN link between sites will be utilized a lot by traffic for these users being sent from the UK to the US (only to fly back to the UK over the tunnel). Setting up a URA server in the UK can not only save money, but also increase the satisfaction levels amongst users.

The considerations for multi-geographic distributions are very similar to those for regular arrays. You will need several servers, of course, and you will configure URA on each of them similarly to how you would with a regular array. The major difference is that with multi-geographic deployment, you define whether clients are automatically routed to an entry point or whether they select their entry point manually (or allow both).

The entry point selection is logic built into the Windows 8 Client. The client knows about all the available entry points via Group Policy and selects the best one by calculating the round-trip time for network traffic to each point. In addition, the administrator can choose to allow the client to choose his entry point manually, overriding the automated process. This mechanism is not present in Windows 7, and so these clients will be tied to a single location, which is assigned to them via Group Policy.

Windows 8 clients come with the **Network Connectivity Assistant (NCA)**, which we've mentioned several times already. The NCA allows the user to see which site they are connected to, and, if the administrator has chosen to allow this, the NCA lets the user manually select a specific site. Since Windows 7 clients are tied to a single site, the administrator will have to decide to which site a Windows 7 client has to connect to. This is done by creating a separate Group Policy for Windows 7 clients, and the policy is linked to a specific site and specific domain. This also means that if there are multiple sites, each entry point will have a separate Windows 7 client policy for that site, and if there are multiple domains in that site, each domain will have a policy that applies to the Windows 7 Client Security groups or **organizational units (OUs)**.

When deploying multi-site, you have the option of whether to use global load balancing or not. Using a load balancer is beneficial because it will distribute the clients between the servers for optimal bandwidth and latency. Naturally, global load balancers are very high-end devices, are therefore very expensive, and can be difficult to set up. For many organizations, you can simply configure URA not to use this option. That way, clients can manually select an entry point, or if it is set to automatic, the client will probe the list of available servers and choose one that is the fastest.

An important consideration for this sort of deployment is internal network routing. As we have mentioned earlier, clients connecting to a site that's far from their normal operational center may experience network latency that is less than optimal, and this may also negatively impact the bandwidth use in your inter-site link. This could be especially impactful if users are allowed to select their own entry point. Sometimes, this leads to the "I can fix it myself" phenomenon, where too-savvy users bounce around between sites looking for the best experience that would allow them the fastest access to servers they want to use. (We're sure you'll enjoy the adventure when one of them calls you at 2 a.m. saying server1 in the UK is 3 seconds slower than server 2 in Japan, and expect you to drop everything and get to the bottom of it!) Seriously though, when dealing with multiple sites, routing can become quite a hassle, and a minor redundant route can cause a lot of havoc. We strongly recommend putting together a detailed and clear network map, and plotting out all possible scenarios.

The things you need to be concerned with, regarding multi-site deployment, are as follows:

- Where are you going to place entry points?

- How many users will be accessing each? Can the entry point handle the expected load?

- Will your clients be selecting entry points manually or automatically?

- If automatically, will you be ok with an automatic probe, or do you want a global load balancer?

- Are your routing tables world-wide ready to handle the possible cross-traffic?

Forced tunneling

When VPN clients connect, it is for the purpose of connecting to corporate resources, but they might still need to use Internet resources for various reasons. With traditional VPN technologies, a connecting client would typically have all traffic forced through the VPN connection once they were connected. Traffic would flow through the corporate network, and that was usually fine because, if the client wanted to do something private, such as a shopping expedition at www.VirusesAreUs.com, they could simply disconnect their VPN and do whatever they wanted.

With URA, things are not so simple. The URA connection is always on, with the client unable to simply disconnect, and so by default URA is configured for split tunneling. This means that the client computer has a setting that defines what traffic should go through the URA tunnel and what traffic should go straight into the Internet (via the user's ISP routers). This is the **Name Resolution Policy Table (NRPT)**, which we mentioned in the previous chapter. The NRPT would typically contain an instruction set approximately as follows:

URL	Action
`*.createhive.com`	Route through tunnel
`Location.createhive.com`	Connect directly
Everything else	Route through ISP

In reality, the table looks more as shown in the following screenshot:

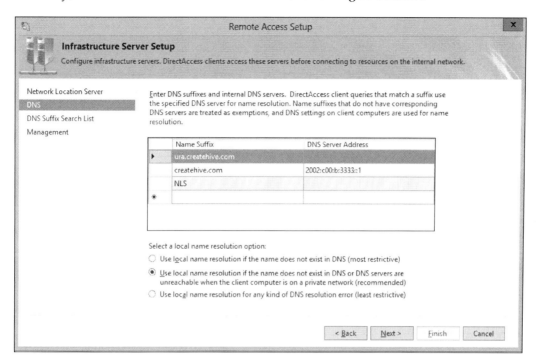

Some organizations would still prefer to configure their URA to have forced tunneling. Usually, the reason would be security. For example, government or military organizations would prefer that any and all Internet access by the client go through the corporate network so that it can be filtered or monitored.

This is a legitimate need for some organizations, but it's a decision that must not be taken lightly. When using forced tunneling, one must keep in mind that it can be extremely restrictive. With forced tunneling, the user has no way of communicating with anything directly, and so if there' s anything wrong with the URA setup, this presents a challenge, and you need to plan on how to provide connectivity to the Internet if the URA service is not functional. In addition, when forced tunneling is used, all connections go through URA, and by nature all will be IPv6 based. This means that if some client applications need to talk to the Internet servers only using IPv4, they may fail and you need to plan around that. If you are concerned about security, consider what it is that you're really trying to block. If you are concerned about clients browsing to websites and introducing malware, keep in mind that they might still get such malware browsing through the company's proxies, via e-mail or via a USB drive plugged into the computer. One can never achieve 100 percent protection, and locking your users in a cage may alienate them more than it would promise safety.

Another important factor to consider is the bandwidth usage costs and the additional load on the URA server for all non-business Internet traffic that users will be creating. Keep in mind that all URA client traffic is encrypted with IPsec, and so even simple Internet browsing adds more load on your URA server's CPU.

How much can my server handle?

Microsoft provides some information to help you assess the hardware that you'll need to meet your client needs, but ultimately, this depends on several factors that are not set in stone. Your users and how they use the connection can make a lot of difference, and the best way to get a clearer picture would be to deploy one server for a pilot group and monitor the server's responses with a performance monitoring tool.

Windows has such a tool built-in, and it's a good way to keep an eye on things. The idea is to set up a pilot and monitor the server over a period of time, and then calculate the capacity for your specific organization and users based on it. With a concrete set of data, one could calculate the server's true capacity and how far it will go. In the following screenshot, for example, you can see a typical graph collected by the **Performance Monitor** tool, allowing us to see how performance varies along a typical work-day:

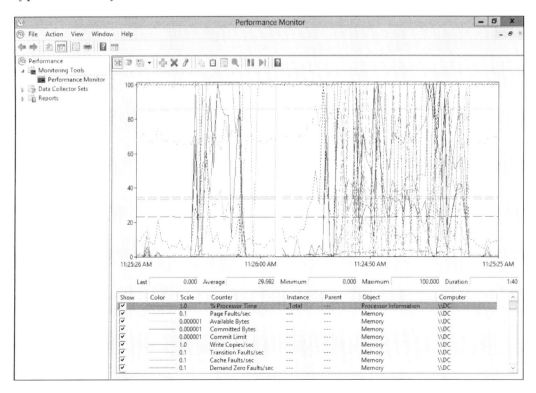

To configure the Performance Monitor for the counters that are related to URA, follow these steps:

1. Open the server manager tool.

2. From the **Tools** menu, select **Performance Monitor**.

3. Expand **Data Collector Sets**.

4. Right-click on **User defined** and select **New** and then select **Data Collector Set**.

5. Give the new collector a name of your liking.

6. Select **Create manually** and click on **Next**.

7. Check **Performance counter** and click on **Next**.

8. Set the interval to one minute.

9. Click **Add** and add the following items. For each, if possible, select **<All instances>**:
    - IPv4
    - IPv6
    - Memory
    - Network Interface
    - Objects
    - PhysicalDisk
    - Processor
    - System
    - TCPv4
    - TCPv6

10. Once done, click on **OK** and and then click on **FINISH**.

11. Right-click on the new collector and click on **START** to start it.

Since usage patterns typically vary over time, it would be ideal to record the performance over a period of at least 24 hours, or even a full week if you can. This will allow you to locate the peak usage times and observe the resource used during them. It will also provide you with invaluable information, such as what percentage of your deployed users actually use the service at various times. Based on these figures, you can see which resources are the most heavily used and estimate how many concurrent users the server would be able to handle. Keep in mind, of course, that some resource use is not, and sometimes there is no perfect correlation between the number of users and the actual resource. For example, if the CPU is at 11 percent utilization with two users, it doesn't mean the server can handle only 18 users before it implodes into a black hole. Also, make sure that you consider the use of all resources. You might find, for example, that the CPU and memory are in low utilization but the network stack is fully saturated. The latter may also mean that your server may be in good shape, but your connection to the ISP is at its maximum, or at any other component along the way.

Summary

This chapter introduced a lot of new concepts and things to think about before even installing your server. You might find yourself scratching your head a bit, not being sure which topology you should select and which features you really need. The good news is that you can start small and work your way up. Many of the scenarios are incremental, so you could start with a simple one and then add on things as you go along. For example, build a simple scenario, without PKI, and add it later, when you want to throw Windows 7 clients into the mix.

In the next chapter, we will discuss Group Policy in more detail and learn how to use it correctly for setting up your URA.

3
Preparing a Group Policy and Certificate Infrastructure

Having read through the planning guide in *Chapter 2, Planning a Unified Remote Access Deployment* by now, you will probably realize just how important **Group Policy** and **Certificates** are for Unified Remote Access. Group Policy is the road through which the connection settings travel to all your clients, and certificates are used for all the advanced scenarios.

In this chapter, we will discuss these topics with a higher level of detail. The topics at hand are as follows:

- Deploying GPO in an organization
- New features with Windows Server 2012 and Windows 8 Group Policy
- Planning group membership for URA clients and servers
- GPO management policies and authorities
- Managing GPO on URA servers and clients
- Basic GPO problems and troubleshooting
- Introduction to certificates and PKI
- Certificates used by URA
- Public versus private certificates
- Enterprise Certificate Authority versus Stand-alone Certificate Authority
- Root Certificate Authorities and subordinate Certificate Authorities

Deploying GPO in an organization

Group Policy was first introduced with the release of the Windows 2000 operating system. It is essentially a group of settings that are configured at the domain level by the administrator, and then applied to clients automatically. When users log in to computers which are domain members, these members apply the current Group Policy to themselves automatically, and it also gets updated automatically every 90 to 120 minutes (the actual update interval has a randomness factor, to prevent all stations updating at the same time, causing an overload on the network and servers). The result of this automation is that as long as the computers have a connection to the domain, they are updated with these settings. If the policy needs to be changed for any reason, the administrator makes the change at the domain level (using the **Group Policy Object Editor**) and he can know that within two hours all the servers and clients will be updated.

This chapter does not presume to be an all-out guide to Group Policy. This topic is complex, so if you would like to tackle this topic more deeply, we recommend reading *Group Policy: Fundamentals, Security, and the Managed Desktop*, Jeremy Moskowitz, Sybex. This 2.6lb, 936 page skyscraper of a book is not for the faint of heart, but will tell you anything and everything there is to know about the topic.

Here are some of the key concepts related to Group Policy that one needs to understand in order to have the right context as we explore how URA works and how it is implemented. This will help you put things together as we go along, as well as address and resolve Group Policy problems, if such arise.

Group Policy Management

The **Group Policy Management Console (GPMC)** is an administrative tool that comes on every domain controller. It's a graphic tool that allows the administrator to manage existing group policies. The following screenshot shows the tool on Windows Server 2012:

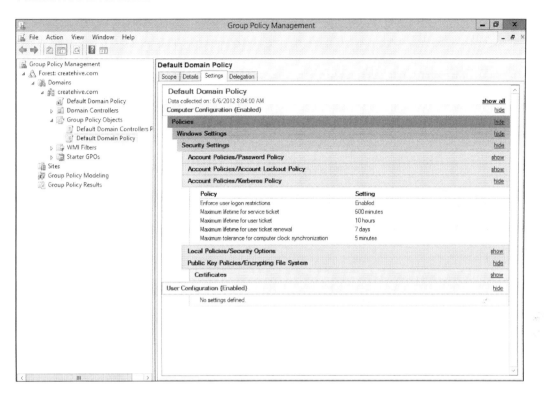

This tool can do a lot of things. It allows you to view existing policies and edit them, and create new ones, of course. Every domain comes with a built-in policy, which we can see in the previous screenshot. The **Scope** tab allows an administrator to "link" it to domains, sites, or **Organizational Units (OUs)**. It also allows you to configure specific **filtering** for a policy, which controls to which groups and users it applies to. You can also right-click on a policy to edit it, which opens the **Group Policy Management Editor** as shown in the following screenshot:

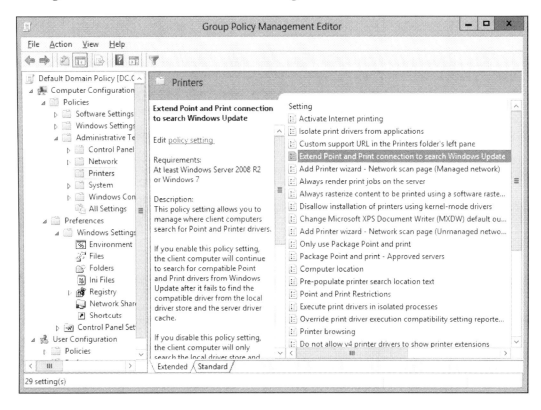

With the editor, you can see the complex tree of options that are in the policy, and configure each and every one you need. It also provides some help regarding each option and what it does. The options available with Group Policy are extensive, from simple stuff like what screensaver to use, to advanced assignment of registry entry collections.

Many administrators go their entire career without ever opening this tool, but knowledge is power, and if you browse through the tree, you might be astonished at the fine control you can achieve over some of the things your users do to destroy their computers. For example, you could block access to a specific drive, or prevent the users from opening the control panel.

In the context of Unified Remote Access, the policy settings to make URA work are all automatically generated and applied by the URA setup wizard, but you might need to view the policy itself, or its scope. This would typically be part of troubleshooting, so we will discuss this in more detail in *Chapter 10, Monitoring and Troubleshooting Unified Remote Access*.

Group Policy and the registry

Essentially, Group Policy is a collection of settings that are applied to the computer's **registry**. The Group Policy editor is a visual tool that shows these settings in a friendly manner. For example, you can edit the Group Policy `User Configuration/ Policies/Administrative Templates/Control Panel/Personalization/ Enable screen saver`, and when it's applied, it creates the registry key `HKCU/ Software/Microsoft/Windows/CurrentVersion/Group Policy Objects/<Your domain>/Software/Policies/Microsoft/Windows/Control Panel/Desktop/ ScreenSaveActive`. The actual locations in the policy settings tree and the registry differ between versions of Windows, so your specific settings may differ. If you are so inclined, you can download a reference document with detailed information about the various settings:

`http://www.microsoft.com/en-us/download/details.aspx?id=25250`

What this means, beyond the fascination we hope you develop with mining your registry, is that a user may be able to change or reverse settings you create by editing his own registry (unless, of course, you have enabled additional Group Policy settings that block editing the registry). This, to some degree, contradicts what we said earlier about the users being unable to damage their settings and destroy their URA connection. It's a lot harder to do, though, and in reality, it's extremely rare.

However, it's important to know that in most domain environments, even if the user does manage to counteract some settings, the computer will automatically refresh and re-apply the policy within a random time period between 90 and 120 minutes. If, however, the URA connection itself has been damaged, then the client won't have a way to refresh the policy (no corpnet connection, no Group Policy refreshes). However, as long as he can access the registry, it's possible to reverse any such damage manually, and you might want to get familiar with the registry branches that are related to the URA connection. Actually, you might even find yourself needing to intentionally "kill" the connection. For example, a URA connection might get tangled in a catch-22 situation, where the connection is working only partially. In such an interim state, it cannot connect to the domain over URA to update the policy, but neither when directly on the corporate network. We will discuss this situation in the troubleshooting section of *Chapter 10, Monitoring and Troubleshooting Unified Remote Access*.

Linking, scoping, and filtering policies

A Windows domain comes with a default policy, but you can create an unlimited additional number of policies. This can come in handy when you have a large and complex organizational structure, and you need different settings applied to different domains or different groups of computers or people. Each policy you create can be **linked**, **scoped**, and **filtered**.

Linking a policy refers to attaching a policy to a domain. You might link one policy to multiple domains, and link multiple policies to each domain. This is usually done when you create a policy. Until you link it to a domain, it's just floating there in active directory limbo, and doesn't affect anybody.

Scoping a policy refers to defining which users and groups the policy is applied to. A policy might be scoped for the entire domain, or to just specific people, depending on the need. For example, the URA policy is often scoped only to a certain group, whose membership is determined by someone such as yourself, or some other powerful being in a high place on the corporate food chain. You know how it is...if you keep it on a tight leash, people will clamor for your attention.

Filtering a policy is done by applying a **WMI filter**, which designates which computers should have the policy applied to them, based on system and hardware level parameters. For example, when configured by the **Getting Started wizard**, the URA policy is by default filtered to only mobile computers, because desktops which are domain members rarely leave the office and need remote access.

Policy replication

Group Policy is edited with the Group Policy editor, and stored in active directory. If your domain has more than one **domain controller**, then all of them need to fetch the updated version from active directory, and this is part of the domain **replication** process. The same process applies to any change that is made on the domain, such as the addition of new users.

Domain replication is an art form, because it needs to take into account things like where changes are made and how to let the updates flow across the network in a way that won't affect it negatively. The replication topology can be quite complicated, and needs to be taken into account with regards to URA as well. If, for example, you make changes to the URA policy, you need to either wait until it replicates across your domain before you expect it to start applying, or you might choose to force a replication. Naturally, the more complex your domain is, the more careful you need to be. If, for example, you make a change to Group Policy that should affect all URA clients, take into account that some may take a while to get updated. First, the change needs to replicate to their domain controller, and the time until their own refresh (which can be up to two hours) passes. Until then, the client is still using the old policy, for better or worse. During initial deployment of URA, you might find yourself twiddling your thumbs, waiting for the replication to complete, or doing a lot of forced ones, so plan ahead in case your domain might be negatively affected.

Manual updates

The URA setup wizard will create the URA policies for you, and that's a big relief as the settings are very detailed. However, there might come a time when you need to edit the URA policy manually, or combine your own policy with URA's. Naturally, you need to be careful not to create a conflict. If a policy in your domain contradicts the URA one, it may become very difficult to find the cause of the problem you are experiencing. Also, your policy may affect other settings that are unforeseen. For example, some organizations disable the Windows Firewall via policy to make room for a third party firewall solution. However, URA requires this service, so having it forcibly blocked prevented URA from working correctly.

There might also be times where you need to manually configure a URA setting that does not have a user-interface option in the URA wizards. Hopefully, these will be rare and far-between. In any case, we recommend you attempt such a thing only after having become seasoned with URA.

New features with Windows Server 2012 and Windows 8 Group Policy

Windows Server 2012 introduces a new feature for Group Policy, which allows an administrator to remotely trigger a Group Policy update at will. This is very useful, because until now, any update required the administrator to either wait between 1.5 to 2 hours for all domain computers to automatically update themselves, or manually run the update command on any computer that he wanted to have updated. Some clever administrators developed their own way of doing this using various automation and remote-management tools, but now this is built right into the operating system.

The feature, called **Group Policy Updates** works by remotely creating a **scheduled task** on each computer in the domain or group. The scheduled task is triggered to run within 10 minutes, with a random offset, so as to not hit your domain controllers with many computers updating at the same time. The task simply runs the **GPUPDATE /force** command, which performs the update.

In addition, the **Group Policy Management** console in Windows Server 2012 has a **Status** tab, which shows valuable information about the status of Group Policy in your domain as shown in the following screenshot:

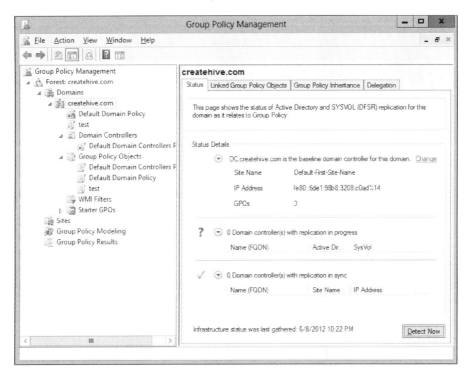

This status is related to the situation we discussed earlier, where you make changes to the policy, and need to wait for it to replicate to other domain controllers. The policy status shows you how many domain controllers are still performing replication, and how many completed it successfully, and additional information about the domain controllers themselves.

 There are additional improvements that also help with troubleshooting Group Policy, and you can read more about them in the following article available at: `http://technet.microsoft.com/en-us/library/jj574108.aspx`.

Planning group membership for URA clients and servers

Even if your organization is small, planning who will get to enjoy URA is important. From a technical perspective, deploying URA has some risks. We discussed the topic of the **Network Location Server (NLS)** in the *Preface*, and in case you missed it, deploying URA with a bad NLS could actually cause havoc. The URA clients use the NLS to detect whether they are on the corporate network or not. If they cannot contact it for some reason, they will think they are outside the network and attempt to initiate the URA connection. Establishing the connection from within the corporate network is not likely to work properly, unless you designed your routing specifically to handle it. If the URA connection is not working, this could lead to these clients being in total network **limbo**. They can't connect with the NLS, and keep trying to establish URA, but the lack of connectivity prevents them from seeing the local network, so you can't even reset their policy. If this hits a few test clients, it's not the end of the world, but if you deployed it to your entire user base, you might be looking at a phone-call tornado. For this reason, it's often best to limit the scope to a test group until everything is confirmed to be working perfectly.

From a political perspective, if your solution is not fully baked yet, because you just finished reading this chapter and are not in full control yet, you might also find yourself under attack. If many users are expecting this new development to improve their life, you would want to have to handle as few disappointed users as you can. For this reason, it's also best to start with some close friends, who are both technically savvy, and have a higher than average tolerance for problems with their connectivity.

As we said in the previous section, by default, the URA server sets a WMI filter to apply URA only to mobile computers, but we recommend that in addition to that, you create a group in active directory, and assign it only to a small group of users' machines as a **Pilot**. It would be best to put users from diverse departments in the company, so that different usage profiles are tested. Keep in mind that if you run into problems, it could be a few weeks until you figure it out, so plan your schedule and milestones accordingly. An initial pilot of two weeks would be an ideal starting point to do some troubleshooting, and if it all goes well, a bigger stretch of about a month will provide ample time to iron out all the kinks and reach a stable stage. It's also important to keep track of performance, so adding more users at this point and forward would be ideal on a weekly basis. For example, add another 10 percent of your users every week to achieve full coverage within about three to four months from the day you started.

How you actually organize the users is up to you, of course, and based on your corporate policy. This is not dissimilar to any other organizational task that you might have done, so your experience should serve you better than anything we can write here. If you're not sure, then the best practices of group membership would be best:

1. Place computers in Global groups.
2. Place Global groups in Domain Local groups.
3. Use the domain local group or groups in the scope of the URA policy.

Lastly, don't forget to figure out a way to notify the users that they are going to be using URA soon, with instructions detailing what it is, how it works, and how it affects their work. You might also want to provide a guide to opting-out or opting-in. Some users are always early-adopters and want to play with the latest toy. Others might be in the middle of a critical project, and cannot risk losing connectivity or suffering from any level of discomfort. Another good idea may be to survey the users routinely, rather than waiting for them to call in. You might find some minor issue that is not big enough to complain about by the pilot group, but may be a bigger deal when affecting dozens or even hundreds of people.

GPO management policies and authorities

Just because you're a Network Engineer or an IT Administrator doesn't necessarily mean you have the right to stick your fingers in the Group Policy pie. This is not uncommon in larger organizations who wish to have a tight control over people's access level. In fact, security best practices do dictate that power and control is distributed among several individuals so that the company has checks-and-balances. Just like our government is split into three bodies in order to restrict power, making sure an individual administrator has only limited power can provide some counter-measures, just in case the guy who runs things has a bad day and decides to barbeque some servers.

The practical aspect of this is that to deploy URA, someone will need the permissions to create the Group Policy objects. If your account has full permissions on the domain to do so, then you don't have much to worry about. During the setup, when it's time to create the policy, the setup wizard will create the policies, populate them with the appropriate settings, and create the domain links, the policy scopes and the WMI filter. For many organizations, this is really as simple as a mouse-click.

 If you don't have the necessary permissions, you are going to have to cooperate with someone who does, or have your permissions adjusted.

Some organizations may prefer that the URA wizard doesn't create new policies, but would rather push the settings into pre-existing policies. For example, this could be because of a naming convention, where you would rather want the policies to have a specific name rather than the generic **DirectAccess Server Settings**. In case this is something that you need to do, the URA configuration console allows you to do this, as shown in the following screenshot:

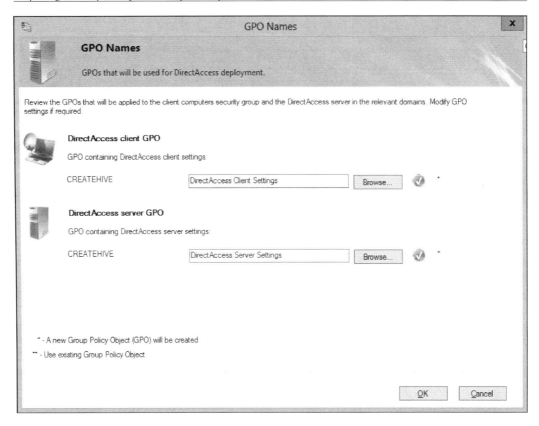

If you plan on doing this, then we should repeat a warning we mentioned in the previous section: the URA GPOs need to be applied carefully, so as not to override each other or be assigned to the wrong resources. The client policy must not be applied to the URA servers, and should not be applied to DCs or the NLS server either. Keep in mind that removing a policy is harder than applying it, because if the policy locks a computer's network access, it may be hard to get it to apply a new policy (or remove one). This is one of those times where it is *harder* to ask for forgiveness than permission, so be careful.

Managing GPO on URA servers and clients

Once you have finished your URA configuration and the new policies have been added to your domain, you might be lucky enough to rarely have to think about this topic again. However, in reality, as your network evolves, you're likely to have at least some administrative tasks to perform.

One kind of change you're likely to need to implement is the URA membership. With a successful deployment, upper management will usually want to deploy the service to more users, and maybe even to the entire organization, or other branches, partners, affiliates, and maybe even guests. When facing this, you need to have a good grasp of how Group Policy plugs into active directory at various levels. Earlier, we discussed the matter of linking GPOs to domains, sites, and OUs, and also defining or editing WMI filtering. These processes are important to practice, and it would also be a good idea to find some way to document the things you have done.

Another thing that's important to keep in mind is that even though you can make changes directly to Group Policy, you should strive to make these changes from within the URA management tool (or by using the URA PowerShell cmdlets) to modify the GPO. Editing the Group Policy directly allows you to reconfigure any and all URA settings, including linking and filtering, and will also push these changes into the domain for you. It's often tempting, especially for those seasoned with Group Policy, to adjust things directly in the policy; but doing so puts you at risk if you later make changes to the configuration within the URA console, and run over the other changes you made directly in the Group Policy. In such a situation, it's easy to lose track of the small stuff, and then find yourself with problems that you don't remember exactly where they started and how.

Protect your stuff

One important task that you need to consider is backing up your Group Policy. This is especially important if you have your own policies, and make frequent changes. Technically, you can always restore the URA Group Policy by simply going through the URA configuration, which isn't that complex, but that may still leave your other policies in pieces.

Backing up Group Policy can be done via the **Group Policy Management** console, and when you do so, you also back up a lot of important data:

- The settings inside the policies
- The policy's permissions
- Links to WMI filters

To perform a backup, right-click on the GPO container, and select **Back Up All...**:

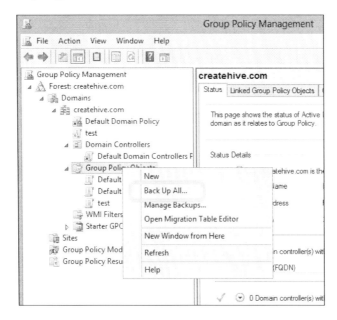

This process allows you to select where to store the backup, and will create a folder for each policy, containing XML files with the various settings and the template for the policy.

Restoring a backup is done from the **Manage Backups...** option (as shown in the previous screenshot, below the **Back Up All...** button). To restore a backup, follow these steps:

1. Open the **Manage Backups..** screen.
2. Pick the backup you want to restore,
3. Click on the backup, and then click on **Restore**.

One thing to know about this is that a restore doesn't link the GP to the domain, and you have to do this manually afterwards.

Basic GPO problems and troubleshooting

In complex domains, Group Policy problems are not unheard of, and it can put a real damper on your day. Troubleshooting URA related Group Policy problems can be more challenging than regular Group Policy issues, because your clients are typically not around and not only will you need to figure out what the heck the user wants over the phone or some cryptic email, you might find it real hard to even know if whatever steps you took have helped or not.

To be clear, we are not going to talk about URA specific troubleshooting here. Don't worry...there will be plenty of that in *Chapter 10, Monitoring and Troubleshooting Unified Remote Access*. For now, we want to discuss generic Group Policy issues, which is something you might need to do even before firing up the URA wizard in the first place.

Some more insight into GPOs

Before we can talk about the kind of problems you might face, it's important to get a good sense of what a GPO really is. People who work in IT are used to looking at folders and files, and configuration consoles that obfuscate them can be annoying. Technically, though, a Group Policy is indeed a collection of files. They are created and stored on your domain controller. Each policy has two parts:

- The **Group Policy Container (GPC)** object, which is stored in the policies folder of the system container in the active directory domain partition

- The **Group Policy Template (GPT)** folder, which is stored in the **SYSVOL** policies directory of the domain controller which is the PDC emulator for the domain

Each GPO has a **GUID**, which has been highlighted in the following screenshot, and which is used to identify and handle the policy:

You can even open the SYSVOL folder on the domain controller (c:\windows\ SYSVOL\sysvol\<your domain>\policies\<GUID>) and observe the files that comprise the policy. For example, the registry.pol file contains registry settings that are part of the policy as shown in the following screenshot:

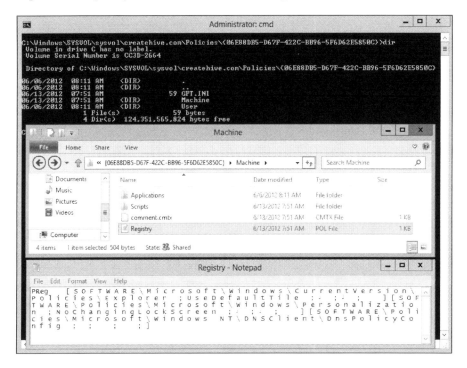

In the **Details** tab of the **Group Policy Management** console, you may have also noticed that lines no. 5 and 6 show a **User version** and a **Computer version** (set to **2** and **4** in the screenshot before the previous one). These numbers indicate the number of times the policy has been changed. Any time you edit the policy and make changes to it, the number advances for the part of the policy you edited. This is important to keep in mind, because unless you write down everything you do, that's the only way to keep track. This is especially true if there are multiple people in your organization who fiddle with Group Policy.

One specific situation where the policy number becomes very important is if you suspect a client isn't receiving the policy. If you remember from previous sections, domain computers trigger an automatic update of Group Policy every 90 to 120 minutes, so whenever you create a new policy or update one, it will take a while for it to apply. Unless you were waiting for a chance to watch the extended version of Lord of the Rings, most people aren't big fans of sitting around and waiting, and would prefer to trigger an update right away. One way of doing this is running the command GPUPDATE on the client, and another is to use Windows Server 2012's new feature to trigger the update automatically. This is done by right-clicking on a Group Policy container and selecting **Group Policy Update** as shown in the following screenshot:

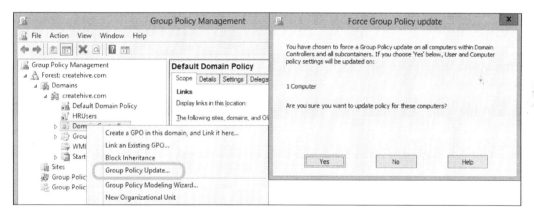

This will automatically create a scheduled task on all affected computers, which would run GPUPDATE /Force on the client within the next 10 minutes, making it pull any and all updates.

For full reference of the GPUPDATE command, visit http://technet.microsoft.com/en-us/library/bb490983.aspx.

Once a policy update has commenced, you might need to check if a specific client has successfully received and applied a policy, and for that, the command GPRESULT is useful. You would typically run the command with the /H parameter, which sets it to produce an HTML-formatted report showing extensive details about the policies that have been applied. In the following screenshot, you can see a snippet of the full report. This snippet shows that the **Default Domain Policy** has been applied, and the **HRusers** policy has not (because its scope did not match). You can also see which revision of the policy is in use, which would allow you to confirm the latest version was indeed applied...or if there's something wrong in there somewhere as shown in the following screenshot:

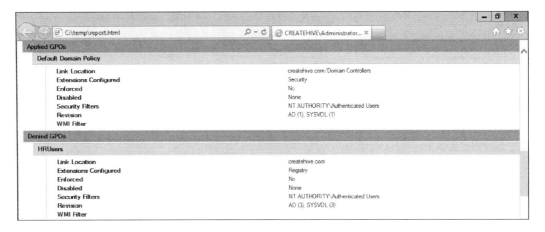

The same report would typically have a sizeable amount of data, which includes a full listing of every setting the policies contain, info about the WMI filtering, errors encountered, and more. All in all, a very useful diagnostic tool that you'll probably find yourself falling in love with. For full reference of this command, visit http://technet.microsoft.com/en-us/library/bb490915.aspx.

Diagnosing and fixing Group Policy problems

If something is failing with your Group Policy system, which would be indicated by errors in the GPRESULT report, or when running the GPUPDATE command, you're going to have to look further and deeper. Unless the error is very specific and well known (such as the ones listed here http://4sysops.com/archives/troubleshooting-group-policy-part-6-common-problems) the first place to look is in the **Event Viewer** administrative tool. In the **Event Viewer**, policy related issues would show up under **Application and Services Logs/Directory Services**, and would have the source of KCC. You should also look under **DFS replication** for events with the source of NTFRS.

If the event viewer shows no clear signs of trouble, a good place to start is with higher-level domain troubleshooting. Windows Server comes with a tool called **DCDIAG**. This tool scans active directory and can reveal many types of problems, as well as fix some of them. For this reason, it's considered to be one of the most powerful and important tools in any administrator's toolbox. The tool is shown in the following screenshot:

```
Administrator: cmd

C:\Windows\System32>dcdiag

Directory Server Diagnosis

Performing initial setup:
   Trying to find home server...
   Home Server = DC
   * Identified AD Forest.
   Done gathering initial info.

Doing initial required tests

   Testing server: Default-First-Site-Name\DC
      Starting test: Connectivity
         ......................... DC passed test Connectivity

Doing primary tests

   Testing server: Default-First-Site-Name\DC
      Starting test: Advertising
         ......................... DC passed test Advertising
      Starting test: FrsEvent
         ......................... DC passed test FrsEvent
      Starting test: DFSREvent
         ......................... DC passed test DFSREvent
      Starting test: SysVolCheck
         ......................... DC passed test SysVolCheck
      Starting test: KccEvent
         ......................... DC passed test KccEvent
      Starting test: KnowsOfRoleHolders
         ......................... DC passed test KnowsOfRoleHolders
      Starting test: MachineAccount
         ......................... DC passed test MachineAccount
      Starting test: NCSecDesc
         ......................... DC passed test NCSecDesc
      Starting test: NetLogons
         ......................... DC passed test NetLogons
      Starting test: ObjectsReplicated
         ......................... DC passed test ObjectsReplicated
      Starting test: Replications
         ......................... DC passed test Replications
      Starting test: RidManager
         ......................... DC passed test RidManager
      Starting test: Services
         ......................... DC passed test Services
      Starting test: SystemLog
         ......................... DC passed test SystemLog
      Starting test: VerifyReferences
         ......................... DC passed test VerifyReferences


   Running partition tests on : ForestDnsZones
      Starting test: CheckSDRefDom
         ......................... ForestDnsZones passed test CheckSDRefDom
      Starting test: CrossRefValidation
         ......................... ForestDnsZones passed test CrossRefValidation
```

The tool, of course, has multiple options to perform deeper checks and various fixes, and you can find full reference at http://technet.microsoft.com/en-us/library/cc731968(v=ws.10).aspx. Even if everything is working perfectly fine, we recommend running this tool on a routine basis, so you can become aware of potential issues early, before your users notice.

If your domain is humming along fine, the next thing to look into is **replication**. A common situation is where the policies themselves are okay, but they are not replicating from one DC to others. Replication is one of the primary functions of Windows Server, of course, and affects a lot more than Group Policy. Windows Server comes with a built-in replication administration tool called REPADMIN. Running this tool with the parameters /replsummary and /showrepl allows you to view diagnostic information about the replication status. You can also use the tool to view the replication queue, trigger a sync on all domain controllers, and much more. For full reference of this command, visit http://technet.microsoft.com/en-us/library/cc770963(v=ws.10).aspx.

Yet another "fix it for me" tool is called...well...Gpfixup. Yeah, if only everything in life was that straightforward, huh? Where's "CarEngineFixUp" when you need it? Anyway, this tool, as its name implies, searches and fixes various issues with Group Policy. It can help with problematic links between Group Policy and your domain, and their dependencies on DNS and NetBios names. For a full reference visit: http://technet.microsoft.com/en-us/library/cc816615(v=ws.10).aspx

Client-specific Group Policy issues

If diagnosing stuff at the domain level shows that everything is fine, and most clients work well, then whatever issue you're dealing with may be a client-specific issue. In reality, many administrators would prefer not to invest their time in digging into the guts of the operating system, and would rather simply re-image the computer, but in case you prefer solving problems, here is some further information and suggestions.

When troubleshooting client GPO issues, you must keep in mind that proper communications with the domain is the key to everything. When Group Policy isn't working correctly, the first thing to check is domain communications. Essentially, when you log in to a computer, it verifies your credentials against a domain controller, but occasionally, this process may fail. Possible reasons for the failure are:

- The computer account has expired in the domain
- The computer's clock isn't synchronized with the domain
- There is something blocking the network connection at some level

In theory, Windows clients are supposed to inform you that there's something wrong, but they are also designed to cache the domain profile, and if the communication breakage is deep enough, they might just assume you're off the network and just log you on locally.

One way to know if the computer was actually logged on is using the NLTEST command, which is included with all Windows clients. You run the command with the parameter /sc_query:<your domain name>, and if it returns an error, something is wrong.

Another way to check is using the KLIST command. It lists the Kerberos tickets that the client currently has. It's normal for a client to have more than one ticket, and the tickets have specific start and end times, which can indicate the status. If there are no tickets, then the client is not really logged on, of course. Also, the start time of the ticket is supposed to match the most recent login, so if it's different, that may indicate a problem too. As you can see in the following screenshot, the last line in the ticket points to which **KDC (Kerberos Distribution Center)** was used to log in and issue the tickets.

In the following screenshot, you can see an example of the output of the KLIST command, showing a valid Kerberos ticket, and the output of a successful NLTEST command and a failed one:

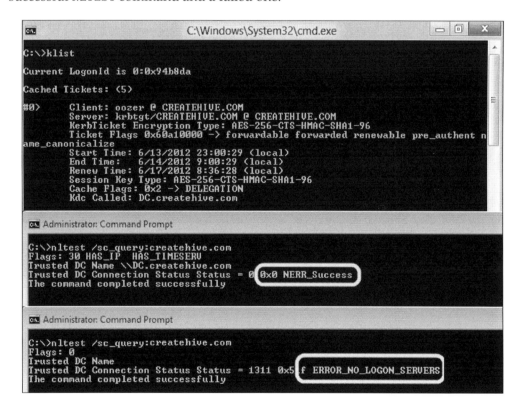

If this shows that the client hasn't logged on, then it calls for networking or domain membership troubleshooting. Sometimes, this happens because of a time synchronization issue—if the client's local time is different than the one set on the domain controllers, this would prevent a successful login. Another option is that some software is blocking communications, such as some security software or some malware. If the computer has not been active for a while, then it could be simply that the computer account has expired, and all it would take to fix it is disjoining the computer from the domain and re-joining it.

A situation that is pretty rare, but has been known to happen is some kind of corruption to the computer's registry that prevents Group Policy from applying, or causes it to apply only partially. This could be quite challenging, as the registry is one of the most complex and intricate storage containers out there. If it got corrupted, you're not very likely to succeed in repairing it on your own, but you could start by examining it, and seeing if anything looks weird. The area in the registry where Group Policy is stored is at `HKEY_CURRENT_USER\Software\Policies` and `HKEY_LOCAL_MACHINE\Software\Policies`. The former is the user settings, and the latter is the computer settings. Alternatively, some applications may choose to use `HKEY_CURRENT_USER\Software\Microsoft\Windows\CurrentVersion\Policies` and `HKEY_LOCAL_MACHINE\Software\Microsoft\Windows\Currentversion\Policies` (user and computer settings, respectively). Rather than digging into these manually, you might consider using a commercial level tool for scanning and repairing the registry such as **Advanced SystemCare** by **IObit** or **WinASO Registry Optimizer** by **X.M.Y. International**.

Introduction to certificates and PKI

Plenty of books have been written about digital certificates, so we won't go too deep into the concept, but it's important to lay down some ground work, so that we are all on the same page about this topic.

PKI stands for **Public Key Infrastructure**, and this refers to the keys used to encrypt and decrypt data that is exchanged between computers over a non-secure medium such as the public internet. The science of encrypting data goes back a long way. (Remember using Pig Latin as a kid? Esyay, atthay isway away udecray ormfay ofway encryptionway!)

Encryption is based on a simple concept. You want to send data to someone without anyone else being able to read it. You take the data, and change it in a way that only you and the future recipient know. If that data falls into the wrong hands, it will look like meaningless garbage. The intended recipient, though, knows how to reverse the process and read it.

With computers, encryption is done by taking a **key**, which is a very long and unique number, and using it to perform a mathematical function on the data, resulting in encrypted data that appears to be meaningless. To decrypt the data, you do the opposite, with the same number, and obtain the original data. For example, you can convert the word "riddle" to a numerical sequence based on the order of letters in the alphabet, and come out with the sequence 18,9,4,4,12,5. A very simple encryption would be adding a known number to each number in the sequence, so if you add 50, you end up with 68, 59, 54, 54, 62, 55. With this example, 50 is our key, and to convert the message back, you simply subtract the key from each number. Naturally, that level of secrecy wouldn't be too hard to break, but real key-based digital encryption is much more complicated. This form of encryption is referred to as **Symmetric encryption**, because the same key is used for encoding and decoding the data.

In old-school espionage, agents would be sent out with decryption sheets or devices, but on the internet, data needs to be encrypted and decrypted with the sender and recipient never meeting, and for that, **Asymmetric encryption** has been developed.

Asymmetric encryption

Asymmetric encryption uses a very advanced mathematical formula that uses *two different* encryption keys, instead of one. One key is used for the encryption process, and the other for the decryption. This is called asymmetric because the encryption and decryption are not the same, and the math is designed such that if you perform the encryption using one key, only the other key can be used for the decryption.

The two keys are referred to as the *public* key, and the *private* key. The public key is, as its name suggests, public and is given out freely. The private key, of course, is the opposite, and is kept very secret. When two computers need to communicate securely, computer 1 retrieves the public key from computer 2, and encrypts data using it. It then sends that data to computer 2. Because of the asymmetric nature of this encryption, even if that data falls into the wrong hands, it's useless, because one would need the matching private key (from computer 2) to decrypt the data.

Computers can do the decryption and encryption pretty fast, but the asymmetric decryption and encryption is actually quite difficult and time consuming even for modern day quad-core CPUs, and so to make things easier, the initiating computer actually generates a symmetric encryption key. Symmetric encryption and decryption are much easier for computers to do, and so the initiating computer encrypts the symmetric key itself, and sends it to the target computer. The target computer decrypts the message using its secret private key, and obtains the symmetric key. Then, for the duration of the session, both computers use the symmetric key to encrypt and decrypt data.

There is one more side to this...trust. Any computer can generate a public key, so how can computer 1 trust that computer 2 is really who it says it is? When you browse to your bank's website, how can you be sure it's not some other website that looks the same? For that, we have **Digital Certificates**.

Digital certificates

A digital certificate, like a real-world certificate, is a way to prove one's identity. In the real world, proving one's identity is based on showing something that's produced by a trusted body, and is hard to forge, and the same goes in the digital world.

A digital certificate is issued by a special server that is operated by world-wide trusted providers such as **VeriSign**, **Thawte**, **Valicert**, or **Entrust**. Even if you never heard of them, every computer comes prepared to accept their digital certificates and consider them to be trusted. You can also install your own **certificate authority** and issue certificates to your computers. Certificate providers typically charge a significant amount of money for their service, so setting up your own can save you some dough, but may make things a bit more complicated for other reasons.

A digital certificate is issued to a specific computer, and that computer will present it when contact is initiated to it, in order to prove its identity. This happens, for example, when you browse to a server over a secure channel (**HTTPS**). When you do so, your browser checks that the server name in the URL you typed matches the one listed in the certificate presented by that server, and will warn you that something's fishy if the certificate isn't presented, doesn't match, or bad in some other way. This is like a TSA agent looking at your passport and asking for your name. If you say a different name than what appears on the passport…you're busted.

The thing that makes a digital certificate trust-worthy is the fact that it is signed by the body that produced it. Remember the whole asymmetric stuff we mentioned earlier? It comes into play here as well. The certificate starts out as a simple piece of text listing the details, like the computer's name and the validity date. Then, the computer that issues the certificate produces a **hash** of that content. The hash is a number that's a result of a computation done on the text of the certificate, so that each certificate has a unique result that's not reversible. This means you can calculate the hash from the certificate, but not vice-versa. Then, finally, the entire thing is encrypted with the issuer's private key. Because the encryption is asymmetric, the public key can be used to decrypt the certificate, and since every computer comes with the public keys of all the major providers, every computer can decrypt and examine the certificate without any additional configuration. If the content of the signed certificate changes by a single bit, it will make it invalid, because the hash is unique to the original content. No one else can forge a known provider's certificates, because no one has the provider's private key.

Authorities, roots, and the trust chain

As we said earlier, a digital certificate is issued by a certificate authority, which can be either a public provider or a privately owned server. In both cases, just because someone gave you a certificate doesn't automatically make it okay. An American TSA agent at the airport will trust a passport issued by the government of Turkey not because he likes thinly sliced poultry, but because he has been instructed and trained to trust certain governments and not others (like Never Never Land, which one should never never trust).

In the world of PKI, a certificate verifies identity, and so even the Certificate Authority itself needs to prove its identity via a certificate of its own. When you install a Certificate Authority (CA) server, part of that process is for the CA to generate a "root" certificate which proves its own identity. Then, someone needs to install that certificate in a special container on computers that will be dancing in this party. When this is done, the process is as follows:

1. Computer 1 wants to connect to computer 2 securely, and initiates the connection.

2. Computer 2 presents its certificate. That certificate was created by CA 1.

3. Computer 1 examines the certificate, and looks for who issued it.

4. Computer 1 examines its own root certificate container (the official name is "Trusted Root Certification Authorities" folder) to see if it has the root certificate for CA 1.

5. If it doesn't, it won't trust the certificate. If it does, there are additional checks, which we will discuss soon.

When dealing with certificates provided by third party providers, you don't need to install the root certificate from the provider…it's built into Windows. If you open your certificate store (you can do so by clicking on **Start**, typing in `certmgr.msc` and pressing *Enter*), you can see a long list of root certificates that Windows comes with as shown in the following screenshot:

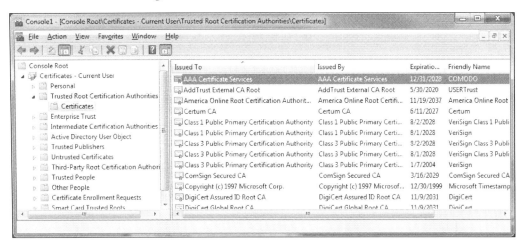

As you can see, these belong to several well-known providers such as **Comodo**, **UserTrust**, **AOL**, **Centrum**, **Verisign**, **ComSign**, **DigiCert**, and there are a few dozen others there. You can also see, from the **Issued By** column, that they all issued their own certificates (as expected). Also, the **Expiration Date** column lists dates that are very far ahead in the future (indeed, if you're somehow able to continue using your Windows 7 computer for the next 16 years without ever updating it, you'll be running into trouble accessing certain websites).

This system, where a certificate authority has a root certificate to prove its own identity, and it issues certificates to other servers, is known as a **trust chain**. Occasionally, you might see certificates that have a more complex chain, where a root CA certifies an **intermediate** CA. In that situation, the verification is a tad more complicated for the computer, though the user doesn't feel a difference. Some organizations need a more complex structure to support the organizations' complexity and management constraints. For example, if an organization has world-wide branches, they might prefer to divvy-up the work with intermediate CAs that are managed by local administrators, rather than have one CA that's worked to exhaustion (or...risking the guy who has to click "issue" for each request going postal). You can view a certification path by opening a certificate from the **Certificate** management console, and going to the **Certification Path** tab as shown in the following screenshot:

In the previous screenshot you can see that the root authority (**Createhive Corporate Root CA**) is okay, but the intermediate authority is not, and showing a red **X**. This also makes the certificate itself bad, because the issuing authority is not trusted for whatever reason.

Certificate revocation and expiration

Certificates are issued by CAs all the time, and they are usually valid for a period of a year or two, and occasionally longer or shorter. When a certificate expires, one needs to have it reissued, and that's pretty simple and easy. If it's a commercial certificate, you simply go to the provider's site, pay up whatever crazy amount they want, and get a new certificate. If it's your own CA, you can usually right-click on the certificate even before it expired, and ask for a renewal:

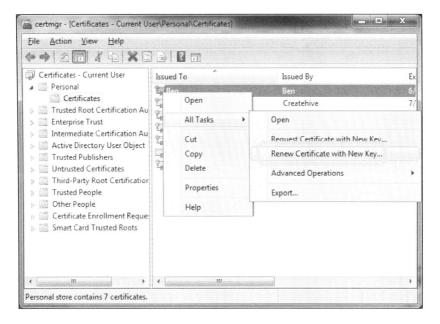

However, there may come a time when you might need to **revoke** a certificate. For example, if you issue one to a user who has left the company, you might want to revoke his certificate in order to make sure he doesn't use it to connect to any corporate resources (usually, closing his domain account would suffice, but it can't hurt to be a tad extra careful). Commercial certificate providers also do this, if a customer decides to cancel after having purchased a certificate, or if a certificate was issued with errors or by mistake, or if a certificate is superseded by a newer one. When a certificate has to be revoked, the provider needs to let potential clients know of this, and this is done with a **Certificate Revocation List (CRL)**.

The CRL is a list of serial numbers of certificates that have been revoked, and every certificate provider publishes that list on the public internet. One of the fields on a certificate is the **CDP**, which stands for **CRL Distribution Points**. When you look at a certificate's details, you can see the location of the list, and this could sometimes be multiple locations. Here's the URL for a typical VeriSign certificate, and a chunk of the list itself:

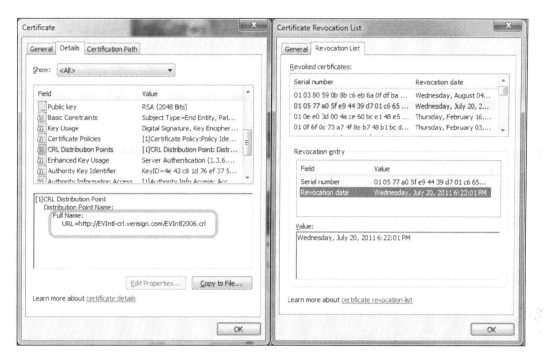

Certificate providers update their list regularly, by replacing the `.CRL` file on the web server that is hosting it. If you have your own CA server, you'll have to worry about that too, because usually, a client that checks for a certificate is also designed to check the CRL, and make sure the certificate being asked to trust hasn't been revoked. One challenge with that is that for the whole thing to work, the client will have to have access to where the CRL is stored. Your CA is typically going to be on your corporate network, so if the client is out on the public internet, you'll need to figure out a way to bridge that gap. One option, of course, is to publish the website to the internet. Another option is to configure the CA to not use a CRL at all, although that is quite insecure and we strongly recommend against it.

Certificate intended purpose

Another property of a certificate is the **intended purpose**. When you create a certificate, one of its properties is the **Enhanced Key Usage**, which governs what the certificate can be used for. For example, a certificate might be intended for proving the identity of a server, and would therefore have **Server Authentication** listed in its Enhanced Key Usage field. Various usages have specific **Object Identifier (OID)**, which are represented as a number like **1.3.6.1.5.5.7.3.1** in the following example:

When a computer presents a certificate to another computer, the intended purpose is checked to make sure it's appropriate. This is important, because the body that issues the certificate issues it with certain configuration options such as key length, and needs to be sure it's used appropriately.

Certificate validation

When a secure communication process that uses a certificate starts, there are several things that happen as part of the certificate validation. It's very important to understand them, so that you can make sure it goes smoothly for everyone, and fix things if it doesn't. These are the things the computer checks:

- The certificate is not corrupted
- The server's name or URL matches the one on the certificate
- The certificate is issued by a trusted authority (which includes the root or intermediate trust chain)
- The certificate has not expired
- The certificate's intended purpose corresponds to the kind of action that is being performed
- The certificate has not been revoked by the authority that issued it

This is not necessarily the order in which these are checked—that changes depending on the implementation of the specific software that is doing the checking. We already discussed the trust checking, but the checker also decrypts the certificate using the CA's public key to check if the certificate is intact and hasn't been altered. The certificate is decrypted using the public key, and then its content is hashed and compared to the hash that came with it. If it's a match, this means the certificate hasn't been tampered with.

In addition, the validity and expiration dates are checked, to check if the certificate has expired or isn't valid yet. Now, the CRL locations are read off the CDP field of the certificate, and the list is downloaded from one of the locations. If the CDP has more than one CRL location listed, the software would start with the first, and move on to the next if it's inaccessible. If all are inaccessible, then the certificate cannot be confirmed to be valid, and the software would reject it as invalid.

Another check is done by comparing the name of the resource that has the certificate to the name listed on the certificate. If the certificate is for a website, then the URL of the website would be compared. If there's no match, the software may decide to reject it, or show some kind of warning. Some certificates are designated to match more than one name. These are referred to as **SAN certificates**. SAN stands for **Subject Alternative Name**, and SAN certificates have a special field that lists the various names the certificate has. A SAN certificate can be installed on several servers, and it's a good way to save money, as it would cost less than a bunch of separate certificates (just like buying your certificates at Costco!). Another special type of certificate is a **wildcard certificate**. With a wildcard certificate, part of the name is replaced with a star, and the star covers any string. In the following screenshot, you can see a wildcard certificate on the left, and a SAN certificate on the right:

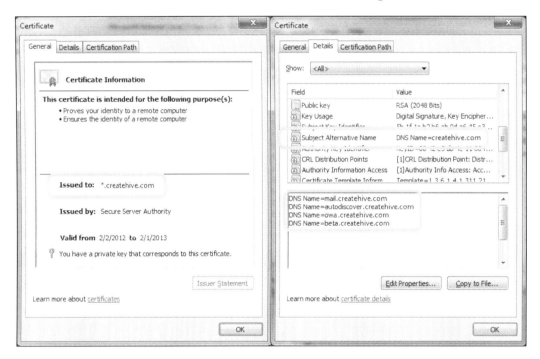

Naturally, part of the check is for the certificate's intended purpose. As we said earlier, not all certificates can be used for any purpose, and that is determined when the certificate is created. In the previous screenshot, the certificate on the left shows that it can be used by a computer to prove its identity to another computer, or, if received from another computer, can be used to ensure its identity is legitimate.

We said earlier that if the CRL is inaccessible, the software might reject it. It's important to know, though, that the decision of whether to accept a certificate or not is not set in stone. Different software check different things, and react differently to problems. **Internet Explorer**, for example, will issue a warning if the certificate name doesn't match the server, but will allow the user to continue, if he so chooses. **Firefox** issues a similar warning, but requires a more elaborate process of setting an exception to allow access. Other situations may not show any warning and block access completely, and we will see some examples of this with URA later on.

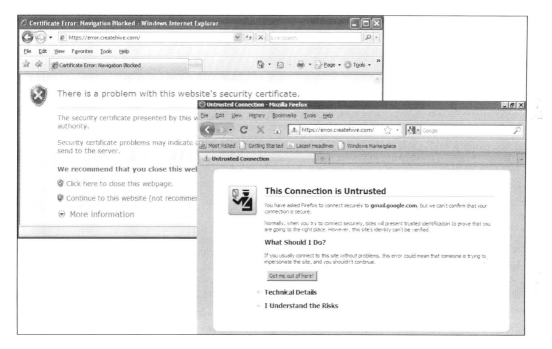

Certificates used by URA

When deploying URA with a full PKI, you are going to require several certificates:

- A certificate for each client computer, which has an *intended purpose* of **Client and Server authentication**

- A certificate for the URA server (for IPsec authentication), which also has an intended purpose of **Client and Server authentication**

- A certificate for the IP-HTTPS connection, which has the intended purpose of **Web server** or **server authentication**

- A certificate for the Network Location Server (NLS), which also has the intended purpose of **Web server** or **server authentication**
- A Trusted Root CA cert to issue the client certificates presented by clients

The client certificates are often the most challenging, because you need to set up a certificate authority server in your domain, and then create and deploy a certificate to each and every computer that will be connecting to URA. Luckily, active directory offers **Auto-Enrollment**, which will take care of this automatically, so once you've set up the infrastructure properly, you should be fine.

The second certificate is used by the URA server itself when establishing IPsec connections with clients, and is pretty simple. It will have to meet some requirements, but can also be deployed by your internal CA.

The IP-HTTPS certificate is a bit trickier. It will be used only by clients that are connecting using this method (which would happen when they cannot use 6to4 or Teredo...if you don't recall what those are, re-read the *Preface*, where these concepts and technologies were introduced). An IP-HTTPS connection, as its name suggests, uses HTTPS, and establishing this connection requires the server to present a certificate just like any regular secure server on the web requires a certificate. The IP-HTTPS certificate can be created by your internal CA, or acquired from an external certificate provider.

The NLS server certificate is probably the simplest of them all. When clients try to contact the NLS server for the purpose of checking their location (inside the corporate network or outside it), they attempt to establish a simple HTTPS web connection to that server. As any HTTPS connection, it requires a simple web server certificate. Such a certificate can be purchased from an external provider, or issued by your own CA, and since the server only needs to be available inside the corporate network, it makes things easier with regards to publishing the CRL.

Public versus private certificates

An important decision regarding these certificates is whether to deploy them using your own internal certificate authority server, or whether to purchase a certificate from an external provider such as Verisign and Thawte. We discussed some of the differences earlier in this chapter, and also in *Chapter 2, Planning a Unified Remote Access Deployment* but if you're not sure yet, here are the considerations again, briefly:

- All the certificates can be issued by an internal CA, and that saves money, but may complicate things, as you need to make sure the CRL is published and accessible by the clients for all the certificates

- If publishing the CRL is difficult or impossible for your organization, you can use a third party provider for the IP-HTTPS connection, and that makes things a bit simpler

- The IPsec certificates (both for the URA server and clients) need to be issued by your internal CA, and there's no getting around that

With most deployments that require a full PKI, organizations typically prefer to use their CA for all the certs and don't rush to dump any more dough on external providers. This does mean you need to set up publishing for the CDP of your CRLs.

Publishing a CDP can be tricky in some organizations, because it requires you to open up unauthenticated access to something produced by one of the most sensitive servers you have. You need to find a way to deliver these important CRLs to the internet, without risking anyone hacking through into the CA itself. To do this safely, it's important to remember that you can configure your CA to push the CRL to anywhere you want. Truly, by default it would just drop these CRLs on its own hard drive, but all that can be changed. A good way to configure this would be to place a server in your dematerialized zone, with a shared folder on which your CA server can drop the CRL files. Then, you publish that folder as a website through your corporate firewall. To make this as secure as possible, make sure the website is published securely using a decent firewall, and with restrictive settings (for example, set the site to not allow scripting or code execution) and make sure the share to which the CA pushes the CRL is also restricted so that only the CA server can write to it remotely. Alternatively, configure the CA to put the CRL on a read-only share on itself, and write a batch file to pull those from the CA into the published web server.

Once you have decided how you want to configure CRL publishing, adjust the CA configuration accordingly. The **Extensions** tab in the CA configuration allows you to set to which folder the CA will push the CRL files to, and also to set the URL that will appear on the certificate's CDP (that would be whatever URL you will publish the CRL files under). To learn more on configuring the extensions settings on a Microsoft CA server, visit the following page:

```
http://technet.microsoft.com/en-us/library/ee649168(v=ws.10).aspx
```

Enterprise Certificate Authority versus Standalone Certificate Authority

When you install a certificate authority server, you can install it as either an **Enterprise CA**, or a **Standalone CA**. As the name implies, an Enterprise CA integrates into your organization's active directory infrastructure, and is designed to make deployments of certificates to all computers as easy as possible. It offers the following advantages:

- The CA's Root certificate is automatically deployed to all clients. With a standalone CA, you would have to do that manually.

- It comes with pre-existing certificate templates, which allow you to select the one you need, rather than create it manually.

- Certificate generation is authenticated and secure, which allows it to be completed automatically, rather than the administrator having to approve each certificate request manually.

- The certificate subject (which would be the computer name for the IPsec certificates you need) is generated automatically, rather than the user providing it manually.

- You can configure auto-enrollment, so the entire certificate deployment process is fully automatic.

So, as you can see, using an Enterprise CA is the easiest and most convenient choice for pretty much any organization. If you do need to use a stand-alone CA for some reason, you will need to have each client manually request a certificate, and then you, or some other administrator, will have to approve the request. The user-side of this is typically done via a website installed by the CA wizard on the CA server. The website wizard does require the user to provide some information, such as the computer name, so make sure you perform this task for your users, or provide them with sufficient guidance as to what information to provide.

To learn more about Stand-alone CAs versus Enterprise CAs, read the following TechNet article:

`http://technet.microsoft.com/en-us/library/cc732368.aspx`

Root Certificate Authorities and Subordinate Certificate Authorities

When installing the Certificate Authority role, another choice you have to make is whether to install it as a **root CA** or **subordinate CA**. Earlier we discussed how sometimes organizations use intermediate CA to help keep things tidy and organized, and a subordinate CA is exactly that. For most organizations, the scale is not sufficient to require anything more than a single CA, so you would simply install a root CA. If your organization spans multiple sites or geographic locations, you might need to design an infrastructure of servers, with a subordinate CA at each location (however, let's face it...if your organization is that large, you probably know a lot about certificate infrastructure design already and don't need this chapter).

Another consideration that might drive you to deploy subordinate CAs is availability. If your CA is a single server, then it introduces a single point of failure. In most deployments, this wouldn't be a big problem, assuming you would be backing up the server as you would any other. After all, certificates are typically good for a long time, so even if the CA server is down for a few days, it wouldn't impact many people. If your company policy dictates that any server has to have a live backup, then your only option is to install at least one subordinate CA to back up your root CA.

Using a subordinate CA improves your security as well. The reason is that if the Root CA is compromised you have to rebuild it and reissue all the certificates for your entire organization. If, however, you use a subordinate CA to issue the actual certificates, it's safer and easier to recover. In such a situation, the Root CA itself is kept segregated (or even turned off) in a secure location.

Summary

Ultimately, there's a lot more to know about Group Policy, and some people spend years mastering its every knob and level. Unified Remote Access, for the most part, requires understanding of the Group Policy and Certificate infrastructure and concepts, but with any luck, you won't need to fiddle with this a lot after your initial deployment. However, do try to keep at least the basic principles in your head, and we also hope this discussion made you more interested in taking advantage of some of the things Group Policy can offer you and your organization. Certificates, on the other hand, are required for all the advanced scenarios for URA, as well as deploying URA to Windows 7 clients, so this information will be of high value as we go further into the innards of URA.

In the next chapter, we will finally go into the actual tasks of deploying URA. We will see the configuration wizard and console, and see how the various options can be implemented.

4

Installing and Configuring the Unified Remote Access Role

Now that we have finished going through the various considerations and planning options, the time has come to take a dive into the real world. In this chapter, we will learn how to install and configure Unified Remote Access, and deploy the basic scenarios.

The topics we will cover in this chapter are as follows:

- Adding the URA role
- Configuring the basic URA scenario
- Editing the configuration
- Network Location Server
- Configuring the Name Resolution Policy Table
- Enabling load balancing

Adding the URA role

The URA server role poses very few requirements, technically. All you have to do is add it, as you would add any other role. The wizard still runs through no less than 13 pages, but unless you intend to add additional roles in the same go, you can simply step through everything quickly. As opposed to some other roles, adding it is simple, with the advanced stuff happening after the role is already installed:

1. Open Server manager by clicking on the server manager shortcut on the bottom-left corner.

2. Click on **Add roles and features**.

3. Click on **Next** three times to reach the **Server Roles** page.

4. Check the **Remote Access** role.

5. Click on **Add Features**.

6. Click on **Next** six more times, and finally click on **Install**.

7. You can close the wizard, or leave it open until the installation completes, and close it then. If you close the wizard before the installation is completed, then you can see the status of the installation from the alerts in the Server manager page:

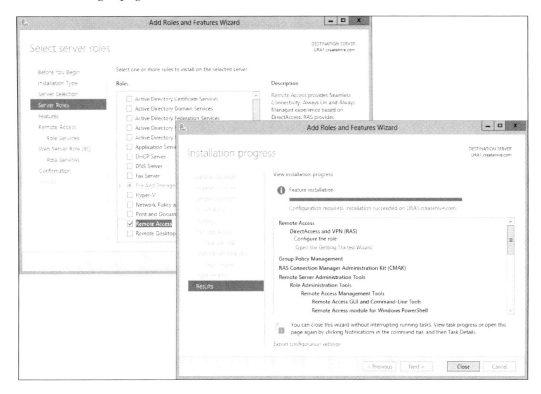

Once the role installation has completed, you can start configuring it from the server manager console.

Configuring the basic URA scenario

To do so, open the **Tools** menu, and select **Remote Access Management**. The remote access console has the main five operational containers on the left (**CONFIGURATION, DASHBOARD, OPERATIONS STATUS, REMOTE CLIENT STATUS**, and **REPORTING**), and following it, a list of your URA servers. At this point, it would only show one, but if you configure multiple sites or arrays, others will show up.

The middle pane is the main operation screen, where you configure options and see information. This is where most of the work is going to be done. On the right, you have a list of categorized tasks, which changes dynamically based on what configuration or monitoring screen you are on.

The console opens on the configuration screen, which would show you two ways to start your deployment. First, you have the **Getting Started Wizard**, which is the easy-peasy, no-brainer, "just get it done" method; though please note that this will not be suitable for many organizations, as it requires that all your clients be Windows 8 clients. Running the **Getting Started Wizard** will configure the most basic scenario for URA, asking you the minimal number of questions. If you're used to installation wizards that take forever to check through two billion options, you'll be surprised at just how easy this thing is—four clicks, one selection, and you're done:

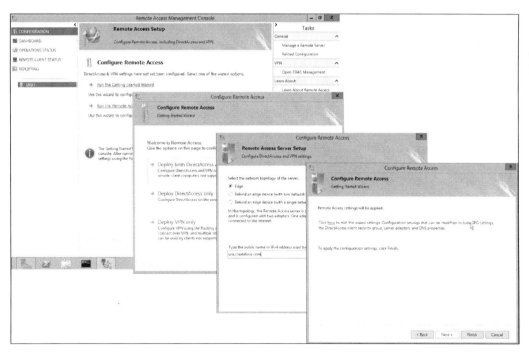

Using this deployment mode can make things very easy for you, and has several advantages, but a few limitations too. The easy part is that you don't need to deploy computer certificates to clients, and that the wizard automatically creates the **NLS** site and creates **self-signed certificates** for it and for the **IP-HTTPS** connection. This also enables the **Kerberos proxy** feature so only a single tunnel is used. The limitation of this mode is that only Windows 8 clients can use it, and that the **Teredo** connectivity method cannot be used, leaving only 6to4 and IP-HTTPS as a connectivity method for clients (though that in itself has no noticeable negative impact on anything). During that simple wizard, you have three selections to make:

1. On the first page, you can select to deploy DirectAccess alone, or also deploy classic VPN options, such as **PPTP, L2TP**, and **SSTP**. We won't talk about VPN here, but know that this option only enables the service needed for VPN, and there's no configuration for it now. In other words, no matter what you choose, it won't make your life any more complicated at this stage.

> As you may recall from earlier in the book, the Unified Remote Access role includes both traditional VPN, and DirectAccess under one roof, which is why this option is offered here. If you do choose to configure VPN, you can do so later on using the RRAS console.

2. On the second page, you need to select your network topology from three possible options. With the first one, your URA server has two network cards, with one connected directly to the internet, and the other going into your corporate network. The second scenario also has two network cards, where one goes to your **DMZ** and out to the internet through a firewall or other edge device, and the other NIC directly into your corporate network. The third scenario is the single-NIC one, where the URA server is connected to the corporate network.

3. On the third page, you need to specify the URL to which URA clients will connect to. This URL is used for IP-HTTPS connections, and needs to resolve to the public IPv4 address of the server, and that's something you'll need to configure in your public **DNS** zone separately. Naturally, if the server is behind an edge device, then it would have to resolve to the public IP on the edge device, with the edge device configured to route the data to the server's IP address. If you are using **split-brains DNS**, where the public hostname and your internal domain have the same domain suffix, then this public hostname will need to be **exempt** from the **NRPT**. In such a case, the URA wizard will do so automatically.

Below you can see a generic diagram of the three topologies. Keep in mind, though, that the scenarios are not very rigid. For example, the 1 NIC scenario can have the URA server either inside the DMZ or inside the corporate network. On a similar note, the edge scenario can be deployed with a firewall sitting behind the URA (separating it from the corporate network). The major differences between the scenarios is whether the URA has one or two NICs (which affects the routing), and whether the NIC that goes to the internet has a private or public IP. It's also important to remember that additional firewalls or routers in various network junctions are permissible, as long as the routing is planned carefully so no packets get lost, and the appropriate ports are open, so all the necessary traffic can go through. Below you can see a diagram of the three basic networking scenarios:

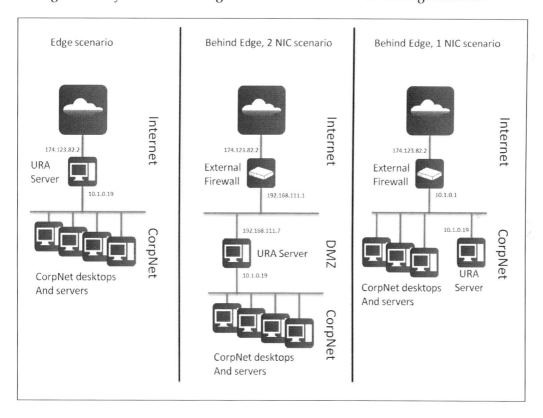

Once that wizard completes, the URA **Group Policy** settings are deployed to your domain, and for most networks, this shouldn't take long. Once that's done and replication across all domain controllers has completed, you can open the domain's **Group Policy editor** and see the new policies:

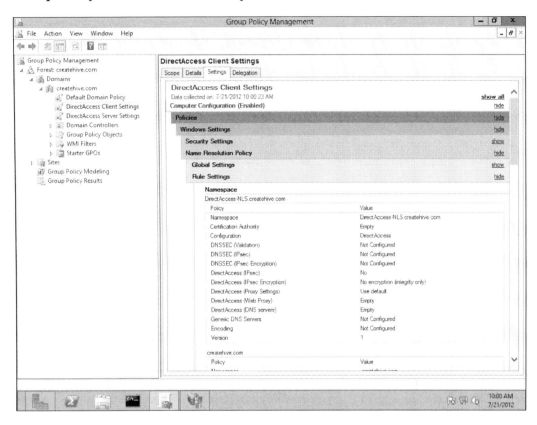

On the left, you can see the two policies **DirectAccess Client Settings** and **DirectAccess Server Settings**. By clicking on the policy itself, you can explore its settings and understand how they relate to things we have discussed. For example, the rule in the previous screenshot refers to the **Network Location Server**, which was automatically named DirectAccess-NLS.createhive.com by the wizard.

Connecting and testing with a client

By default, the URA policy **scope** for clients is set to **all domain computers**, but it also has a **WMI filter** that sets it to apply only to **mobile computers**. To test this, you would need a mobile computer that has an internet connection outside of your corporate network. This phase often throws administrators off, because typically, getting an appropriate network connection is a challenge. We're sure you have plenty of laptops around, but you're not driving home to test it, right? In such a situation, a wireless network card using a cellular network is what you would pick, but it may not be the ideal way. If you recall, we mentioned earlier in the book that cellular connections are sometimes managed in a way that restricts connectivity. It's not very common, but if that's the case, you might find that your URA connection isn't working not through any fault of yours. Without some advanced troubleshooting skills, you might not be able to tell if it's your URA server's fault, your routing, your ISP, or the client. To make it easy on yourself, our recommendation is to either do this initial testing in a lab environment, or to do this from home. From home, you could use a VPN connection to connect and configure the URA server, and then connect the test client over VPN to receive the Group Policy. Another option, of course, is to install a DSL or cable connection in your office just for this purpose, though many companies have various policies against that kind of thing.

Warning!

If you are thinking of removing the WMI filter in order to test this with a desktop, keep in mind that you should also remove the domain computer's group and add a specific group with just your test client or clients. If you don't, the client settings will apply to the URA server and DCs as well, and may disrupt your network. Also, see about forcibly removing the URA policies from the registry in *Chapter 10, Monitoring and Troubleshooting Unified Remote Access*.

Assuming you have not changed the client group or scope, every laptop computer that is connected to the corporate network will receive the URA Group Policy when it does an update the next time. This would take up to two hours to reach all clients, but you can trigger an update manually by typing the command GPUPDATE /FORCE on the client (this has to be in a command prompt that is running as **administrator**). You can run the command gpresult /f /h report.html to generate a report that shows you the applied policies, and it too needs to be run in an administrator command prompt. If the policy was successful, it would show that the **computer policy** for DirectAccess client was applied and you can also expand it to see the settings:

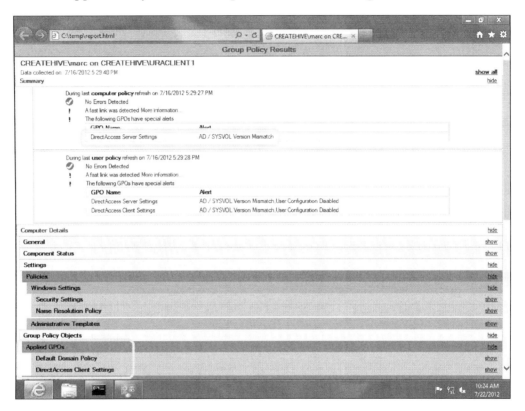

As you can see in the previous screenshot, the **DirectAccess Server Settings** policy has an alert about **AD/SYSVOL Version Mismatch**. This is perfectly normal and doesn't mean anything is wrong, because we don't expect a **client** to receive the settings destined for the **server**. There is also a warning about both the server and client policies below it, but that part is about the **user policy**. The URA settings are in the **computer** policy and not in the **user**, and so this is to be expected as well. The positive confirmation that the policy was applied lies below, where the **Applied GPOs** show, and you can see the **DirectAccess Client Settings**. You can also click on **show** to expand the view and observe additional settings contained in the policy.

Now, disconnect the client computer from the corporate network, and connect it to the public internet. To see the status of the URA connection, click on the network icon on your system tray, which will open the **View Available Networks** UI on the right. It would show at least two network items—one is your regular network card and the other is the URA connection. The URA connection might already be established and shown as **Connected**, or still trying to connect to the URA server. You can right-click on it and view the status, which opens the connection properties (the NCA user interface). Another way to see this is by running `DAProp.exe` from an admin command prompt.

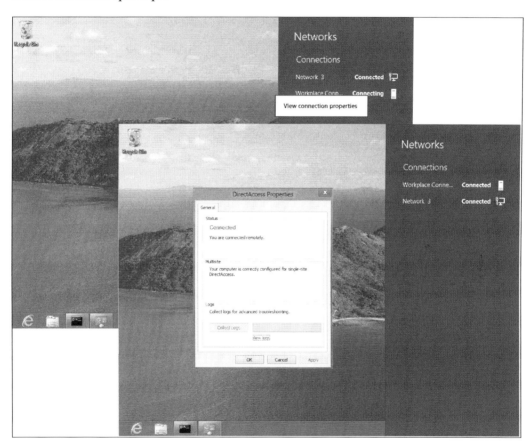

Editing the configuration

In case you haven't noticed it earlier, the last step of the **Getting Started Wizard** says **Click here to edit the wizard settings**. If you were to click on that link, you could edit some of the default settings, such as the URA policy scope or the public name of the URA server. Naturally, you can still edit the settings now, using the configuration console, but there is one setting that you won't be able to change later—the URA policy target GPO. By default, the wizard creates two new GPOs. The one for client settings is named **DirectAccess Client Settings**, and the server policy is named **DirectAccess Server Settings**. If you would rather have a different name or store the settings in an existing GPO, you can only change it during the wizard, before the settings get applied. This doesn't mean this is irreversible, but if you do decide later you need to change it, the only way would be to clear the URA settings and run the wizard from scratch.

To edit the GPO, click on the link in the last step of the wizard, and have a look at the various options you can edit. It's an interesting read, but do keep in mind that all the others except the GPOs can be edited later. Click on **Change...** next to **GPO Settings**, and edit the GPO names. You can also click on **Browse** to see a list of existing policies on the domain, and choose one of them as the target.

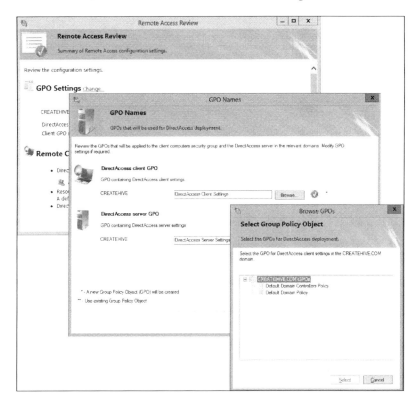

As we said, the other settings can be edited later as well, so let's move along and see how you can do that. After the configuration has been applied, the URA configuration console goes to the **Configuration screen**, where you can edit the four main configuration containers:

- **Remote Clients**: This container includes the following options:
    - Full DirectAccess, or just remote management
    - URA client groups selection
    - Enable or disable the WMI filter for mobile computers
    - Enable force tunneling
    - Connectivity probes servers and URLs for the NCA/DCA
    - E-mail address for the **send logs** button in the NCA/DCA
    - Label for the URA connection, as shown by the NCA/DCA
    - Enable or disable the option to let the user enable local name resolution (which appears, on the client, as a disconnect button)

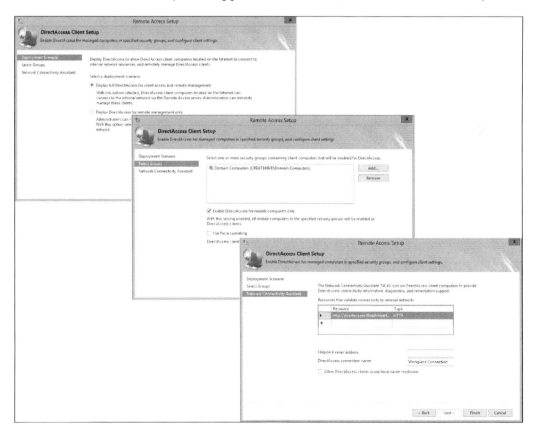

- **Remote Access Server**: This container includes the following options:
    - Topology (you cannot change it, but you can observe the settings)
    - Public URL or IP that clients use to connect to the server when using IP-HTTPS
    - Internal and external network card selection (in the one NIC scenario, you can only select one NIC, of course)
    - Certificate selection for the IP-HTTPS interface
    - Enable two-factor authentication with a smartcard or one-time password (OTP). If OTP is enabled, several other configuration screens will be added, and we will discuss these in *Chapter 9, Deploying NAP and OTP*
    - Enable and configure use of computer certificate (advanced PKI), if you are deploying a scenario that requires it
    - Enable support for Windows 7 clients
    - Enable Network Access Protection (NAP)

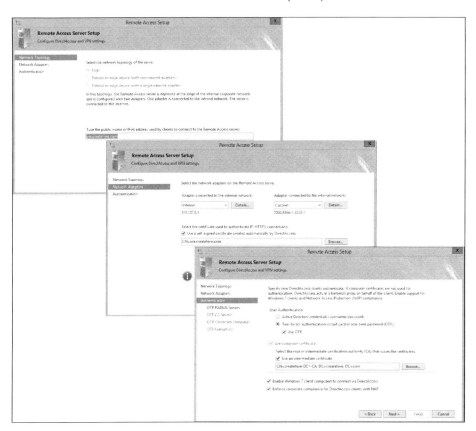

- **Infrastructure Servers**: This container includes the following options:
  - Selection of a local NLS on the URA server, or point to a separate server
  - Certificate selection for a local NLS
  - Configuration of the Name Resolution Policy Table (NRPT)
  - List of additional domain suffixes for the NRPT
  - List of management servers that are included in the first IPsec tunnel

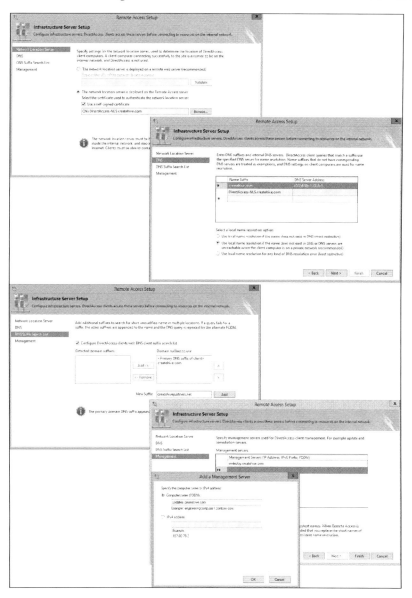

- **Application Servers:** This container includes options for IPsec end-to-end authentication to specific servers within the corporate network, and related options.

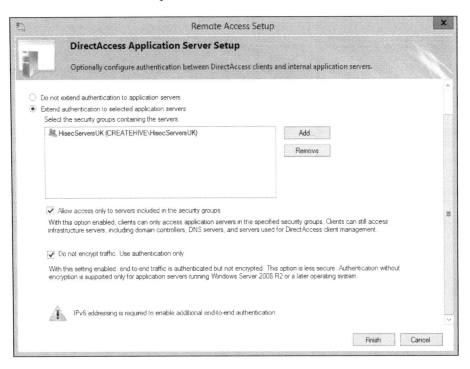

In addition to the configuration containers, the **tasks pane** also offers the following tasks:

- Manage a remote server
- Remove configuration settings
- Add an application server
- View configuration summary
- Refresh management servers
- Reload configuration
- Open RRAS management
- Enable VPN
- Enable site-to-site VPN
- Enable multisite
- Enable load balancing

Now, let's discuss some of the options in the configuration containers and tasks that are less obvious and may require more background to configure correctly. Naturally, we'll probably miss the one item that's most confusing to you personally, so we'll have to apologize in advance! The other options and tasks are self-explanatory, but if you require more information, you can find it in the TechNet documentation:

```
http://technet.microsoft.com/en-us/library/hh831416.aspx
```

Remote client options

Remote client options pertain mostly to things the client would see on his screen, or governing client behavior. Let's take a look at these options.

Full DirectAccess or just remote management

The Remote Management Only option deploys URA using just the first tunnel, which permits access only to Domain Controllers (and other servers you may have listed as management servers in the *Editing the configuration* section). When using URA this way remote clients can obtain Group Policy updates, change their passwords in the domain, and be remotely managed; but nothing more.

Enable force tunneling

Forced tunneling is a mode that routes all traffic through the URA connection. Some organizations prefer to use this, though it has far reaching implications on the connection and the users. We discussed this in *Chapter 2, Planning a Unified Remote Access Deployment* and will discuss this in more detail in *Chapter 8, Enhanced Configurations for Infrastructure Servers*.

Helpdesk e-mail address

This setting is not only about setting up which e-mail address will be used by users to send in logs, but also enables this button on the client side. If you don't specify an e-mail, the **Collect Logs** button on the NCA will be greyed out.

Remote Access Server options

Remote Access Server options pertain to how the server behaves. Let's take a look at these options.

Topology

In case you're wondering why you can only see the topology but not change it, the reason is that the topology selection is very fundamental to the other configuration. Changing it here would require so many other things to be changed, that it's not feasible to allow it as a change. To make a change to this, you would need to disable URA (by clicking on **Remove Configuration Settings** on the task pane) and re-run the wizard from scratch.

Public URL or IP that clients use to connect to the server

In case you're wondering, the URA client will try to connect to that IP or URL, so if it's a URL, the public DNS server that the clients use needs to resolve it to the right IP (though you can use a **HOSTS** entry instead as a temporary means for testing purposes). The IP this entry resolves to, or if you just specify an IP address, has to be the public IP the URA server listens on for the IP-HTTPS traffic. If it's behind a NAT device, the host name should be pointing to the Public IP of the NAT device and then the device needs to forward data coming to that IP address to the URA server's public facing NIC.

 Note that if you use an IP, the certificate will need to have that IP as its name, and that may be confusing to deal with.

Certificate selection for the IP-HTTPS interface

If you configure URA using the **Getting Started Wizard**, a self-signed certificate will be created and assigned to this function if there is no pre-existing certificate for the public name (the wizard will look for available certificates that match the name entered). For advanced scenarios, you can deploy a certificate to the URA server, and then use the **Browse** button to select the certificate you want to use instead.

Enable and configure use of computer certificate

If you configure URA using the **Getting Started Wizard**, URA will use the **Kerberos proxy** instead of computer certificates. If you prefer to use certificates after all (or if you need to enable support for Windows 7 clients, which mandates this), then you need to choose the certificate of the Root CA that will be trusted by your domain clients. By knowing which CA it is, the URA server configures itself to use it to validate the certificates presented by clients during the mutual certificate authentication.

Enable Network Access Protection (NAP)

Network Access Protection is a technology that allows you to inspect and monitor domain computers, and prevent them from connecting if they don't meet your security compliance policy. For example, you might want to keep out computers on which antivirus software hasn't been updated, or not running the latest updates for Windows or another software. With NAP, you set up some infrastructure to check this status, and then configure URA to use it. NAP is also useful for regular network access, and this is a great way to keep your network neat and tidy. We will discuss this in detail in *Chapter 9, Deploying NAP and OTP*.

Infrastructure Servers options

The Infrastructure Servers options pertain to the servers and services that serve as the infrastructure to URA, such as the NLS and DNS. These include:

Selection of a local NLS on the URA server, or point to a separate server

As we've discussed, the NLS is the server which URA clients use to determine where they are. By default, the URA wizard sets itself to be the NLS, but it's often a good idea to set up a separate NLS, which is highly available. If you have such a server, this would be where you set it.

Certificate selection for a local NLS

The **Getting Started Wizard** assumes you want to keep things simple, and generates a **self-signed certificate** for the NLS role. To remind you, the NLS works by running a secure website which clients connect to and the secure site requires a certificate for the HTTPS connection. If you'd prefer using a real certificate rather than the self-signed one, this is the place to choose that certificate (you would have to issue it using the regular methods, via a CA server).

Configuration of the Name Resolution Policy Table (NRPT)

The NRPT controls which destination names the client will connect to via the URA tunnels, and which would go through the regular internet connection, so this setting is very important. We will discuss the NRPT and how to set it up a tad later in this chapter.

List of additional domain suffixes for the NRPT

This is also related to the NRPT, so read on to learn all about it.

List of management servers that are included in the first IPsec tunnel

The management servers are servers to which URA gives access through the first access tunnel, and so they are of particular interest. By default all the domain controllers are added to this list. Even though all the DC names don't appear in the UI, all the DCs are added when the **Apply** button is clicked or when the admin clicks on the **update management servers** task in the task pane of the console.

Application Servers options

As you may recall, the **IPsec** protocol is used for establishing the secure tunnels from URA clients to the URA server, and this is referred to as **end-to-edge**. The client is the "end", and the URA server is the "edge". However, sometimes organizations want the connection to be highly secure all the way from the client to target servers. In this case, you can create an active-directory group containing internal servers for which you need this to happen, and add the group, or groups, here.

When you define this option, you can also elect to allow only the specific servers that are members of this group to be reachable via the URA connection. Another option you can set here is for the IPsec tunnel to not be encrypted. This means that the IPsec will be used to authenticate the URA client to the target internal servers, but the data from the URA server to the internal servers won't be encrypted. One thing to keep in mind is that since the IPsec connection is based on IPv6, this means that the target servers need to fully support IPv6, and be configured with an IPv6 address. Also, this end to end is a new tunnel (a third tunnel!) inside the end-to-edge tunnel and so even if you choose the **authenticate only** it means the traffic is not encrypted for the traffic flowing through the third tunnel. Since the third tunnel is inside the end-to-edge traffic, the unencrypted traffic is not visible on the internet.

The considerations for choosing this option or not are beyond the scope of this book, but generally speaking, organizations who have elected to deploy IPsec for internal communications between computers would be candidates to consider using this as well. On the other hand, one must keep in mind that encrypting everything puts an extra burden on every computer that has to participate, and for older computers, that may be a noticeable performance drop. Also, an encrypted network can be harder to troubleshoot.

Unified Remote Access tasks on the task pane

The task pane provides several options that are peripheral to the configuration. The options will be discussed in the following section.

Remove configuration settings

This option reverses the URA server to its default clean state and clears the URA GPOs from the domain. It's a great way to get back to starting point in case you toyed with the settings too much and things quit working. Also, we're sure you're relieved to know that you can do this without having to uninstall the role or go through other complicated steps.

Warning!

It's important to know that performing this requires a Group Policy update on the clients to apply. If the clients are off-site, this won't affect them until they come into the office or connect using another type of VPN and get a Group Policy refresh. The main problem here is that the cleanup also removes the NLS website and DNS entry. Remote clients that are brought into the network after this won't be able to see the NLS and detect they are inside the network, and won't be able to apply the GPO update to clear the URA configuration. This is one of those catch-22 situations, so make sure all clients are inside the network before you run this, or be prepared to perform a manual cleanup of the NRPT on these clients. We will discuss clearing up the NRPT manually in *Chapter 10, Monitoring and Troubleshooting Unified Remote Access*.

Add an application server

This opens up the application server options to add end-to-end encryption, just like what we discussed in the previous section.

Refresh management servers

Generally, when you make changes to the URA configuration, you need to click on the **Finish** button at the bottom of the screen, which updates the GPOs in the domain. However, if you are only adding additional management servers (see the, *Editing the configuration* section) as the update to the policies is small, this button only updates that portion of the policy. Another situation where this is very important is if you add new domain controllers to your domain or remove them. In such a case, this button updates the policy to allow access to new ones or remove old ones from the policy, and you should keep in mind to run it as soon as you can after such a change to the network.

Reload configuration

This button loads the current URA configuration from disk, and refreshes the view. The URA configuration is stored in a file named `RemoteAccessServerConfig.xml`, located in `c:\windows\DirectAccess`. If the configuration in the console goes out of whack, clicking this button re-loads the file. This is a typical configuration file:

Enable site-to-site VPN

Since the Unified Remote Access role also includes **VPN**, the above two options are related to enabling and configuring these two types of VPN.

Enable multisite

Multisite allows you to configure URA servers in different locations, which could be very useful for organizations that have branches in different places and want to have clients connecting to their nearest location. We will discuss this scenario in more detail in *Chapter 5, Multisite Deployment*.

Enable load balancing

This task opens a configuration screen which allows you to configure several URA servers to work in tandem as a **cluster**. We will discuss this in more detail later in this chapter.

Network Location Server

The NLS is one of the most important things in the URA configuration because it's what allows URA clients to detect that they are connected to the corporate network when they are in the office. If they cannot connect to the NLS, they will assume that they are still on the public internet and try to establish the URA connection, and that's not a very good idea while inside the office, just like you wouldn't want people to use their VPN connection in that situation.

The NLS is simply a web server that listens for HTTPS requests and replies to them. It does not need to contain any specific content, so a blank site is perfectly fine. Essentially, you can use any internal web server for that role, but the URA **Getting Started Wizard** assumes you want to keep things simple and uses itself for it.

The automatic setup chooses a distinct name to represent this role, as it cannot be the same name used by URA clients to access it. The reason for this is that since the URA clients access the URA server from the internet by its name, the same name cannot be used to determine if they are outside the network or inside it. In other words, as the old saying goes "you can't judge a book by its cover" (not even this amazing book!). The **Getting Started Wizard** then proceeds to create a DNS entry for the chosen name, generate a self-signed certificate for the same name, and add an HTTPS **binding** to the **IIS server** running on itself for that name. The name that the wizard chooses is **DirectAccess-NLS** appended with its domain suffix.

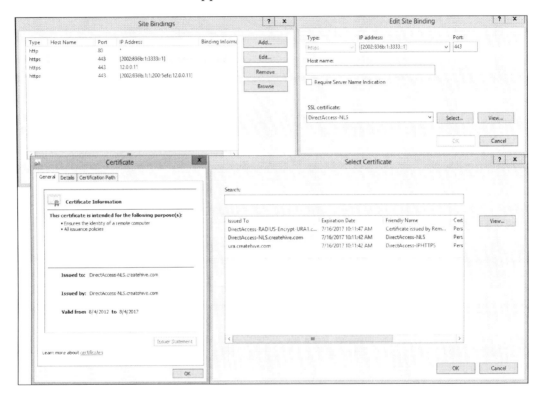

In the previous section you can see the three HTTPS bindings that the **Getting Started Wizard** creates on the local IIS server on the URA server. The bindings are established for the three internal IPs used by the server (the internal IPv4 address, the internal IPv6 address, and the internal ISATAP address). The certificate assigned to them is the DirectAccess-NLS self-signed certificate for the hostname `DirectAccess-NLS.createhive.com`.

Your own NLS?

There are several reasons for you to prefer to use your own NLS server. The primary one would be **availability**. As we said before, this role is pertinent in letting your clients know where they are, so if this website stops responding, you might be in trouble. Keeping the site on a separate server would provide you with more options for reliability. For one thing, if it's another server and it dies for some reason, it would be relatively easy to move this function to another server—all you have to do is point DNS to the "new" server's IP, and configure a website with the appropriate certificate. If you are a planning type of person, you might even prepare such a site and keep it offline until it might be needed. An even better plan would be to set up a cluster of servers with this role.

To set up a website for this function, all you have to do is run an IIS website, with a binding for HTTPS, and a certificate that matches the name you intend to use for it. The name itself doesn't matter—it can be a short-name or an FQDN, as long as you make sure your DNS has an entry to resolve to the bound IP address, and that the certificate you assign to it matches it as well. One drawback is that you cannot use a **wildcard** certificate for that site, so keep that in mind. The site doesn't have to have any content—it can be blank, or the default IIS website, or anything else—as long as a request to the root of the site is successful (with an HTTP **200 OK** response). It might be a good idea to put some meaningful page on it, to allow you to be able to test the site if you suspect there's a problem with it.

Once you have the site prepared and tested, you can configure your URA server to use it by going to the **Infrastructure Server Setup Network Location Server** page (Step 3, page 1 of the URA configuration console), and selecting **The network location server is deployed on a remote web server (recommended)**. Then, type in the FQDN of the server and click on **Validate**. The target server will be checked to make sure it responds correctly. If you get a green checkmark, you're good to go. When you finish the wizard, URA will update the group policies in the domain, and once your clients update their policies, the new NLS server will come into play.

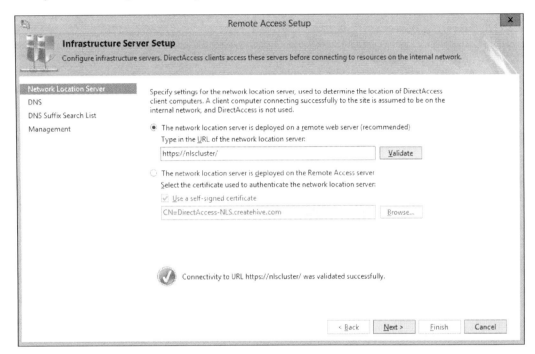

Configuring the Name Resolution Policy table

The NRPT is another thing that has crucial importance with URA; because mistakes in it cannot only cause problems—they could cause some serious issues in your entire network. The NRPT can have two types of items:

- A domain suffix, which defines a pattern for resources that should be accessed through the URA connection
- An exception entry, which is a name of a resource that should never be accessed through the URA connection

Your NRPT may include more than one entry of each of the previous items, depending on your network configuration. As part of the **Getting Started Wizard**, the NRPT would be configured to contain two or three items. The wizard will assume that the domain it's joined to is to be used as the domain suffix, and will add it to the list. This entry also includes the IP address of the DNS server that will resolve names for URA clients, and that DNS will be the URA server itself. The URA server includes the **DNS64** service, which can take care of resolving names for IPv6 and IPv4 resources on the internal network.

If the public URL for URA (the one you set in step 2 of the **Getting Started Wizard** as mentioned in the *Configuring the basic URA scenario* section) uses the same domain suffix as your internal domain, then it needs to be listed in the NRPT as an **exception**, because the clients need to access it through the internet to establish the URA connection. If the URL you listed in step 2 does indeed match your domain suffix, the wizard will automatically add an entry for it.

The wizard will also add an entry for the NLS server. The **Getting Started Wizard** sets up the URA server itself to be the NLS, and also assigns it a URL. That URL is automatically added to the NRPT as an exception. If you are using your own NLS, then you need to configure an exception entry for it.

When the URA clients make decisions about how to access a network resource, they use the NRPT, and anything that's not specifically listed in it is assumed to be an internet resource. That is why accessing any resource by using its IPv4 address directly does not work through DirectAccess because the NRPT expects a name to determine whether the resource is in corpnet or not. That is also why you can't test connectivity to internal resources by simply pinging their IPv4 address directly.

The **Getting Started Wizard** is supposed to take care of things for you, so with any luck, you might not need to make any adjustments. Situations where you might need to change things are as follows:

- If your network has multiple domains, you need to add the domain suffixes for all of them to the table
- If you intend to use a separate server as the NLS, you need to add it as an exception (and remove the exception that was created for the NLS running on the URA server)

To make changes to the NRPT, you need to open the **Infrastructure Server Setup** configuration (Step 3) and click on **Next** to move to the **DNS** page. Here, you can right-click on any of the entries to edit or delete it, and you can also right-click on the blank line to add a new item. When you want to add a domain suffix, type it in, and then click on **Detect**. This prompts the wizard to fill-in the IP of the DNS server that would service requests pertaining to this domain (which would typically be the URA server itself). If this is supposed to be a different server, you can input the IP manually. Either way, you should click on **Validate** afterwards, to make sure that the server is responding correctly.

If you need to add an exception to the table then make sure you do **not** specify any DNS server in the exception entry. This has to be left blank for the client to treat the entry as an exception.

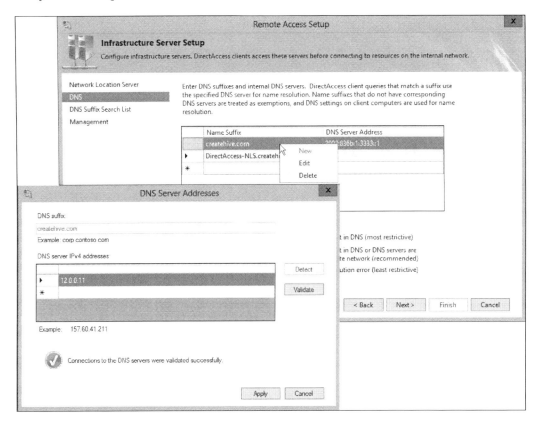

Exceptional exceptions

You might be wondering for what situations you might need to add exceptions other than the NLS server. Remember that exceptions are specific resources to which the URA client will resolve and connect through its regular internet connection, and not through the URA tunnel. Normally, you would want any connection to corporate servers to go through the tunnel, but if you are using **Split-brains DNS**, these exceptions could be really handy.

Split-brains DNS is a situation where you are using the organization's DNS suffix both internally, and externally. This is something that many companies do. In such a situation, you might have some servers that are accessible on the public internet using the same domain suffix as the internal servers. One common scenario for this is **OCS** or **Lync**. Companies that deploy Lync or OCS typically place the Lync **Edge server** on the internet, so that partners, customers, and guests can join meetings from the outside.

In such a situation, you would want to add the Lync public URL to the exception list, so that URA clients can connect to it directly. Using split-brains DNS could require other exceptions, such as a case where you need users to access the organizations public website, or if you have another type of VPN connection as backup to URA, and the public access URL for the VPN uses the same domain suffix.

If you are using split-brains DNS, and you specified an entry URL for URA that matches your domain suffix, then the URA wizard will detect this, and issue a warning:

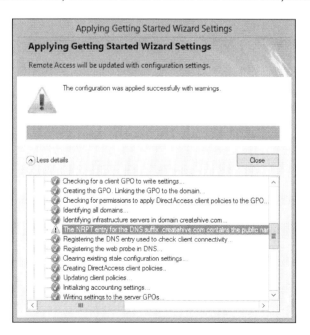

The full text of the warning is **The NRPT entry for the DNS suffix .createhive. com contains the public name used by client computers to connect to the Remote Access server. Add the name ura.createhive.com as an exemption in the NRPT**. The message suggests that you add an exception, but in fact, the wizard will have already added one for you, so there's nothing to worry about. Also, the wizard would prevent you from entering a duplicate item.

Enabling load balancing

For any IT-savvy organization, setting up any service without some form of redundancy is not an option, and this is where **load balancing** comes into play. Setting up load-balanced URA servers provides two benefits:

- It allows you to provide service to more users than what a single server can handle
- It allows the service to function continuously even if one server goes out of commission for some reason, either planned or unexpected

Load balancing means setting up one public IP and hostname that represents multiple servers, and having some mechanism that forwards incoming requests to these servers and distributes them equally (or as per the ratio of load you want each to handle). This can be done in two ways:

- Using the built-in Network Load Balancing (NLB) service in Windows Server
- Using a third party device, such as those sold by F5 Networks, Cisco, Radware, Barracuda, and others

There's one more option, referred to as **Global Load Balancing (GLB)**, and it is used when you have URA servers in different sites (while regular load balancing is for servers in the same location). We will discuss GLB in *Chapter 5, Multisite Deployment*, which is dedicated to **multisite** configuration. To load balance URA, you essentially install the URA role on two or more servers, configure URA on one of them, and then add others as load-balanced servers. The steps are as follows:

1. Configure your first server with your URA settings, whatever they are.
2. Install the URA role on additional servers.
3. If you wish to use the Windows integrated NLB, install that feature on all servers.
4. Run the load balancing wizard on the URA console on the primary server.

5. As part of step 4, choose whether you wish to use the Windows integrated NLB service, or another method.

6. Add the additional server or servers from the load balancing configuration page.

 If you have used NLB to load balance other servers or services in the past, know that with URA, the NLB console is used only to manage the servers in the cluster, but not to create or configure the cluster. You will be using the NLB console to stop or start the service on the members, as well as fine tune some settings, but the initial configuration is done from the URA console.

With load balancing, you can cluster together up to eight servers. This limit applies to both Windows NLB and external load balancers. Before you actually go into this, there are some considerations, decisions, and possible configuration to be made.

Considerations for load balancing with Windows NLB

Windows NLB makes life relatively simple. Not only do you not need to deal with a third party device (some of which can be quite challenging to configure well), but it also makes life simpler with regards to addressing.

In *Chapter 2, Planning a Unified Remote Access Deployment* we discussed some of the concepts and challenges with windows NLB, such as the issues of **DIPs**, **VIPs**, **re-convergence**, **datalink layer routing**, **network throughput,** and others. If these don't ring a bell, you should re-visit that topic. You might also want to read up on NLB here:

`http://technet.microsoft.com/en-us/library/hh831698.aspx.`

Before starting the NLB wizard, you should pick your **DIPs**. When the URA wizard runs, it will use the current IP addresses assigned to the internal and external NICs on the URA server as the **VIPs**, and ask you to provide the DIPs. The DIPs and VIPs should all be on the same subnet.

Lastly, if you are running your server as a guest on a **Hyper-V** server, keep in mind that you need to enable **MAC address spoofing** on the servers' NICs. Otherwise, you won't get very far. In Windows Server 2012 Hyper-V, the MAC spoofing configuration is under the **Advanced Features** section of the virtual network adapter.

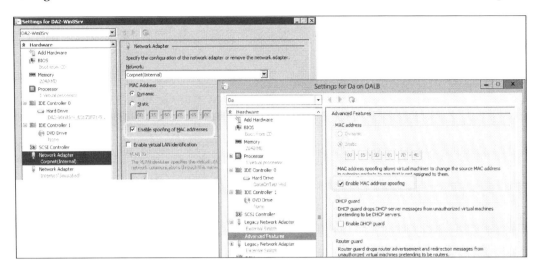

Load balancing with external load balancers

With the release of Windows Server 2012, using an external load balancer is supported, but the configuration requires you to configure your network with IPv6 addressing as well as several extra steps which are beyond the scope of this book. If you attempt to configure this option directly, you are likely to encounter errors that would prevent you from completing the setup. The Windows Server product team has published information about this topic under known issues in the following article:

http://technet.microsoft.com/en-us/library/jj134175.aspx

Installing the NLB feature

To add the NLB feature to a server, use the **Server Manager**, and click on **Add Roles and Features**. You don't need to configure anything, so it's pretty straight-forward:

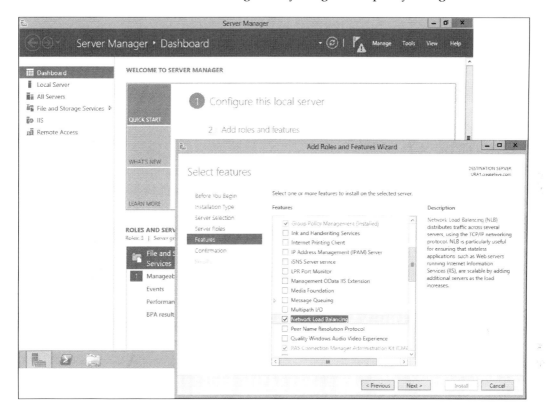

Now, click on **Enable Load Balancing** on the task pane in the URA configuration console. After the introduction page, select whether you wish to use Windows NLB or an external NLB. If you choose to use Windows NLB, the next steps are pretty simple:

1. Provide the DIP and subnet mask for the external interface.

2. Provide the DIP and subnet mask for the internal interface.

3. After the summary, click on **Commit**!

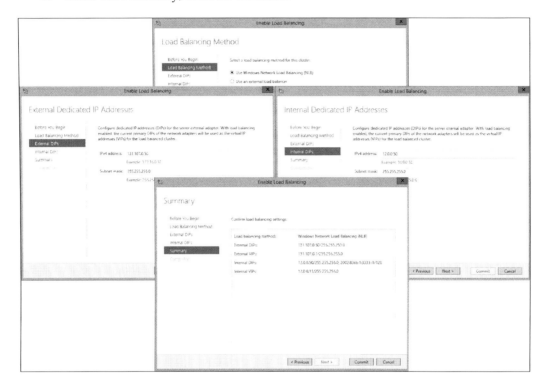

As you can see, the wizard uses the currently configured address as the VIP, and asks you to enter a new address to be used as a DIP. The reason for this is because your current address will typically be mapped in DNS already, so "promoting" it from a DIP to VIP allows keeping the name resolution as it is, making life a bit easier. At this point, your first server should be ready to go, and now, you need to add your other server (or servers) as array members. The task pane should now have a new area named **Load Balanced Cluster**, with buttons to configure load balancing settings and to add or remove servers from the array. The settings button allows you to switch from Windows NLB to external load balancing, but that's about it.

On the **Add or Remove Servers** wizard, you can see a list of your array members, and you can click on any of them to remove it, or click on **Add Server** to add a new one.

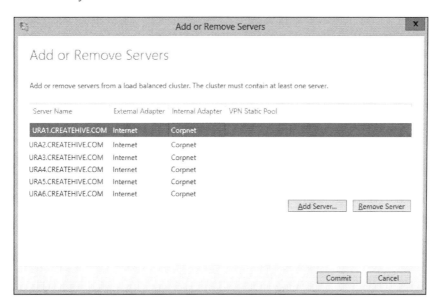

When you add a server, the wizard will contact it and validate that it has the NLB feature installed. On the next page, you need to select the network adapters for the internal and external connection, and the IP-HTTPS certificate. The NIC and Networking configuration on the server that you are adding needs to match the one on your first server: if it's a two-NIC scenario, the new server must have two NICs as well, connected to the same networks. There is some room for variations in the network configuration, but do keep the routing in mind, as each member of the array must receive all incoming traffic, and they need to be able to communicate with each other at all times.

The certificate for IP-HTTPS can be either a real certificate, or a self-signed one, but all array members must have the same type. Also, the target server has to already have a certificate installed during the wizard.

The next page of the wizard is for selecting the certificate for the NLS server, and same as IP-HTTPS, it can be of either type, as long as the added server matches it and has it pre-installed already.

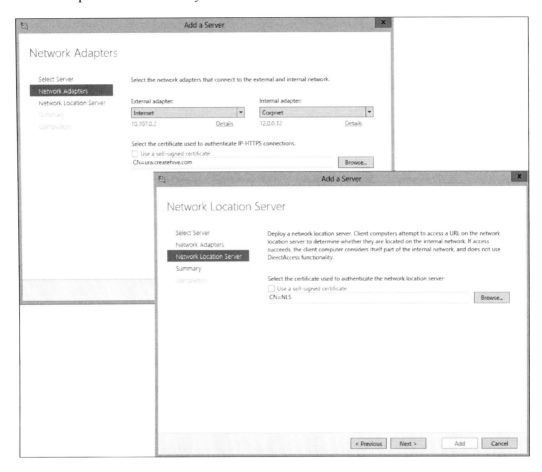

Once you've finished adding or removing servers from the list, clicking on **Commit** configures the NLB settings and adjusts the **Group Policy** settings in the domain—but that's not all. You also need to start NLB on the cluster members using the NLB manager.

Managing the NLB cluster

While the URA wizard configures NLB automatically, it doesn't start the NLB on the members, which you need to do yourself using the **NLB manager**. The NLB manager is also useful if you need to manually manage your cluster. For example, if you are doing some maintenance on a member, you might want to temporarily take it out of the cluster. Another situation is troubleshooting (if you suspect a certain member is malfunctioning, or if you want to focus your efforts on a single node).

You can launch the NLB manager from within the Server Manager, under the **Tools** menu. When it opens, you might be surprised to find not one but two clusters—don't worry—this is perfectly normal. The reason for having two clusters is that URA needs to make sure that traffic is load balanced not only when it comes from the URA clients on the internet, but also when it leaves the corporate network towards the clients. This is essential for things like **remote-management**. So, one cluster will be the external NICs, and the other is the internal NICs.

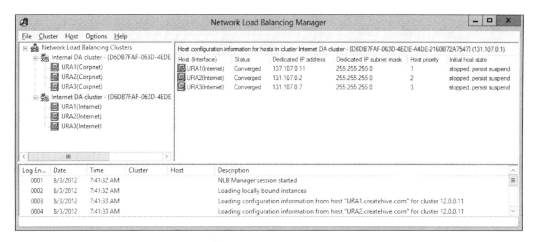

As you can see in the previous section, the console lists the servers you've added to the array, and on the **Status** column, you can see them all as **Converged**, which is what we want! If something is wrong with the configuration or the network, you might see one or more of the servers in other states, such as **Stopped**, **Misconfigured**, **Pending**, **Converging**, or **Suspended**. We will discuss troubleshooting in the final chapter of this book, but generally speaking, virtually all NLB issues are networking and routing related, so if something is not right, triple-check your settings and make sure you didn't miss anything like entering a wrong subnet mask or IP.

Other than seeing what's going on with your cluster, you can use the NLB manager for other things. If, for example, you need to take a server offline for some reason (maintenance, for example), you can click on the server, and from the **Host** menu, select **Control Host** and **Stop** or **Suspend**. When you do this, the cluster performs a re-convergence, where the remaining active members decide how to re-distribute the load between them. When the member stops, users will be disconnected and then reconnect to another of the members. Later, when your maintenance is done, you can use the same menu to resume or start the member back.

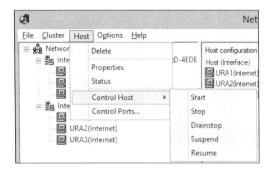

If you're a responsible administrator (or at least one who prefers to keep his job!), you probably want to avoid stopping a cluster member with no warning and kicking off all its users. As opposed to other services, URA is actually very friendly with that kind of thing, because the connection establishment is automatic. Even if you pull the power cable, users' tunnels will automatically establish on another cluster member very quickly, and unless the user is in the middle of a file-transfer or a remote-desktop session, he is unlikely to feel anything. However, best practices are, after all, to move users gradually, and for that, NLB has the **Drainstop** option, which you can also see in the previous screenshot. **Drainstop** is like the "closed" sign that they put up in the bank at closing time. It sets the member to not accept any new connections, but it doesn't drop existing connections. The member will continue to function and service these users until they drop on their own account. Naturally, if your users are workaholics who never leave their computers, they might stay on indefinitely, but usually, within a few hours the server will have only a handful of users, at which point you might feel it's reasonable to completely stop it or perform your maintenance.

Another thing you might need to do with the NLB manager is adjust the cluster **NLB method**. NLB has three modes of operation—**IGMP MULTICAST**, **MULTICAST**, and **UNICAST**. The difference is the way the NIC's MAC addresses are used. With the Unicast method, all the servers are assigned an identical UNICAST MAC address. With the MULTICAST method, each server retains the original MAC address of the NIC, but the NIC is also assigned a MULTICAST MAC address, which is shared by all servers. When using MULTICAST, incoming client requests are sent to all the servers by using the MULTICAST MAC address.

Unfortunately, the shared MAC addresses on multiple hosts can cause **flooding** on the network. This happens because the network switch, which usually forwards traffic only to the appropriate ports, is forced to forward the UNICAST or MULTICAST traffic to all its ports, which effectively turns your clever switch into a dumb hub. Ideally, you should prefer MULTICAST to UNICAST, if your networking hardware supports it (most modern devices do).

However, MULTICAST can cause flooding just like UNICAST, unless you specifically configure the switch with static entries so that it will send the packets only to members of the NLB cluster and not all of its ports. What's even better is IGMP MULTICAST. It is similar to MULTICAST, except that it allows capable network switches to perform IGMP snooping on the traffic, and know on their own to which ports to forward the traffic. This makes the switch's life harder, but allows your network to run better.

By default, NLB is set to UNICAST for both clusters when you create it. To change it, follow these steps:

1. If you wish to change both clusters, start this with the internal cluster.
2. Right-click on the cluster you wish to adjust.
3. Stop the cluster.
4. Select **Cluster Properties**.
5. Switch to the **Cluster Parameters** tab.
6. Select another cluster operation mode.
7. Click on **OK.**
8. Start the cluster back.

9. Repeat for the other cluster, if you want.

Summary

In this chapter, we explored the various scenarios and options that URA offers, from the very basic to some of the advanced, enterprise-ready solutions. However, there's plenty more to learn, and in the next chapter, we will discuss multi-site deployments, which is one of the most sought-after features introduced with Windows Server 2012. With multisite, you can deploy URA servers in various locations, to provide faster access to local clients, as well as higher availability in case of a disaster in a local site.

5
Multisite Deployment

One of the most significant new abilities of Windows Server 2012 Unified Remote Access is multisite deployments. Many customers have requested this feature, which allows an organization to deploy several URA servers in different geographic locations that serve as alternate access points; and now it's finally available! Multisite deployment can make life better for administrators, by providing an off-site backup entry point, in case of a major disaster to the primary site. It also makes life better for users, because they can now access URA from a location that is closer to them, providing the best performance. In this chapter, we will discuss the following:

- What is multisite deployment and how does it help?
- Multisite scenarios
- Network infrastructure considerations and planning
- DNS considerations
- Deploying load balancing
- Windows 7 clients and multisite
- IP-HTTPS and NLS certificates
- The multisite configuration wizard
- Adding more entry points

What is multisite deployment and how does it help?

Multisite deployment describes a situation where you install several URA servers, and place them in different places, as opposed to a simple array where all the servers are in a single location. The big deal that makes multisite more significant is three-fold:

- If you have users in different locations, you can set up entry points that are closer to them. This can reduce **network latency** and provide better performance.

- If you have servers in different locations, you can set up entry points in these locations rather than in other sites. This reduces network latency as well and provides better performance.

- In case some kind of disaster happens, thus hurting the operation of a single site and impacting the local network or the internet infrastructure in that location, having an alternate access point can provide immediate relief both to remote users and employees who may be unable to reach the office and can resume their work remotely.

However, if not planned carefully, setting up multiple sites can make things very confusing for some users. An important term here is **entry point**. An entry point is a single or **load-balanced** URA server in a physical location, so by setting up a URA server or servers in multiple locations, you're creating additional entry points. Once you have those, you can set up certain users for certain points, or allow the users to make the selection when they connect.

The question here is: *can you really trust your users enough to let them play with this toy?* That question is for you to answer, and for us to snigger at, but it's quite important, really. In a perfect world, John Nash's Game theory may lead us to think that all users will connect to the fastest entry point, and will form equilibrium. In reality, though, people tend to play around, looking for a sweeter deal. Just like we try different routes, looking for the fastest way to get to work and beat the traffic, people will experiment with the various entry points to find the best one. With internet performance being affected by many factors, from a microwave polluting the Wi-Fi signal to swarms of aNthusiasts rushing to order a new aNtenna for their aPhones, you can bet that your users will be disconnecting and reconnecting to the various entry points all the time, trying to find the best one.

Making these decisions may not be easy at this point, and you might find that your best laid plans aren't working out. It would be ideal to plan things based on your intimate knowledge of your own organization and users, but include some metrics in the plan, so that you can clearly see and react if things are turning out differently.

Multisite scenarios

Multisite scenarios are not always mutually exclusive, but in essence, they might include:

- A single server in each site, with users assigned to a specific site
- A single server in each site, with the user's computer detecting the fastest or closest entry point
- A single server in each site, with **global load balancing** directing the traffic
- A single server or an array at a main site, with other sites being on stand-by in case of disaster recovery
- A scenario involving backward compatibility for Windows 7 clients

A variation, which could apply to any of the previous scenarios, is one where one or more of the sites have a load-balanced array of servers instead of a single server.

The primary difference between all of the above is how traffic is directed, based on the options we listed earlier. A URA entry point is associated with the **active directory site** in which it is placed, and clients which connect to that entry point are considered to be connected to that site. You don't have to have an entry point in every site, but you also cannot have one entry point belonging to more than the site it's in. You can however have more than one entry point in a single site, so if your network is designed as one single site (with fast links between physical locations), this is perfectly fine.

The addition of Windows 7 clients to the mix complicates things, because they would not be able to choose which entry point to use. Windows 7 clients are assigned a single entry point, and that may mean more work when deciding how to assign those. Here is a diagram depicting a classic two-site scenario:

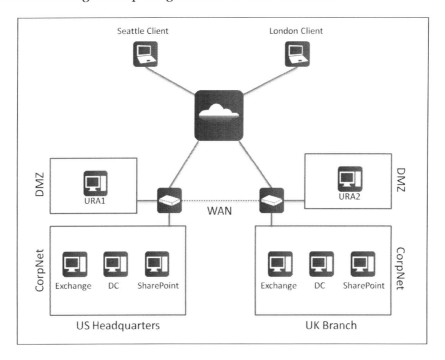

At this point, you probably already know which of the previous scenarios best suits your organization. If you're not sure, keep in mind that whatever you choose is not set in stone, and you can take an incremental approach—start with a simple deployment, and add a secondary site with another entry point later on, or wait for things to work smoothly with Windows 8 clients before adding support for Windows 7 clients. You can also adjust your entry point selection settings at any time.

Network infrastructure considerations and planning

The most important aspect of planning this type of deployment is realizing how it will affect your network. As you may recall from *Chapter 2, Planning a Unified Remote Access Deployment*, one of the primary design considerations is the **routing**. When a URA client connects to a site, the routing on the URA server will determine where packets are going to be sent to, and if you are not careful, problems could arise. A simple example of such a problem could be a situation where the URA server doesn't have the appropriate **routes**, and traffic destined for certain target networks or computers would simply be discarded. A more complicated one is if the routes are inappropriately set, causing the traffic to get to its destination indirectly, which could result in slow performance, or over-utilization of your network. For example, a URA server located in New York sending traffic destined to a local server through a router in California instead, which would both delay the arrival of the data and overload the router and WAN links. Yes, we consider a "no connection" situation the lesser evil, because at least then you know what to look for. When the routing "works", it might be a while before you even see a link between your URA setup and network degradation; and even then, you might not even know how to begin troubleshooting it.

Planning the routing can become tricky in this situation, because you would be using a mix of IPv4 and IPv6 networking. The IPv6 portion of things should take care of itself, unless you are actually involved with your IPv6 network configuration (for example, using **DHCP** to assign stateful addresses rather than stateless configuration). If your corporate network is using global IPv6 addresses, and each of the sites also uses a global IPv6 range for IP-HTTPS, a URA client may enter via an entry point in the US and access a resource in the Europe site. In such a situation, if the routing infrastructure is not planned properly the return traffic to the URA client from the resource in Europe may try to go back via the entry point in Europe instead of the one in the US. This can cause trouble because the Europe entry point will not have a matching IPsec Security Association for the IP-HTTPS client and will drop the traffic. Also, if you have intrusion detection devices at the Europe entry point, they may not have seen the original incoming traffic (because it came to the US entry point) and so may break the connection. This needs proper planning for the corporate network to route the respective client ranges within the corporate network.

Regardless of the situation, we recommend preparing a network map that lists your resources not just logically, but from a routing perspective. For example:

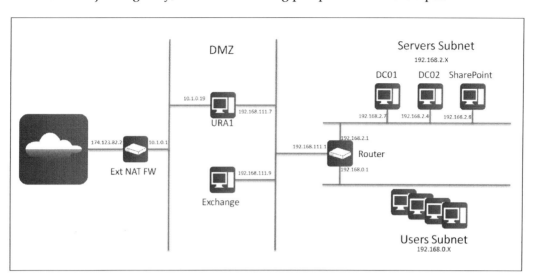

The IPs above may be hard to read, but this is just an example, so they have no particular significance. This kind of drawing would allow you to "think like a packet", or at least brain-storm with others if things don't work out.

Default gateways and routes

A topic that is still source of confusion to many is how setting up routes and default gateways affects technologies such as URA. A URA server is fundamentally a router—it routes traffic coming from the URA clients on the internet to computers on the corporate network and back. A router needs to know what to do with any packet it receives, and we (the administrators) provide the instruction in the form of routes and a default gateway (DG). Without any routes or a DG, a server is only aware of the IP subnets that are configured on its own network interfaces, and would ignore any other traffic that it might receive. In the case of a URA server, if the corporate network contains IP subnets that are outside of the subnet it itself is configured with, we need to provide a route rule (possibly more than one) to tell the server what traffic it should route, and through which router. Usually, the public internet contains all other IP subnets, so instead of creating routes to cover all of them, we set the default gateway, which says "anything not covered by the routes goes through there". It's very important not to confuse the server by setting up two default gateways—it can only be configured on the interface that sends traffic to the public internet.

Group Policy planning

With multisite, the Group Policy infrastructure becomes a little more complicated. As opposed to single-site, where everything goes into two policy objects (server and clients), multisite needs a separate GPO for the server of each entry point, and a separate client GPO for each domain. If Windows 7 clients are also a part of this, then you would need a client GPO for each entry point and each domain for the Windows 7 clients. Let's say, for example, that your company has a site in the US, Europe, and Africa, each with its own domain and servicing both Windows 8 and Windows 7 computers, and with two entry points in each continent. In that case, you would have:

- six server GPOs (one per entry point)
- nine client GPOs (three GPOs for Windows 8 clients and 6 GPOs for Windows 7 clients)

When you create the multisite configuration, the URA wizard creates everything automatically, unless you specify otherwise. This could become a little tricky, because creating all the policies and links may require permissions that you, the person running the configuration wizard, might not have. Setting up multisite requires that each entry point administrator be an administrator for each of the other entry points. A good way to handle this is to create a **security group** in **active directory** that covers all admins for all entry points. If there is a permission problem, the wizard will inform you of this, but it cannot automatically recover. You'll have to take care of the cross-domain permissions and run the configuration again.

If you don't have the permissions required for creating the **GPOs** or **linking** them to the domain, you can have someone else create the GPOs manually, so that the multisite wizard only needs to update them with the settings. The wizard will still need edit, delete, and modify security permissions to do its job, though. If it's not permitted to link the GPOs, it will issue a warning, and then the linking can be done by someone else afterwards (naturally, URA won't work until that's done). Another reason for creating the GPOs manually is if you want to control the naming of the GPOs.

DNS considerations

DNS is an important consideration for every URA deployment, but particularly so for multiple geographic locations. As you may recall from *Chapter 2, Planning a Unified Remote Access Deployment*, the **Name Resolution Policy Table (NRPT)** is the mechanism by which URA clients know which resources are to be accessed via the URA tunnel, and which are to be contacted directly over the internet. For example, if your domain is Createhive.com, then the NRPT rules would typically say that any resource related to that domain, except the network location server, would go through the tunnel. What could make this a bit more complicated is that if you're looking into this, you are likely running a complex domain environment. If you have a large forest with multiple domains, each separate name space will have to be distinctively added to the NRPT.

Network Location Server concerns

Another significant thing to consider is the **Network Location Server (NLS)**, which allows your clients to know they are connected directly to the corporate network, when the user is in the office. The clients look for the NLS server by name, and try to connect to it to make this determination. With remote offices or sites, you will need to place a network location server in each site so that local clients have their own NLS rather than going through the WAN to other offices.

When you configure URA, you need to provide the name for the network location server, and the same name will be used by all URA clients everywhere, to connect to one of the multiple servers that will be set up by the wizard. Since the NLS servers in all the sites will answer to the same name, you need to set up your **DNS name resolution** appropriately, so that in each site, it will resolve to the IP of the local NLS:

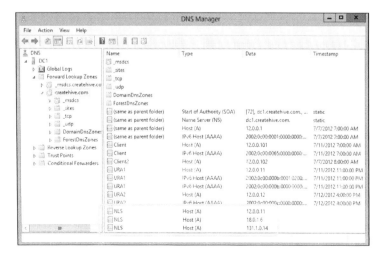

The multiple servers will also need to have certificates for this, and we will discuss this shortly, later in the chapter.

Deploying load balancing

As we've discussed, when you set up multiple entry points, you have several ways of configuring an entry point selection. If one of your goals is **disaster recovery**, then you might want to deploy **global load balancing** solutions, such as those provided by F5 Networks, Radware, Citrix, and others. A **global load balancing** solution monitors the status of your URA servers world-wide, and in case one of them becomes unavailable, reroutes client connections to other servers based on rules you define. The advantage of global load balancing over regular local load balancing is that the monitoring and rerouting are done on a global scale, and therefore provide protection against larger-scale disasters. With regular load balancing, array members take over failed members, but if your ISP connection goes out, or the site itself suffers a major disaster, your users are left wagging their network cables. A global load balancer works one level above, and can compensate for an entire site going offline.

The actual deployment of the global load balancer differs between products, and is beyond the scope of this book. We will, however, soon see how the URA wizard handles this configuration.

Certificate authentication

If you have already installed the URA role on one or more of your servers, you might have selected the easy option of using **Kerberos Proxy** for authentication, instead of **Certificate authentication**. Unfortunately, this option is not available for the multisite scenario, and therefore, you are going to have to configure and deploy a certificate infrastructure. To do this, follow these steps:

1. Install the **Certificate Authority** role on a server of your choice in your domain.

2. Configure an **auto enrollment** policy to issue certificates to clients (either all clients, or at least those which will be using URA).

3. Verify that clients have received the CA's **root certificate** (after the clients Group Policy has been updated, you should see the root certificate in the **Trusted Root Certification Authorities** container on all clients).

4. Verify that clients have successfully enrolled and received a certificate.

5. Verify that the URA server itself has been issued a certificate as well.

Then, in the URA configuration console, edit **Remote Access Server settings** (step 2) and in the **Authentication** page, enable **Use computer certificates**. Click on **Browse** and select the CA that you configured earlier:

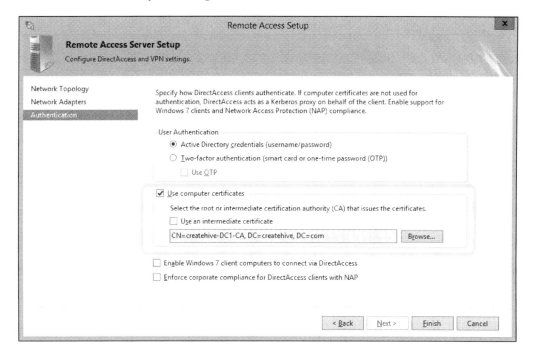

The other URA servers that you will deploy will also need an authentication certificate, so make sure you issue one for them as well.

IP-HTTPS and NLS certificates

As you may recall from previous sections, one of the three available client connectivity options is **IP-HTTPS**, with which the IPv6 packets are encapsulated inside **HTTPS** traffic. To establish the HTTPS connection, the URA server requires a certificate, and you will need to get one from a commercial certificate provider, or from your own certificate authority server. When we discussed this topic earlier, we noted that the URA wizard can generate a **self-signed certificate**, but unfortunately, this option does not apply to multisite deployments, and therefore, you'll have to deal with it. Using the **Certificate Authority** role in Windows is perfectly fine for this, but do keep in mind that the clients need to trust this CA server. If you configure it as an **Enterprise CA**, then its trust chain is automatically deployed to clients via active directory, so that could be easy, but the CAs CRL also needs to be made available on the public internet, and that may be harder to achieve. Using a third party provider is a lot easier, because all Windows clients come preconfigured with the root certificates of all providers, and the public providers do publish their CRLs regularly, taking that concern off your plate.

It's important to remember that since you will be configuring multiple URA servers, you have to have an IP-HTTPS certificate on each and every one of them. Each entry point needs to have a different **public hostname** than the others, but if they are all using the same domain suffix (for example, `USA.createhive.com`, `Europe.createhive.com`, and so on), then one nice shortcut is using a **Wildcard Certificate**. This way, one certificate can be used on all your URA servers.

 If you are purchasing your certificates from a commercial provider, this is also more economic because one wildcard certificate is cheaper than a bunch of regular ones. If you have your own CA, then issuing a gazillion certificates doesn't cost anything, so the cost doesn't matter as much.

If you intend to use a Windows CA server for either or both certificates, you will need to use the **Web Server certificate template** for this IP-HTTPS certificate. You can get a certificate using the web interface that Windows CA servers come with, or use the certificate management console on the URA server to request one. Either way, if your CA server is a newly installed one, then by default, the web server template's security settings won't let you enroll a certificate using the certificate management interface. To get around that, edit the security settings for this template:

1. On your CA server, open the Certificate Authority management console.
2. Right-click on **Certificate Templates** and choose **Manage**.
3. In the list of templates, find **Web Server** and double-click on it.
4. Switch to the **Security** tab.

5. Click on **Domain Computers**.

6. Check the option **Enroll** and click on **OK**.

Note that this will allow any computer to request a certificate of this type. If you don't like that idea, you can instead create a special security group for this. To do so, create such a dedicated group in active directory Users and Computers, and add the URA servers to it. Then, edit the template security settings as described in the previous section, but instead of adding the **Enroll** option to **Domain Computers**, add the new group you created and check that option only for that group.

Once your first URA server has the appropriate IP-HTTPS certificate, select it in the URA configuration console:

1. In the URA console, edit **Remote Access Server settings** (step 2).

2. Go to the **Network Adapters** page.

3. If the wizard hasn't been automatically configured with the appropriate certificate, click on **Browse**, and select it.

4. Click on **Next**, and then **Finish** the wizard.

5. Click on **Finish** at the bottom of the screen to apply your configuration.

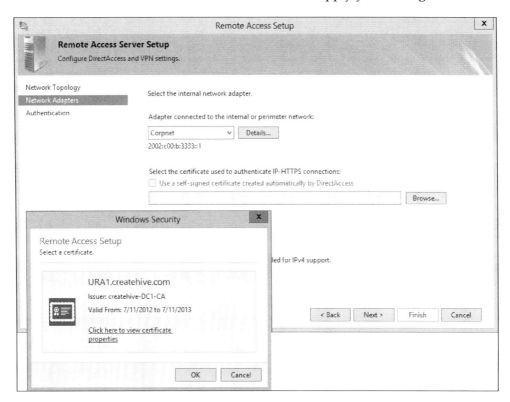

Similar principles apply to your network location server (NLS). It too requires a full certificate issued by either an internal or external CA; so if you have configured your URA settings with the easy start wizard that sets this to use a **self-signed certificate**, you'll have to issue the certificate, and set it in the URA configuration. The NLS certificate is also generated using the web server template, but unlike the IP-HTTPS one, it cannot be a wildcard certificate. Each and every site needs to have its own NLS, and they will all answer to the same name using the special DNS entries you configured earlier. This means that the certificate you issue for the multiple NLS servers needs to cover the same name. If you're using your own CA, then you simply issue a web server certificate with the common name set to the FQDN of the NLS (for example `nls.createhive.com`). If you are getting your certificate from a commercial provider, you can get one certificate, and then export it and import it on all the other URA servers.

To change the NLS certificate in URA from the self-signed to the regular certificate, follow the steps as shown:

1. In the URA console, edit **Infrastructure Servers** (step 3).

2. The wizard starts with the **Network Location Server** page.

3. Click on **Browse** and select your NLS certificate.

4. Click on **Next** through the rest of the wizard, until it's finished.

5. Click on **Finish** at the bottom of the screen to apply your configuration.

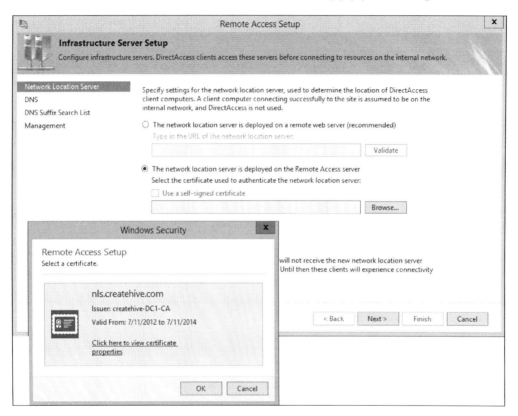

Connectivity verifier considerations

An important part of URA operations are the **connectivity verifiers**, also known as **probes**, which are used by clients to confirm that their connection is working. With a single-site, URA sets up a single probe, but as you can imagine, with multisite, you need one for each entry point. The default probe address is `directaccess-WebProbeHost`, and the URA wizard will attempt to create it in the DNS. The idea is that in each site that has an entry point, the DNS will resolve that address to the internal IP address of the entry point for the site. If the DNS entry is missing, clients won't be able to tell their connection is working and would misinform the end-user about this fact. If the entry resolves the wrong IP, the client might think it's correctly connected even if it's not (misinforming the end-user as well). Another problem could arise if the entry resolves to the wrong URA server. If clients connected to one entry point get the wrong name resolution, and use another entry point mistakenly, the probing traffic might go over your **WAN** link between these sites, and waste considerable bandwidth.

When you run the URA multisite wizard, it will attempt to create the DNS entries for the probes on each site. If it fails because of connectivity or permission issues, it will warn you, and you'll have to then create the entries yourself. It would be a good idea to verify the entries, and see that in every site, they indeed resolve to the internal IP address of the URA server that services that site. The default web probe name is `DirectAccess-corpConnectivityhost`, and it should resolve to ::1. Another point to keep in mind is that if you have **DNS scavenging** enabled, you need to configure it so that the **directaccess-WebProbeHost** entry is not scrubbed automatically. If it's gone, the clients will not know they are able to reach the corporate network and may show incorrect status to the user.

Windows 7 clients and multisite

If you intend to deploy your URA with **backward compatibility** for Windows 7 clients, you must keep in mind that it complicates your setup somewhat. The hard part is not in the multisite wizard, but in the fact that multisite selection is not available for Windows 7 clients, and so this will require you to plan your security groups.

During the multisite wizard in URA, you will be specifically asked whether you wish to provide this service to Windows 7 clients. If all the other requirements are met, this will be rather simple. As you may recall from *Chapter 2, Planning a Unified Remote Access Deployment* and *Chapter 3, Preparing a Group Policy and Certificate Infrastructure*, Windows 7 clients cannot choose which entry point to connect-to, and so you'll have to make that decision for them. This is done via security groups in active directory. For Windows 8 clients, you need only one security group to contain all of them, but with Windows 7 clients, you'll need one group for each entry point, and membership in that group will determine the site that the computer connects to.

To do this, simply create a security group for each entry point you plan on creating, and assign the appropriate Windows 7 clients to that group. If you wish to move a certain computer from one site to the other, you'll have to move the computer from the security group for its current site to the other, and then update the Group Policy on the computer, so that the client can have the appropriate Group Policy for the new site. You also need a separate Windows 7 client GPO that applies to the Windows 7 client security group for the domain and is tied to the specific entry point. If you have more than one domain from which you will have Windows 7 clients, then you will need the GPO for each of these domains that is tied to that specific entry point.

The multisite configuration wizard

Hopefully, you now have everything planned out and ready to deploy. The general order of things is that you first configure your first URA server separately and independently. Then, you install the URA role on other servers that you want to use as entry points in other sites. Once they are ready, you enable the Multisite option on the first server and define some general settings such as entry-point selection options and support for Windows 7 clients. After this step is complete, you add the other URA servers as entry points. At that point, you can also enable **Global Load Balancing**, if you have the appropriate hardware and want to use it for this purpose.

Assuming you have your URA servers installed in all sites, with each having an IP-HTTPS certificate of its own, and an NLS certificate as well, you should be ready to begin. To be clear—you don't need to configure URA on the other servers—just install the role on them, and the rest will be done later.

To start the process, click on **Enable Multisite** on the far-right, on the URA console:

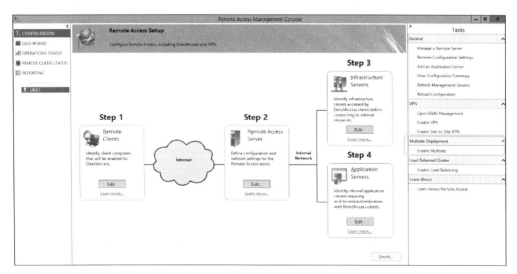

After you start the wizard, you will be presented with a generic welcome page, notifying you how this affects Windows 7 clients. This informs you that if you have previously configured security groups containing Windows 7 computers, in order to apply URA to them, you need to remove the Windows 7 computers from this group, and that you will be able to add them as part of the multisite wizard. The reason for this change is because the way URA allows clients to select their entry point cannot be used on Windows 7 computers, so it's important that these new settings don't get applied to them.

The next step requires you to provide a name for this configuration, which you will use to identify this configuration and refer to it. You also need to type in a name for the first entry point, which is this URA server, of course:

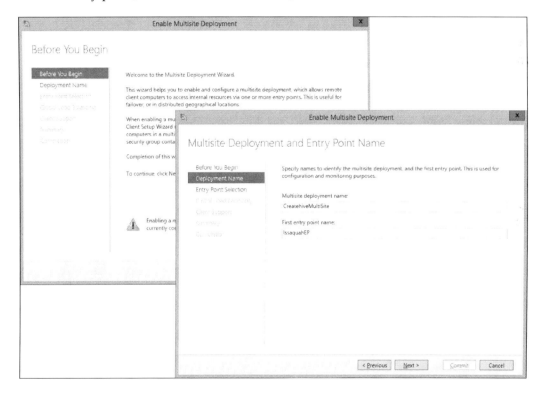

The next step is particularly important, as it pertains to how entry point selection will be done. Entry point selection is automatic, but you can also choose to allow clients to make their own selection. Then, you can configure a global load balancing option, if it is relevant. A global load balancing configuration requires you to type in a single URL that will be used as the main access URL for all balanced URA servers. You will also need to type in the IP address that will represent this particular URA server in the global array as shown in the following screenshot:

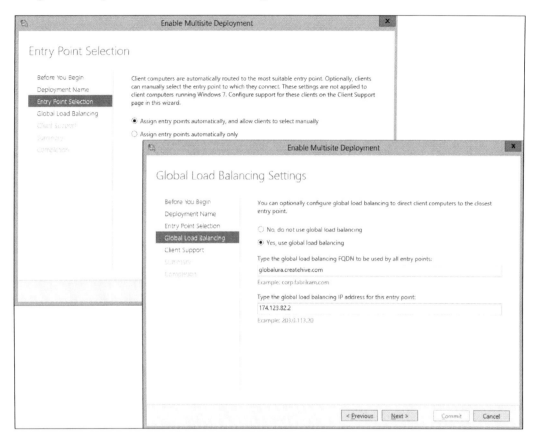

On the next screen, you have the option of enabling support for Windows 7 clients. If you choose to enable it, then you also need to specify a group of computers for which this will apply to. If you haven't created such a group yet, then you can switch to the **Active Directory Users and Computers** to create it, and add Windows 7 computers to it, as shown in the following screenshot:

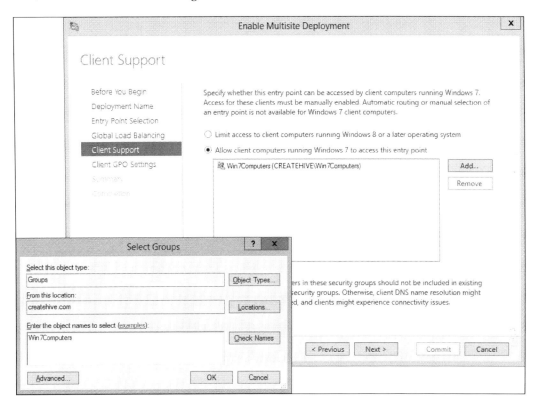

If you did enable Windows 7 client support, the wizard will next go to the **Client GPO** settings dialog, which requires you to create or choose a Group Policy object for this. This is important because, as we said, Windows 7 computers have a separate collection of settings, and need their own GPO for these settings. You can click on **Browse** to choose from an existing GPO, if you have one already, or simply type in a name for a new GPO, and the wizard will create and populate it for you.

Lastly, the **Summary** page lists the choices you made, and allows you to commit them to Group Policy. Once you complete this, the wizard will update the domain's Group Policy configuration, and it will start getting applied to clients which perform a Group Policy update. Naturally, if you have multiple DCs, you might need to wait for replication to other DCs to complete before you can start things moving. If you recall from *Chapter 3, Preparing a Group Policy and Certificate Infrastructure*, you also have the option of triggering a Group Policy update on your clients remotely using the **Group Policy management console**.

If you look at your URA configuration console, you will notice that the tasks pane on the right-hand side of the screen now has the option to **Configure Multisite Settings** and **Disable Multisite**. The latter is self explanatory. The other allows you to change the options you selected for the entry point selection mode, and to edit the global load balancing options.

Adding more entry points

Now that multisite is running, it's time to add more entry points. To do so, click on **Add an entry point** in the URA configuration console, under the **Multisite deployment** area in the tasks pane on the right. On the first page of the wizard, you need to specify the hostname of the other URA server you are adding, and give the entry point a name. This name is what users will see when they are connecting to it, so a descriptive name would be a good idea (for example, **US East** would probably be better than **SrvURANYSvr01**). When you click on **Next**, your server will try to contact the new server and verify it's running the URA role. To remind you, you must have administrative privileges on each entry point server you are adding.

The next few steps are somewhat similar to the configuration steps for a regular URA setup, except the fact that they are done remotely to the new server. First, you configure the **Network Topology**, during which you select whether the new entry point will be on the edge or behind an edge firewall, and whether it has two network cards or just one. Next, you need to type in the public name or the IP that will be used by the new entry point:

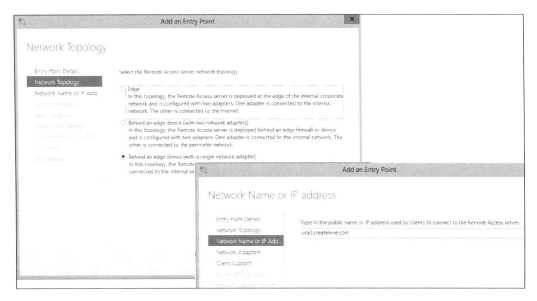

Note that using an IP here is tricky, because this is where the clients will attempt to connect when using IP-HTTPS. Part of the HTTPS connection, of course, has the client comparing the subject name on the certificate the server sends it to what it was trying to connect to. If that target is an IP address instead of a hostname, the subject name on the certificate needs to be the IP as well and that's already highly unusual (some certificate providers will refuse to provide such a certificate). If your URA server is not really on the edge, but behind an edge device, then the IP it has on its NIC is probably different than the actual public IP that the edge device listens on. For these reasons, we strongly recommend using host-names, both in the certificate and in the wizard. If that's out of the question, than make sure the IP you specify is the public one, and that the subject name of the certificate is that same IP as well.

On the next page, the network card that will be facing the internet is selected, and if the computer has more than one card, you might need to pick the correct one. On this page you also select the certificate that will be used for IP-HTTPS connections. As opposed to the **Getting Started Wizard**, the configuration console doesn't have the option of creating a self-signed certificate, but if you already have one, you can use it. Naturally, you can also use a certificate issued by your CA or a public CA. If you haven't taken care of that earlier, you can still pause now and obtain a certificate now. Once ready, click on **Browse** and select the appropriate certificate. Note that the common-name on the certificate has to match the public hostname you used in the previous page (ura2.creahive.com in our example). The wizard will contact the other server, and will look for certificates that match the name, and show only those as available.

On the next page of the wizard, you can elect to allow Windows 7 clients to use this entry point. As you may remember from us repeating it a gazillion times, Windows 7 clients cannot choose their entry point, and therefore, you need to create a domain group for this purpose, and assign specific Windows 7 computers to it. Based on the group membership, the URA Group Policy will be assigned to those computers, instructing them where to connect to. You will not be able to choose the same group for use with other entry points, so plan your groups, your group membership, and group naming carefully.

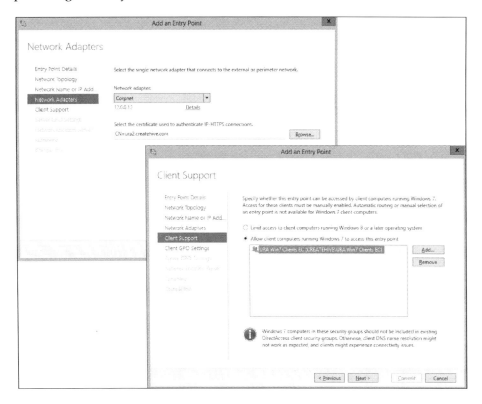

If you elected to enable Windows 7 clients to use this entry point, the next page will allow you to select the Group Policy used for them. Again, since this Group Policy is unique to this entry point, make sure you use a unique name for it. You can click on **Validate GPO** to make sure the name is fine and doesn't conflict. If a green plus appears next to the group, it means validation was successful. If not, you will see a red **X** and a message indicating the failure at the bottom, as you can see in the following screenshot:

The next page is for selecting the Group Policy for the server settings. The GPO you create in that step will apply only to the server you are adding, because it has unique settings that apply only to it, and so it also needs to have a unique name. As before, click on **Validate GPO** to confirm that it's all good.

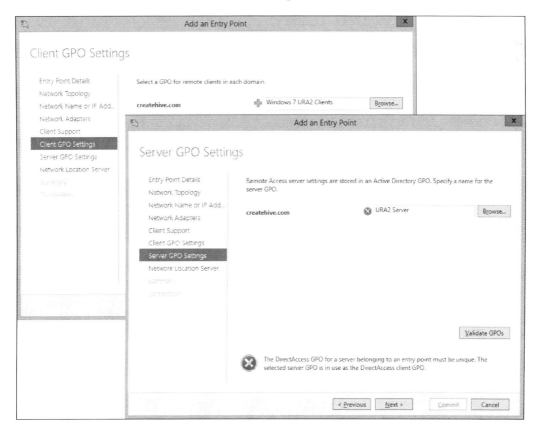

On the next page, you need to select the certificate that will be assigned to the NLS server which the URA wizard will configure on the new entry point. If you recall from previous sections, clients will be trying to contact the NLS to check if they are on the corporate network or not, and since the clients using the new entry point will typically be working in the same office where that entry point is located, they will need a local NLS server to connect to. If you have not yet issued a certificate to the server, you can go ahead and do so now. When you click on **Browse**, the server will contact the new server and look for a certificate that can be used for this purpose. That certificate needs to be for the internal hostname of the NLS server and match the DNS entry you created for it, otherwise, you will get an error informing you of this.

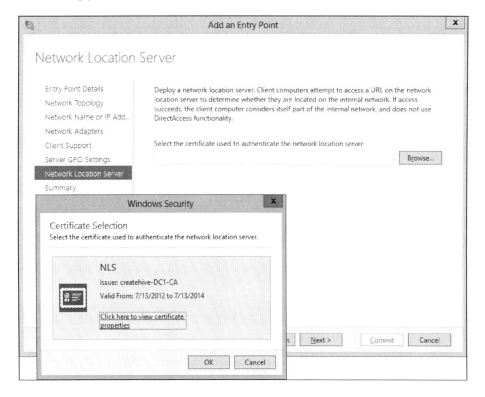

The next page of the wizard confirms all your settings and allows you to commit them, which updates Group Policy on the domain. Once this is completed, and GPO replication has completed, the new policies will apply to clients based on the regular GPO update schedule, and your clients can start using the new site when they leave the office.

Using PowerShell in complex environments

If you need to add many entry points, doing this via the user interface might take a long time. Thankfully, many of these operations can be automated using PowerShell. For example, with PowerShell, you can add an entry point by running the cmdlet `Add-DAEntryPoint` with a few parameters rather than multiple steps we just spent four pages describing, although the complex syntax of PowerShell makes this more suitable for the more experienced, or for situations where you need to add a large amount of entry points and doing so via the console would take an unreasonable amount of time. In *Chapter 8, Enhanced Configurations for Infrastructure Servers*, we will go into PowerShell with more detail. If you're already familiar with it, you can find the multisite specific examples here:

```
http://technet.microsoft.com/en-us/library/jj134167
```

You can also find the full URA PowerShell reference here:

```
http://technet.microsoft.com/en-us/library/hh918399
```

```
http://technet.microsoft.com/en-us/library/hh848426.aspx
```

Summary

Having completed this chapter, you now know how to deploy a multisite environment, and hopefully, also expanded your understanding of certificates and how they work in the real world. In the next chapter, we will see how you can take URA even further, into the cloud, and extend your network securely.

6
Cross-premise Connectivity

Cross-premise connectivity (also known as cloud connectivity) is the ability to establish secure connection between two sites. It could be between a head office and a branch office or from an office to a cloud data center. Before we go into the details of cross-premise connectivity let us take a moment and talk about the connectivity challenges that an enterprise faces. In this chapter, we are going to talk about what cross-premise connectivity is, why it is needed, and how to go about establishing it. The topics we will discuss are as follows:

- Evolving remote access challenges
- Migration to dynamic cloud
- The needs of modern data centers
- Dynamic cloud access with URA
- Adding a cloud location using Site-to-Site
- Basic setup of cross-premise connectivity
- Configuration steps
- Configuring Site-to-Site with PowerShell

Evolving remote access challenges

In order to increase productivity of employees, every company wants to provide access to their applications to their employees from anywhere. The users are no longer tied to work from a single location. The users need access to their data from any location and also from any device they have. They also want to access their applications irrespective of where the application is hosted. Allowing this remote connectivity to increase the productivity is in constant conflict with keeping the edge secure. As we allow more applications, the edge device becomes porous and keeping the edge secure is a constant battle for the administrators. The network administrators will have to ensure that this remote access to their remote users is always available and they can access their application in the same way as they would access it while in the office. Otherwise they would need to be trained on how to access an application while they are remote, and this is bound to increase the support cost for maintaining the infrastructure. Another important challenge for the network administrator is the ability to manage the remote connections and ensure they are secure.

Migration to dynamic cloud

In a modern enterprise, there is a constant need to optimize the infrastructure based on workload. Most of the time we want to know how to plan for the correct capacity rather than taking a bet on the number of servers that are needed for a given workload. If the business needs are seasonal we need to bet on a certain level of infrastructure expenses.

If we don't get the expected traffic, the investment may go underutilized. At the same time if the incoming traffic volume is too high, the organization may lose the opportunity to generate additional revenue. In order to reduce the risk of losing additional revenue and at the same time to reduce large capital expenses, organizations may deploy virtualized solutions. However, this still requires the organization to take a bet on the initial infrastructure.

What if the organization could deploy their infrastructure based on need? Then they could expand on demand. This is where moving to the cloud helps to move the **capital expense (CapEx)** to **operational expense (OpEx)**. If you tell your finance department that you are moving to an OpEx model for your infrastructure needs, you will definitely be greeted by cheers and offered cake (or at least, a fancy calculator).

The needs of modern data centers

As we said, reducing capital expense is on everyone's to-do list these days, and being able to invest in your infrastructure based on business needs is a key to achieving that goal. If your company is expecting seasonal workload, you would probably want to be able to dynamically expand your infrastructure based on needs. Moving your workloads to the cloud allows you to do this. If you are dealing with sensitive customer data or intellectual property, you probably want to be able to maintain secure connectivity between your premise and the cloud. You might also need to move workloads between your premise and the cloud as per your business demands, and so establishing secure connectivity between corporate and the cloud must be dynamic and transparent to your users. That means the gateway you use at the edge of your on-premise network and the gateway your cloud provider uses must be compatible.

Another consideration is that you must also be able to establish or tear down the connection quickly, and it needs to be able to recover from outages very quickly. In addition, today's users are mobile and the data they access is also dynamic (the data itself may move from your on-premise servers to the cloud or back). Ideally, the users need not know where the data is and from where they are accessing the data, and they should not change their behavior depending on from where they access the data and where the data resides. All these are the needs of the modern data center. Things may get even more complex if you have multiple branch offices and multiple cloud locations.

Dynamic cloud access with URA

Let's see how these goals can be met with Windows Server 2012. In order for the mobile users to connect to the organizational network, they can use either DirectAccess or VPN. When you move resources to the cloud, you need to maintain the same address space of the resources so that your users are impacted by this change as little as possible. When you move a server or an entire network to the cloud, you can establish a **Site-to-Site (S2S)** connection through an edge gateway. Imagine you have a global deployment with many remote sites, a couple of public cloud data centers and some of your own private cloud. As the number of these remote sites grow, the number of Site-to-Site links needed will grow exponentially. If you have to maintain a gateway server or device for the Site-to-Site connections and another gateway for remote access such as VPN or DirectAccess, the maintenance cost associated with it can increase dramatically.

One of the most significant new abilities with Windows Server 2012 Unified Remote Access is the combination of DirectAccess and the traditional **Routing and Remote Access Server** (**RRAS**) in the same Remote Access role. With this, you can now manage all your remote access needs from one unified console. As we've seen, only certain versions of Windows (Windows 7 Enterprise and Ultimate, Windows 8 Enterprise) can be DirectAccess clients, but what if you have to accommodate some Vista or XP clients or if you have third-party clients that need CorpNet connectivity? With Windows Server 2012, you can enable the traditional VPN from the Remote Access console and allow the down-level and third-party clients to connect via VPN. The Unified Remote Access console also allows the remote access clients to be monitored from the same console. This is very useful as you can now configure, manage, monitor, and troubleshoot all remote access needs from the same place.

In the past, you might have used the Site-to-Site demand-dial connections to connect and route to your remote offices, but until now the demand-dial Site-to-Site connections used either the **Point-to-Point Tunneling Protocol** (**PPTP**) or **Layer Two Tunnel Protocol** (**L2TP**) protocols. However, these involved manual steps that needed to be performed from the console. They also produced challenges working with similar gateway devices from other vendors and because the actions are needed to be performed through the console, they did not scale well if the number of Site-to-Site connections increased beyond a certain number.

Some products attempted to overcome the limits of the built-in Site-to-Site options in Windows. For example, Microsoft's Forefront Threat Management Gateway 2010 used the **Internet Key Exchange** (**IKE**) protocol, which allowed it to work with other gateways from Cisco and Juniper. However, the limit of that solution was that in case one end of the IPsec connection fails for some reason, the **Dead Peer Detection** (**DPD**) took some time to realize the failure. The time it took for the recovery or fallback to alternate path caused some applications that were communicating over the tunnel to fail and this disruption to the service could cause significant losses.

Thanks to the ability to combine both VPN and DirectAccess in the same box as well as the ability to add the Site-to-Site IPsec connection in the same box, Windows Server 2012 allows you to reduce the number of unique gateway servers needed at each site. Also, the Site-to-Site connections can be established and torn down with a simple PowerShell command, making managing multiple connections easier. The S2S tunnel mode IPsec link uses the industry standard IKEv2 protocol for IPsec negotiation between the end points, which is great because this protocol is the current interoperability standard for almost any VPN gateway. That means you don't have to worry about what the remote gateway is; as long as it supports IKEv2, you can confidently create the S2S IPsec tunnel to it and establish connectivity easily and with a much better recovery speed in case of a connection drop.

Now let's look at the options and see how we can quickly and effectively establish the connectivity using URA. Let's start with a headquarters location and a branch office location and then look at the high-level needs and steps to achieve the desired connectivity. Since this involves just two locations, our typical needs are that clients in either location should be able to connect to the other site. The connection should be secure and we need the link only when there is a need for traffic flow between the two locations. We don't want to use dedicated links such as T1 or fractional T1 lines as we do not want to pay for the high cost associated with them. Instead, we can use our pre-existing Internet connection and establish Site-to-Site IPsec tunnels that provide us a secure way to connect between the two locations. We also want users from public Internet locations to be able to access any resource in any location.

We have already seen how DirectAccess can provide us with the seamless connectivity to the organizational network for domain-joined Windows 7 or Windows 8 clients, and how to set up a multisite deployment. We also saw how multisite allows Windows 8 clients to connect to the nearest site and Windows 7 clients can connect to the site they are configured to connect to. Because the same URA server can also be configured as a S2S gateway and the IPsec tunnel allows both IPv4 and IPv6 traffic to flow through it, it will now allow our DirectAccess clients in public Internet locations to connect to any one of the sites and also reach the remote site through the Site-to-Site tunnel.

Adding the site in the cloud is very similar to adding a branch office location and it can be either your private cloud or the public cloud. Typically, the cloud service provider provides its own gateway and will allow you to build your infrastructure behind it. The provider could typically provide you an IP address for you to use as a remote end point and they will just allow you to connect to your resources by NATting the traffic to your resource in the cloud.

Adding a cloud location using Site-to-Site

In the following diagram, we have a site called Headquarters with a URA server (URA1) at the edge. The clients on the public Internet can access resources in the corporate network through DirectAccess or through the traditional VPN, using the URA1 at the edge. We have a cloud infrastructure provider and we need to build our CloudNet in the cloud and provide connectivity between the corporate network at the Headquarters and CloudNet in the cloud. The clients on the Internet should be able to access resources in the corporate network or CloudNet, and the connection should be transparent to them.

The CloudGW is the typical edge device in the cloud that your cloud provider owns and it is used to control and monitor the traffic flow to each tenant.

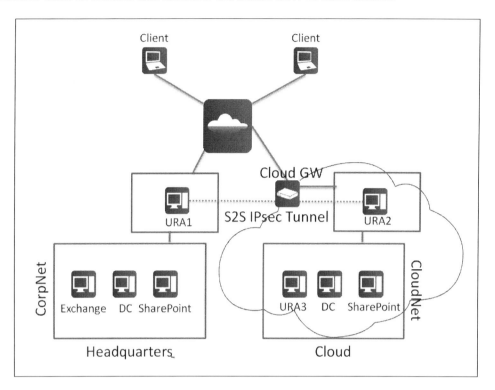

Basic setup of cross-premise connectivity

The following steps outline the various options and scenarios you might want to configure:

1. Ask your cloud provider for the public IP address of the cloud gateway they provide.

2. Build a virtual machine running Windows Server 2012 with the Remote Access role and place it in your cloud location. We will refer to this server as *URA2*.

3. Configure URA2 as a S2S gateway with two interfaces:

   ° The interface towards the CloudGW will be the IPsec tunnel endpoint for the S2S connection. The IP address for this interface could be a public IPv4 address assigned by your cloud provider or a private IPv4 address of your choice.

   If it is a private IPv4 address, the provider should send all the IPsec traffic for the S2S connection from the CloudGW to the Internet-facing interface of URA2. The remote tunnel endpoint configuration in URA1 for the remote site will be the public address that you got in step 1.

   If the Internet-facing interface of URA2 is also a routable public IPv4 address, the remote tunnel endpoint configuration in URA1 for the remote site will be this public address of URA2.

   ° The second interface on URA2 will be a private address that you are going to use in your CloudNet towards servers you are hosting there.

4. Configure the cloud gateway to allow the S2S connections to your gateway (URA2).

5. Establish S2S connectivity between URA2 and URA1. This will allow you to route all traffic between CloudNet and CorpNet.

The preceding steps provide full access between the CloudNet and CorpNet and also allow your DirectAccess and VPN clients on the Internet to access any resource in CorpNet or CloudNet without having to worry whether the resource is in CorpNet or in CloudNet.

DirectAccess entry point in the cloud

Building on the basic setup, you can further extend the capabilities of the clients on the Internet to reach the CloudNet directly without having to go through the CorpNet. To achieve this, we can add a URA Server in the CloudNet (URA3). Here is an overview of the steps to achieve this (assuming your URA server URA3 is already installed with the Remote Access role):

1. Place a domain controller in CloudNet. It can communicate with your domain through the Site-to-Site connection to do Active Directory replication and perform just like any other domain controller.

2. Enable the multisite configuration on your primary URA server (URA1) in similar way that we discussed in *Chapter 5*, *Multisite Deployment*.

3. Add URA3 as an additional entry point. It will be configured as a URA server with the single NIC topology.

4. Register the IP-HTTPS site name in DNS for URA3.

5. Configure your cloud gateway to forward the HTTPS traffic to your URA2 and in turn to URA3 to allow clients to establish the IP-HTTPS connections.

Using this setup, clients on the Internet can connect to either the entry point URA1 or URA3. No matter what they choose, they can access all resources either directly or via the Site-to-Site tunnel.

Authentication

The Site-to-Site connection between the two end points (URA1 and URA2) can be configured with **Pre Shared Key** (**PSK**) for authentication or you can further secure the IPsec tunnel with Certificate Authentication. Here, the certificates you will need for Certificate Authentication would be computer certificates that match the name of the end points. You could use either certificates issued by a third-party provider or certificates issued from your internal **Certificate Authority** (**CA**). As with any certificate authentication, the two end points need to trust the certificates used at either end, so you need to make sure the certificate of the root CA is installed on both servers. To make things simpler, you can start with a simple PSK-based tunnel and once the basic scenario works, change the authentication to computer certificates. We will see the steps to use both PSK and Certificates in the detailed steps in the following section.

Configuration steps

Even though the Site-to-Site IPsec tunnel configuration is possible via the console, we highly recommend that you get familiar with the PowerShell commands for this configuration as they make it a lot easier to configure this in case you need to manage multiple configurations. If you have multiple remote sites, having to set up and tear down each site based on workload demand is not scalable when configured through the console. We will provide the PowerShell commands to set up the Site-to-Site connection later in this chapter.

Enabling the Routing and Remote Access Server service

Assuming the URA role is already installed, the first step is enabling the **Routing and Remote Access Server (RRAS)** service. To do so, follow these steps:

1. From the Server Manager open the **Routing and Remote Access** console

2. Right-click on your server name and click on **Configure and Enable Routing and Remote Access**:

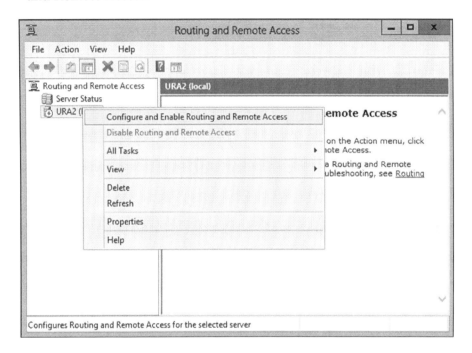

3. If the option is grayed out, this is because you configured DirectAccess by choosing the **Deploy DirectAccess Only** option. In such a case, you need to click on **Enable Site-to-Site VPN** on the task pane of the URA console, and then skip ahead directly to the *Configuring the demand-dial interface* section discussed later in this chapter.

4. Click on **Next** on the **Welcome to Routing and Remote Access Server Setup Wizard** page.

5. Select the **Secure connection between two private networks** option:

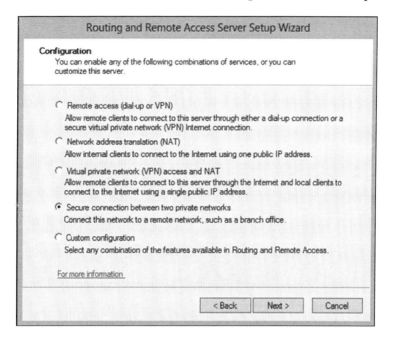

6. The IPsec tunnel will be established only when there is a need for traffic to flow between URA1 and URA2 and so this is called a **demand-dial connection**.

7. Keep the default option **Automatically** checked and click on **Next**:

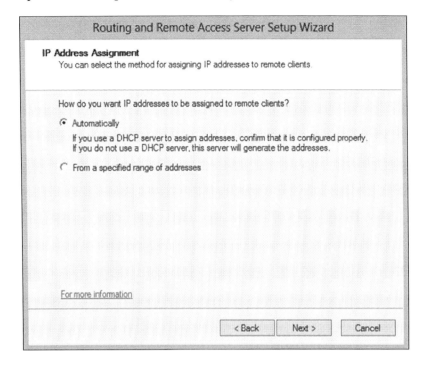

In this section, the wizard provides an option on how to assign IP addresses for the demand-dial interfaces. While this step suggests that we either provide an IP address by using a DHCP server (the **Automatically** option) or configure a static pool of IP addresses from which the demand-dial interface gets an IP, you don't need to do so. Both these options are relevant if we use **Point-to-Point Tunneling Protocol (PPTP)** or **Layer Two Tunneling Protocol (L2TP)** for demand-dial connections. Both PPTP and L2TP use the **Point to Point Protocol (PPP)** interfaces and they require an IP for the demand-dial interface to route the traffic between the two private networks. In our case, however, we use IPsec tunnel mode using IKEv2 protocol and so we do not need to have an IP address for the demand-dial interface. This means that we can simply take the default and move on.

8. Click **Finish** to enable RRAS and start **Demand-Dial Interface Wizard**.

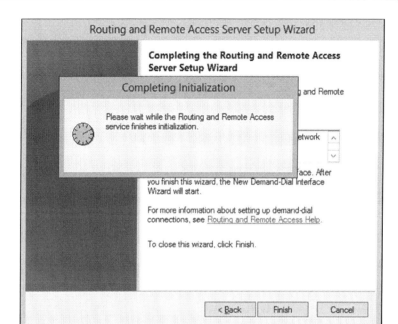

Configuring the demand-dial interface

Once the RRAS service is enabled, we now have to create the demand-dial interface to establish the IPsec tunnel between URA1 and URA2. In this section, we will configure the demand-dial interface on the URA2 server and so the remote end point for URA2 will be URA1. When traffic from CloudNet needs to reach CorpNet, it will automatically use this demand-dial interface.

Completing the RRAS wizard earlier should automatically start the demand-dial interface wizard. If you click on **Cancel**, it will stop the RRAS service and you will have to repeat the previous steps again. If you had to skip the earlier wizard because that option was grayed out, you can start the add-interface wizard by right-clicking on the **Network Interface** node and choosing **New Demand-dial Interface**.

To configure the interface, follow these steps:

1. Click on **Next** on the wizard's welcome page.

2. Enter a name that you can use to identify the remote site.

> While you can enter any name, it would be easier if you enter either Headquarters or Corpnet or URA1 to identify this interface is connecting the remote side. However, if you use PPTP or L2TP connections, the name used in the interface will have to match a username that you will use to reach the remote side. Since we are not using PPTP or L2TP, we will stick to the name URA1. When you have multiple remote sites, it will be easier to keep track of things and manage the server comfortably if you have named them with the site name it is connecting to.

3. Choose the option **Connect using virtual private networking (VPN)**:

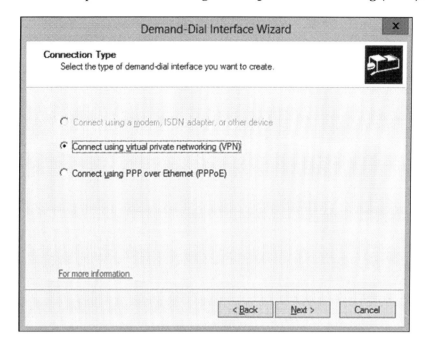

4. Select the option **IKEv2** (it is new in Windows Server 2012!):

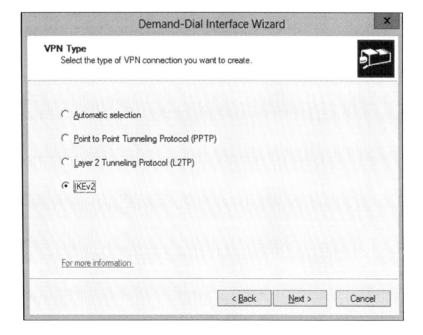

5. Enter the IPv4 address, IPv6address or FQDN of URA1 (we are configuring URA2 to connect to it). Later on, configure a similar setup on the other server (URA1) and then use the IP or FQDN of URA2:

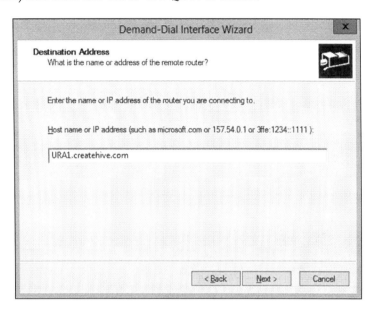

6. Check the **Route IP packets on this interface** option (as discussed earlier, the S2S IPsec tunnel does not need any username for the demand-dial interfaces and so we don't have to select the second check box to add a user account):

7. On the **Static Route** page, you need to specify the addresses of the remote network. Since we are configuring URA2 to connect to URA1 on CorpNet, you need to configure the IP address range used on your corporate network. Later, when configuring the same screen on URA1, you will need to specify the IP range on CloudNet. You can specify as many IPv4 and/or IPv6 routes as you need. If you make a mistake, you can also edit this configuration later via the RRAS console.

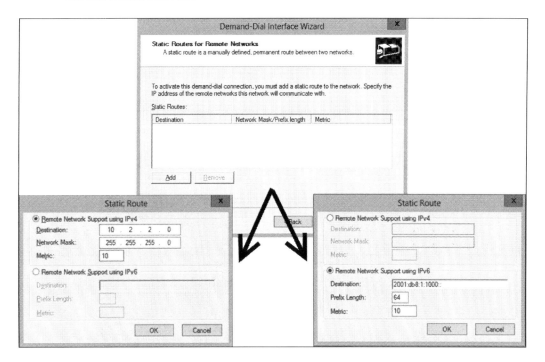

 The **metric** is the route metric that will be used to select the best path, and the path with lower metric is chosen if there are multiple options. This metric value will be useful if you want to create redundant connection to the same destination. If you have two links to the Internet, you can use one of them as the default link with lowest route metric and the other as a backup by configuring with a higher route metric.

8. Leave the **Dial-Out credentials** page blank (as discussed earlier, we do not have to specify a username and a password for the demand-dial connection when we use IPsec tunnel mode S2S connection).

9. Click on **Finish** to complete the demand-dial configuration and return to the RRAS console.

10. Repeat the same procedure on your other server (URA1), but using different destination address and static routes appropriately.

Once you finish configuring both servers, the connection should establish automatically as soon as a computer on either side of the tunnel attempts to send data to a resource on the other side. You can inspect the status of the connection by going to the **Network Interface** node of the RRAS console. The right-hand pane will have a **Status** column, which will show you whether the interface is connected or not. As you may recall, this is a demand-dial interface, so as long as no one on either side is trying to access IPs on the other side, the connection will be disconnected, and that's perfectly fine. To test it, you can try initiating traffic to a resource on the other side, or you could simply right-click on the connection you created and choose **Connect**.

Editing the connection

If you need to view or edit the S2S settings, the RRAS console allows you to do so as well. The **Network Interfaces** node allows you to see all directly connected interfaces including the demand-dial interface (URA1) we just created; and you can double-click on it to edit its properties:

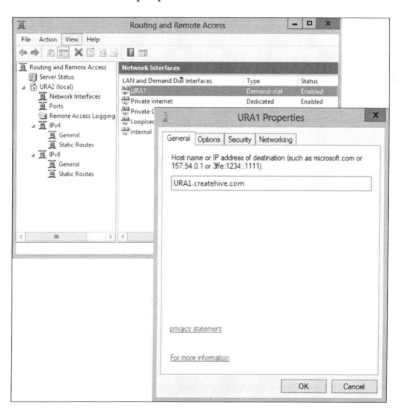

As part of the **Security** tab, you can see the **IKEv2** option that we chose for the S2S connection. The authentication option is set by default to use machine certificates, but allows you to switch to PSK, if you like (the **EAP** option is a legacy setting for RRAS and does not pertain to S2S). The certificate here should match the computer name of the URA server. If you use PSK, you have to configure the same PSK in both sides of the tunnel endpoints. While PSK is an easy way to set up the tunnel, it is not considered to be very secure.

In the RRAS console, you can also expand **IPv4** or **IPv6** to view and edit the static routes that you configured as part of step 7 of the wizard earlier in the preceding section. Normally, the demand-dial connection already knows what the other end point is and so there is no gateway address configured (as you might expect to see with routing configuration):

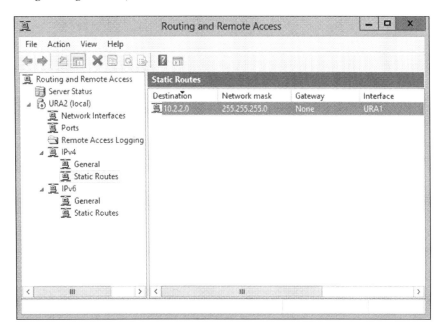

Configuring S2S with PowerShell

As we said earlier, when you have multiple sites, using the console to create the multiple connections can easily become cumbersome and prone to user error, and in such a case, using PowerShell can make things easier. This is not only about speed, but also about the fact that writing your commands in a text file can help eliminate typos and mistakes that could occur during the wizard. Here are the PowerShell commands and cmdlets that you can use to establish the Site-to-Site IPsec tunnel between URA1 and URA2.

Adding the feature

The following commands add the remote access and routing features and need to be executed in a PowerShell prompt on all your URA servers:

```
ipmo servermanager
Install-WindowsFeature RemoteAccess -IncludeManagementTools
add-windowsFeature -name  routing -IncludeManagementTools
ipmo remoteaccess
install-remoteaccess -vpntype vpns2s
```

Adding the S2S interface

To add the S2S demand-dial interface on each of your servers, run the following command:

```
Add-VpnS2SInterface  <interface name> <IP or FQDN of target server>
-Protocol IKEv2 -AuthenticationMethod PSKonly -SharedSecret "<secret>"
-IPv4Subnet <subnet>/<CIDR>:<metric>
```

Other options of this command include using `MachineCertificates` instead of `PSKonly` to use a certificate, using `-Ipv6Subnet` to specify an IPv6 subnet (either with or instead of an IPv4 one). If you need to specify multiple subnets, you can specify them as comma-separated inside the structure `@("<subnet 1>","<subnet 2>")`. Here are two examples:

For additional information about other options of this command, visit the following guide:

http://technet.microsoft.com/en-us/library/hh918397.aspx

As with the console, you would need to add the S2S interface on both the URA server in your corporate network and on the one in your cloud network. If you like, you can also configure URA3 as an additional entry point, as well as any other servers or connections you require based on your site topology. Easy, isn't it?

Note. In our example, we have placed the URA2 server behind the CloudGW gateway. If the interface facing CloudGW on URA2 has a routable IP (as opposed to a NAT IP), you will need to enter that as the remote tunnel endpoint when configuring S2S on URA1. Your cloud provider who is setting up CloudGW simply routes the traffic to the external interface of URA2. If the cloud infrastructure provider NATs the Public IP of CloudGW and has made you configure the external facing interface of URA2 with a private address range, your tunnel end point IP in the URA1 configuration will be the IP of the CloudGW, but it should still send the incoming IKEv2 traffic to the external interface of URA2. If you also configure the URA3 server as a single NIC DirectAccess server, it will work only through the IP-HTTPS connection. In that case, both CloudGW and URA2 should send the incoming traffic on Port 443 to URA3.

Summary

In this chapter, we have seen how by combining the DirectAccess and Site-to-Site VPN functionalities we are now able to use one single box to provide all remote access features. With virtual machine live migration options, you can move any workload from your corporate network to cloud network and back over the S2S connection and keep the same names for the servers. This way, clients from any location can access your applications in the same way as they would access them if they were on the corporate network. This gives you the ability to move the workload easily between the corporate network and the cloud network without much configuration change and keeping it transparent to the client.

In the next chapter, we will explore the client side of URA and learn how to make the best of the available options.

7
Unified Remote Access Client Access

In recent years, we have gone from having one type of operating system running on our clients to hundreds of variations. In addition to that unlimited diversity, our clients are also running hundreds and thousands of applications. Unified Remote Access, however, has some limitations regarding client and application support, and it's important to understand them before you start your deployment and have the right level of expectation. In this chapter, we will discuss:

- Supported clients
- Client configuration options
- Supported client software and IPv4/IPv6 limitations
- Interoperability with Windows 7 clients
- Network Connectivity Assistant options
- Client manageability considerations
- User guidance

Supported clients

Historically, DirectAccess was implemented in Windows 7 as a client, but even then, it was perceived to be the type of service an organization would most benefit from, and therefore it was only enabled on the two high-end editions of Windows 7 – the *Ultimate* edition, and the *Enterprise* edition. It was also implemented in Windows 2008 R2 Server, acting as a client. Truly, not many users install this operating system on their laptops and lug it around all day, but for those who do, it's there.

So far, Microsoft has elected to support DirectAccess only on the previously mentioned platforms, and it doesn't provide a solution for non-Microsoft operating systems either. There has been some confusion in the market surrounding certain software called **SecureDirect** by *Centrify* that provides integration of Linux into DirectAccess, but it's actually only integrating backend Linux and Unix servers and does not allow Linux or Unix clients to connect to DirectAccess.

With the release of Windows Server 2012 and Windows 8, Unified Remote Access will be targeted primarily at Windows 8 as the client platform, and as such, several of the improvements to it over DirectAccess will apply only to it. For example, the ability to use multisite, which was covered in *Chapter 5, Multisite Deployment*. **Unified Remote Access (URA)** is still considered to be an organization-targeted solution, and so will be supported only on the Enterprise edition of Windows 8. Windows Server 2012 itself can also be used as a client, if one is so inclined.

URA also provides backwards compatibility with Windows 7. This does require setting up some additional options and adjusting the server configuration, as we have discussed earlier.

Client configuration options

When DirectAccess released, one of the advertised benefits was that it does not need a client installation and configuration, as opposed to most other remote-access solutions. Indeed, the software that establishes the DirectAccess connection is built into Windows in the form of Group Policy (for transferring the settings to the client) and the Windows Firewall (to establish the tunneled connection). However, some of the advanced options do require the user to install an additional client component – the **DirectAccess Connectivity Assistant (DCA)**. The DCA is required for scenarios that use **One-Time Password (OTP)**, but even for other deployments it could be quite beneficial. The reasons are as follows:

- It provides a visible confirmation to the user that his/her connection is working correctly (or that it isn't)

- It allows the user to select his/her entry point, if `multisite` has been enabled, and if the administrator has chosen to allow clients to select a site

- It can provide a link to send an e-mail to an administrator or a support helpdesk to notify of a problem or request help

- When there is a problem, it can gather a collection of logs to help a support engineer diagnose and resolve the problem

- If the administrator permits it, DirectAccess allows the user to disconnect the URA connection

Most DirectAccess deployments do not use OTP, and so it could be deployed without the DCA at all, but in reality, most organizations elected to go ahead and install it on all clients. To make things easier, Microsoft has integrated the new version of the DCA, now called **Network Connectivity Access (NCA)**, into Windows 8. It appears as a service as shown in the following screenshot:

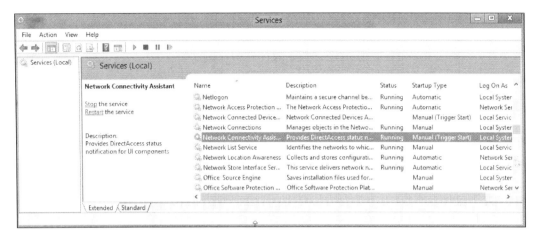

As you can see in the previous screenshot, the service is set to a startup type of **Manual (Trigger Start)**. The trigger is the configuration of URA, so once a client has received a Group Policy update that contains the URA configuration, the service will start and remain active. When a client has been configured with URA, it will show up as a **Workplace Connection** item when the user clicks on the network notification icon on his/her system tray, as shown in the following screenshot:

Then, right-clicking on the **Workplace Connection** item allows the user to open the **DirectAccess Properties** window, which provides additional information about the situation, as we described earlier (status, e-mail help link, log gathering button, multisite selection, and info). The following are several of the dialogs you might see on the NCA user interface:

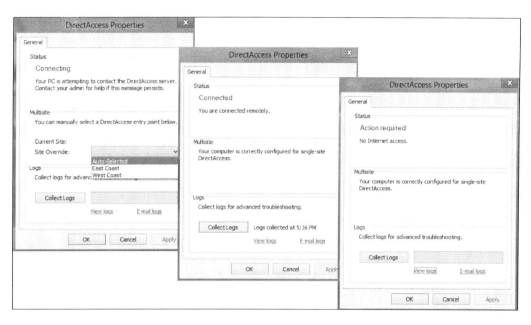

The first image shows the interface when using the **Multisite** feature, where the user can select an entry point. The second image depicts the display when the client is successfully connected to URA, and the third shows a situation where there is no Internet connection and URA cannot connect. **Action required** may also be displayed in an OTP scenario, where the user needs to enter his/her OTP. At any point, either in a successful or unsuccessful connection, the user can click on **Collect Logs** at the bottom to generate a collection of logs and traces for analysis. The logs are actually one single HTML file containing a lot of information and organized into groups. In the following screenshot, you can see an example of the content of such a file. We will discuss this with more detail in *Chapter 10, Monitoring and Troubleshooting Unified Remote Access*.

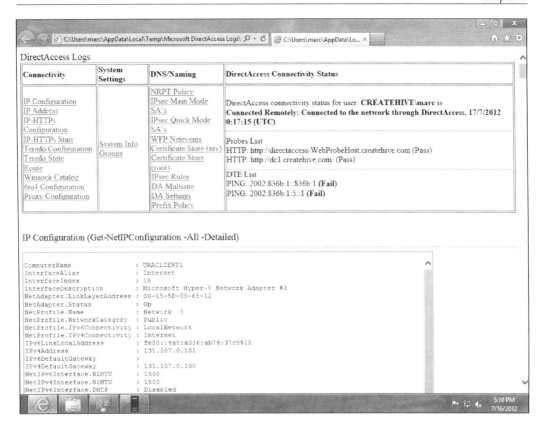

Supported client software and IPv4/IPv6 limitations

Unified Remote Access provides a connection that is very seamless, giving access to the corporate network that is designed to feel, almost, indistinguishable from being in the office and hooked up to the wall. This is indeed the case, for the most part, but there are a few limitations that you might need to consider.

The fundamental connectivity technology driving URA is IPv6, because it allows connectivity between the URA clients and server regardless of the type of NAT the client may be using. This allows URA to work seamlessly in almost all networking environments, and allows the remote-management of clients that is so important to organizations. However, in some parts of the world, IPv6 is still in the early stages of adoption, and this could lead to challenges. The operating systems themselves (Windows 7, Windows 8, and Windows Server 2012) are fully IPv6 compliant, and in fact, Microsoft's operating systems have been so for quite a while, but keep in mind that other application software not always are. Generally speaking, applications that are developed using standard networking **APIs (Application Programming Interfaces)** should work just fine, as the operating system's networking components are supposed to make everything transparent. An application tells the operating system that it needs to send certain data to a certain server, and the networking stack in the operating system's job is to find that server and transmit the data to it. In such a situation, the application shouldn't care if the communication is done over IPv4, IPv6, or something more exotic. It should care neither what the IP address of the target is, nor if it is on the local network or on some remote computer. This is the way things work for a large percentage of the applications. If you remember your networking essentials training, the **OSI (Open Systems Interconnection)** model provides the concept around which operating systems, networking components, and applications are developed:

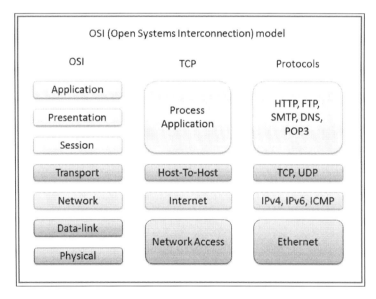

Sometimes applications are written differently, and use legacy APIs or use hardcoded IPv4 source and destinations, rather than relying on the underlying layers. For example, an application might try to contact a server by using its IPv4 address, rather than contacting the server by its name and have the operating system's *Network* layer perform the name resolution. Other times, applications use outdated networking API calls (for example, the `sockaddr` structure) which cannot handle IPv6. Some applications use certain protocols that need hardcoded IP in the headers. For example, the `SIP` protocol used in many **VoIP** (**Voice over IP**) applications uses hardcoded v4 IPs in its `SIP` header to travel across NAT devices. As a result, such applications will fail to work through URA. In fact, this is not just through DirectAccess, they simply fail to work on IPv6. This is one of the reasons why Lync 2010 or older does not work over DirectAccess. Similarly some **Citrix Xen** applications do not work through IPv6.

> If you are an application developer, the following article discusses porting code to be IPv6 compatible:
>
> `http://technet.microsoft.com/en-us/subscriptions/ms737579(v=vs.85).aspx`

Compatibility issues, such as those previously mentioned, may lead to some applications being unable to run through the URA connections, and no configuration change will help. Sometimes, software makers update their code and perhaps upgrade to a later version to resolve any such issues, but otherwise, you might be stuck. Fortunately, Windows Server 2012 supports additional remote access technologies (hence it's called *Unified* Remote Access and not *Constricted* or *Annoying* Remote Access), so you could possibly get around that by concurrently deploying a secondary connection option, such as **SSTP** VPN (**Secure Socket Tunneling Protocol**). The URA role supports the various VPN options that Windows Server offers, making this easy to deploy on the same server you are using for the DirectAccess connection. VPN deployment is beyond the scope of this, but you can learn more about these options here:

`http://technet.microsoft.com/en-us/library/jj613768.aspx`

In addition, Microsoft's Forefront **Unified Access Gateway (UAG)** supports a range of remote-access technologies that might suit your needs, so you might want to take a look at it as an option. At the time of writing, the three major software products **Office Communication Server (OCS)**, **Lync 2010** or older, and **Citrix** are known to be incompatible with URA, although with the increased adoption of IPv6, things may change. In general, keep in mind that OCS, Lync, and virtually all VoIP solutions are designed with the mindset that they would be used by people outside your organization. For example, Lync meetings would have participants from your own customers or partners. For this reason, virtually all companies deploy Lync with the edge role, connected directly to the public Internet. When this is done, your users will be able to use it if you simply configure exclusion for their name, so that the **name resolution policy table (NRPT)** determines the destination is to be reached outside of the DirectAccess connection. Thus, connections to the Lync server would go to the Internet directly, rather than through the DirectAccess connection. You can read about this here (the article talks about 2008 R2 DirectAccess, but applies to URA as well):

```
http://refraction.co.uk/blog/2012/01/16/directaccess-and-ocs-lync-
edge-services/
```

Interoperability with Windows 7 clients

While several of the features of URA are compatible with Windows 8 only, many organizations will take a while to upgrade their clients and will need to deploy URA with Windows 7 compatibility. We already discussed earlier about the configuration options this requires, and saw how you can select this option in the URA wizard and configuration.

For the most part, Windows 7 clients behave exactly like Windows 8 clients as far as URA is concerned. They too inherit the configuration when Group Policy is updated, and use the Windows Firewall to establish the IPsec tunnels. One thing that is different is the fact that they don't have the NCA built into them, so the visual side of that is a little different. As we said earlier, a similar software called the DCA (DirectAccess Connectivity Assistant) is available for installation on Windows 7 URA clients, which provides the same functionality.

The DCA is not actually required for the regular DirectAccess connection to work, but it does make for a better user experience, so we recommend installing it on all your Windows 7 URA clients. The advantages that it provides are as follows:

- Provides a user-friendly interface that shows whether the connection is successful or not

- Allows the user to generate a diagnostic log that can be easily sent to support

- Allows the user to enter additional credentials in case two factor authentications using smart card or OTP is used

The DCA is available for you to download from the Internet at:

`http://www.microsoft.com/download/details.aspx?id=29039`

You can deploy it to your Windows 7 clients manually, or use any of the standard deployment methods such as a **login script**, or Active Directory **Application Publishing** via Group Policy. You can read more about application publishing in the following guide:

`http://technet.microsoft.com/en-us/library/bb742421`

Visually, the DCA on Windows 7 looks a little different. It shows as an icon on the system tray that looks like a computer, clicking on which shows the main interface that indicates a successful or failed connection, and a button to collect logs, if relevant:

Network Connectivity Assistant options

As you may recall from setting up URA earlier, there are some specific options related to the Network Connectivity Assistant. This was part of the **remote client** (step 1) setup, where the final page is the **Network Connectivity Assistant** page. That page has four configuration options you should consider.

The first one is the **validation probes**. These are servers within the corporate network which the NCA attempts to contact once it establishes the URA connection. If the NCA is able to connect to these resources, it determines that the connection is successful. The reason for needing the validation probes is because in some situations, a URA connection may actually work only partially. If you recall , the URA connection in the advanced mode uses two tunnels, where the first one allows a connection only to the domain controllers and allows the client to perform NTLM authentication against the DCs, and that's what allows the second tunnel to connect. Sometimes, that authentication process fails which leaves the client in VPN limbo. The first tunnel allows it to connect to DCs, but it can't actually connect to any other server. In such a situation, the probes are what allows the NCA to know if the connection is working only partially, or fully.

By default, the URA role registers a DNS entry for **DirectAccess-WebProbeHost**, which resolves to the URA server itself and sets it as an HTTP probe. If you like, you can add additional probes, although it should be noted that the connectivity check tests all probes and if a single one fails, it will conclude that the URA connection is not working. This has the potential of creating false negatives if the probe target is simply offline for some reason. The additional probe should be an internal server, and you can set the probe to be either an HTTP probe, or a PING probe (based on the type of server you are using to probe, of course). Keep in mind that if the probed servers go offline for any reason, your URA users will fail the probe and the users may see this and think their URA connection is not working, even though it actually is. If you don't appreciate those 3 A.M. phone calls, it would be a good idea to make sure the servers listed are reliable ones and possibly even use a clustered server. Also make sure that the probes are servers that will only be accessible if the URA connection is fully successful. This is particularly important for PING probes, because **ICMP** traffic is exempted from the IPsec rules and may lead to false positives. Using a domain controller for this would not be a good idea, because your domain controllers should be accessible via the first tunnel, and therefore, a successful connection to them doesn't really indicate that the URA connection is fully operational.

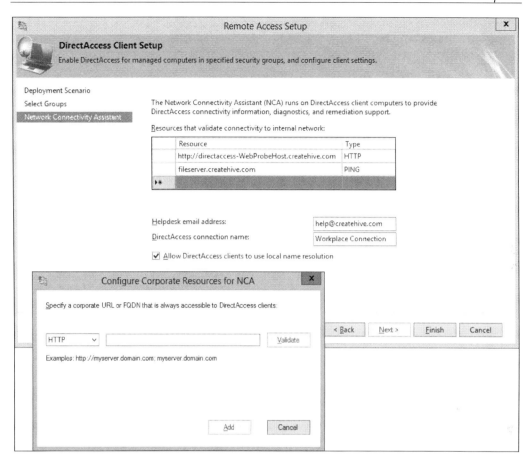

The second option is the e-mail that will be used if the client generates troubleshooting logs and clicks on **Email Logs**. That would typically be your organization's generic support e-mail mailbox, or your URA support expert. Note that if you leave this blank, the **collect logs** button on the client will be grayed-out, preventing your users from collecting logs.

DirectAccess connection name is the text that will show up in the list of available connections in the **View Available Network (VAN)** UI, when you click on the network icon in the system tray. Ideally, you would set it to something that makes sense to the users, such as URA connection or URA VPN.

The fourth option is one of the more important ones, because it allows the user to effectively *disable* his/her URA connection. This is not a simple decision to make. On one hand, you would want users to be able to disable the connection in case there is some problem with it, but on the other hand you might want them connected at all times for manageability reasons. If you do decide to set this option, then the client will see a **Disconnect** button if he opens the VAN interface, as shown in the following screenshot:

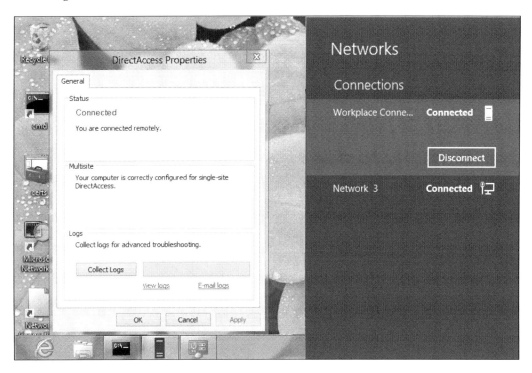

It's important to note that when the URA connection is *disconnected*, it doesn't really disconnect the IPSec tunnels or disable them. What really happens is that the local name resolution is enabled. This means that instead of consulting the NRPT to decide whether to use the Corporate Networks DNS server to resolve hostnames or not, every name resolution is done using the DNS server originally configured for the computer (this would typically be the ISPs DNS, but could also be the DNS server setup on the local network). Another important difference between this and a real tunnel disconnection is that even with local name resolution enabled, the client still has the tunnels up, so it can be remotely-monitored and managed by the organization's administrators.

Client manageability considerations

One of the main benefits of DirectAccess over most VPN technologies is the fact that it allows you to manage your remote clients (this is often referred to as **Manage Out**). With other VPN connections, you can only remote-manage a client if the user has established the connection because he has some work to do. Often times, this means that some users may go on for days without connecting, thus keeping you away. In times of peace, this may not be so terrible, but if there's a sudden outbreak of a virus or some other security related issue, you may not be able to protect such clients.

> Remotely managing clients is about the ability of IT administrators to actively monitor and configure clients over the network. For example, you can read a remote computer's registry or disk drives to see what programs are installed on it, and even use remote-assistance to take control over the console of the client and fix issues or provide guidance. Essentially, any such thing that you would normally do while the client is on the corporate network can be done over the URA connection.

With URA, however, this is much better. URA clients connect to the corpnet all the time, and since many users leave their computers on constantly, this means you can manage them more easily. One of the key enablers for this is the fact that clients have unique IPv6 addresses that can be reached from the corporate network, and this allows you to connect to them no matter where they are. With other VPN technologies, even when the client is online, you may not be able to willfully establish a connection to it, if it's behind a NAT router (like things are in almost every household and corporate network these days).

To be able to establish a connection from a computer on the corporate network to a remote URA client, the management server needs to use IPv6, and this bring about the **ISATAP** concept to the table once again. If you remember, ISATAP is a system of assigning IPv6 addresses to corporate computers, and thus it's very important here. If your corporate network does not have either a full IPv6 deployed, or ISATAP, then your management servers will not have a functioning IPv6 stack, and won't be able to connect to them (although tasks that are initiated from the client itself, such as installing Windows updates or pulling an updated Group Policy will work just fine). What this means is that if managing-out your clients is high on your to-do list, then you might need to reconsider your foray into IPv6. If you weren't sure ISATAP or going full-IPv6 was the best idea, this information may bring it back to the table. If so, re-read the introduction chapter, so that you can prepare for this.

We should note that ISATAP is, after all, considered to be a transition technology, so it's not ideal as a long-term or permanent solution. If you're not ready to deploy full IPv6, then using ISATAP is your only option for remote-management of URA clients, and it's a legitimate need. However, if that is the case, we urge you to study up on IPv6, and formulate a plan to convert your network to it. If you feel it's too confusing, then don't hesitate to ask your Internet Service Provider for help. ISPs deal with this on a daily basis, and would have experts to help architect a move and hold your hand along the way.

Another thing you need in order to enable remote management is to configure the Windows Firewall on your client computer to allow the remote management traffic into the computer. Most of the types of remote management are done using some sort of agent installed on the clients, and so depending on the direction (client initiated, or server initiated), and type of traffic, the configuration required may vary. If you are already managing your remote clients on the corporate network or via a different VPN technology, then these steps may not be required at all. The configuration entails creating inbound rules that allow edge traversal for the management traffic, or editing existing rules to allow edge traversal.

If you already have existing rules, then simply edit them, and add `edge=yes` to them. For example, if you use the NETSH command to create the rule, you would adjust the syntax like as follows:

```
netsh advfirewall firewall set rule name="Remote Desktop (TCP-In)" dir=in
new edge=yes
```

This setting can be done as a separate GPO, or added to the GPO for URA (see *Chapter 8, Enhanced Configurations for Infrastructure Servers*, for information about editing the URA GPOs). To configure NETSH in the context of a GPO, visit the following article:

```
http://technet.microsoft.com/en-us/library/cc947798(WS.10).aspx
```

User guidance

As we have shown, the user interface for a URA client is pretty straightforward and does not have many options. However, you must keep in mind that users can still get confused, especially if they suffer from PCPhobia, or are used to classic VPN technologies. In addition, network conditions out in the wild vary, and it's hard to guess what kind of trouble your users will have to deal with. Therefore, it's very important to plan the deployment and provide users with the guidance they need.

One way to do this would be to prepare good support infrastructure, and provide preemptive guidance. Some customers prepare pamphlets or booklets with screenshots, explaining to users how the new technology works and providing steps to follow in case of a problem. Others set up a public web page on the company's website with troubleshooting steps and suggested alternatives in case nothing works. You probably know your users better than anyone, so it would be your prerogative and responsibility to decide how to prepare. One thing that pretty much everyone does is set up a pilot group, which will allow you to estimate the scale of things to come without risking too much "heat". Another thing is to dedicate a single expert to this topic, so that he/she can provide the best possible support, and also gain visibility as to the success of the project.

Summary

In this chapter, we discussed the client side of things, and how things work. Having gone through it and the previous chapter, you are now ready to deploy URA in your organization with full service.

In the next chapter, we will explore some of the advanced scenarios and enhanced configuration options that can help IT savvy organizations to fine-tune and tweak URA to their needs.

8
Enhanced Configurations for Infrastructure Servers

In the previous chapters we discussed the various basic and advanced scenarios, and how to deploy them successfully. Now, you might want to fine-tune certain advanced aspects of your configuration that go beyond a simple click in the console. Some of these options will allow you to better fit URA to your environment, as well as meet more complex security requirements such as forced tunneling, specific IPSec options, and a deeper IPv6 integration. We will also see how you can take advantage of PowerShell to configure some things via scripts and save yourself the time and effort. Our topics at hand are as follows:

- Tweaking the Management Servers list
- URA and PowerShell
- Configuring IPSec policies with advanced options
- Fine-tuning SSL and PKI
- Configuring forced tunneling
- Advanced options with the NCA
- Tweaking IPv6 for complex networks

Tweaking the management servers list

As you may recall from the section *Editing the configuration* in *Chapter 4, Installing and Configuring the Unified Remote Access role*, the *Infrastructure Server configuration* (step 3 – page 4) is about management servers, so what does that mean?

Well, management servers are servers that are specifically listed in the URA policy as accessible through the first tunnel, in a scenario where the two tunnels model is used (as opposed to the one with the Kerberos proxy, and only a single tunnel). As you may recall from the preface, the purpose of the first tunnel in the 2-tunnel scenario is to provide access to your domain controllers, so that the client computer can perform Kerberos authentication and obtain the Kerberos ticket as part of establishing the second tunnel.

The **Management Servers** option allows you to specify servers that will be granted access through the first tunnel, in addition to DCs. This means that these servers will be fully accessible to clients as soon as they establish the first tunnel and even if they fail to establish the second one.

Adding such servers would be beneficial because even if your clients fail to fully establish the connection, you might still want to give them access to some critical services. For example, you might have some smartypants dude from your tech-support group who "accidentally" deleted his smartcard certificate while on a trip to Hackistan, and now cannot access the rest of the corpnet. You might not be able to (or want to) fix it remotely, but you still want his computer to receive updates to his antivirus, so that he won't be a menace and bring down the network upon his return. In such a case, you might want to provide the access to your server that hosts AV updates as part of the management servers list.

To add a server, simply go to the wizard, double-click on the blank line, and type in an IP address or FQDN name, as shown in the following screenshot:

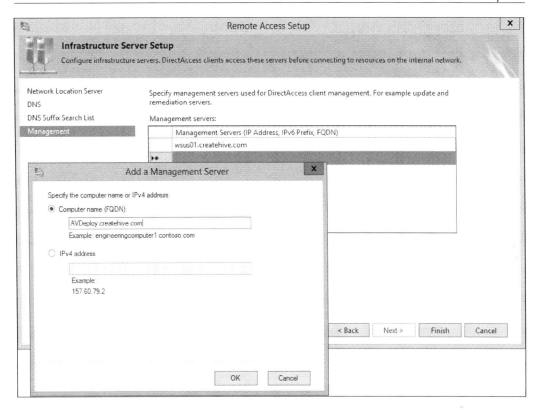

When finished, click on **Finish** to close the wizard, and then click on **Finish** at the bottom of the screen to update Group Policy with the new settings. As usual, when Group Policy is applied to clients, the new settings will take effect.

Now, let's see how you can make your life easier with PowerShell scripting.

URA and PowerShell

PowerShell is a task automation framework that's been around for over five years, but is still a mystery to many. If you're a serious and experienced IT administrator, you've no doubt performed a lot of work using classic shell in the form of CMD or batch files, and probably written quite a few of those yourself to help you automate certain things. PowerShell is the successor to the classic shell, and offers advanced options that rival and even surpass many scripting languages and platforms. Before PowerShell came along, people needing advanced automation turned to VBScript or PERL to achieve their goals, and many use the third party automation platform AutoIt as well. With Windows Server 2012, Microsoft has implemented many advanced URA functions and tweaks with PowerShell, and this is an opportunity for you not only to use them, but also jumpstart your PowerShell knowledge and experience. In other words, anything that could be done from the management console can also be done using PowerShell.

In PowerShell, you use cmdlets (pronounced command-lets) to perform tasks. A cmdlet is a program that performs certain operations. PowerShell comes with a set of cmdlets, and when you install other roles, features and software on the server, additional cmdlets may get added as part of that. You can also write scripts that use cmdlets, and your scripts can also run executables and use COM objects.

COM (Component Object Model) is a standard that enables software to interact with other software. When someone writes a piece of software, they may choose to implement some or all of the software as COM objects, and then, other software can communicate with it directly. Most software written by Microsoft, as well as the Windows operating system itself includes many COM objects which other programs use. For example, a very popular COM object is **FileSystemObject** (**FSO**), which allows direct interaction with files and folders. By using that object, any software can read, write, copy, move, or delete files and folders very simply.

A COM object comes in the form of a DLL file, which needs to be registered. The operating system comes with tons of these, ready for use, and when you install other software, it registers other objects as part of the installation. For example, when you install Office, it registers the `Excel.Application` object, which allows other programs to automatically create and edit excel files directly.

Most of Microsoft's COM objects are heavily documented and referenced, and this makes it easy to use them in your scripts. Many other software vendors produce COM objects as part of their products, though it may take more research and experimentation to successfully interact with theirs.

Windows Server 2012 comes with hundreds of cmdlets, though only a handful of them pertain to Unified Remote Access. We will discuss these here, but we recommend reading about other cmdlets too. For example, the system has 65 cmdlets pertaining to managing network adapters. You could use the cmdlet `Set-NetAdapter` to set the properties of the NIC and automate the setup of new computers in your organization. For more information:

`http://technet.microsoft.com/en-us/library/hh801904`

If you'd like to really learn PowerShell through-and-through, we recommend the book *Learn Windows PowerShell in a Month of Lunches*, authored by *Don Jones*, and published by *Manning Publications*. Another good resource is *Windows PowerShell in Action* also by *Manning Publications*, and authored by *Bruce Payette* though its 1016 pages could also be used for weight training.

Using PowerShell

To use PowerShell cmdlets, you need to start by opening a PowerShell window. On Windows Server 2012, you can find a shortcut for it on the start screen, and also a shortcut icon on the taskbar as shown in the following screenshot. You can find a shortcut for it on the **Tools** menu in **Server Manager** as well, or simply type `powershell` in a regular CMD window. On a Windows 8 client, you can get to it by typing **powershell** on the start screen, as shown in the following screenshot, or typing **powershell** in a regular CMD window:

The PowerShell window is blue, by default, and inside it, you can simply go ahead and type the various available cmdlets. PowerShell also supports the classic CMD commands such as DIR, COPY, CD, MD, and so on. In the following screenshot, you can see the result of the DIR command, as well as the Get-DaServer cmdlet, which shows information about the URA Server configuration:

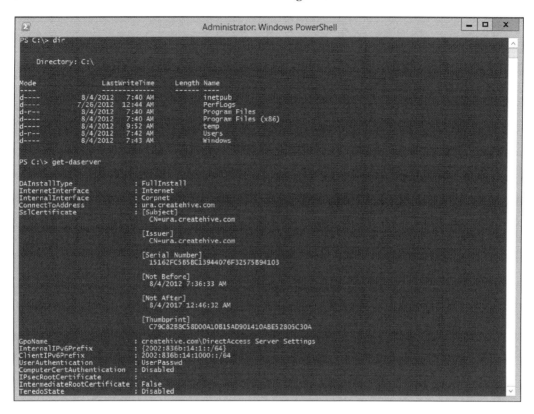

Writing PowerShell scripts

Just like the classic DOS Shell, PowerShell allows you to write your own scripts, to execute several commands or cmdlets in batches. To create a PowerShell script, simply create a text file with notepad, or your favorite text editor, type the command and cmdlets into it, and save it with the extension .ps1. Note that by default, PowerShell restricts running scripts, as a security mechanism. To allow your scripts to run, you must first reduce the restriction by using the cmdlet Set-ExecutionPolicy. Ideally, you would set it to RemoteSigned, which will run your own scripts, but prevent scripts downloaded from the internet from running.

You can also set this option by editing the registry key `HKLM\Software\Microsoft\` `PowerShell\1\ShellIds\Microsoft.PowerShell\ExecutionPolicy` and setting it to `RemoteSigned`. If you would like this to apply to all your domain computers or servers, you can configure this via Group Policy as well, under `Computer` `Configuration/Administrative Templates/Windows Components/Windows` `PowerShell/Turn On Script Execution`.

If you do decide to venture into writing your own scripts, a helpful tool would be the PowerShell **Integrated Scripting Environment** (**ISE**). You can find it in your start menu, and it allows you to write, test, and debug scripts in a single interface. It makes life easier, because it has multiline editing, tab completion, syntax coloring, selective execution, and context-sensitive help. You can use menu items and keyboard shortcuts to perform many of the same tasks. When debugging your scripts, you can create break-points to make it easier to find problems as shown in the following screenshot:

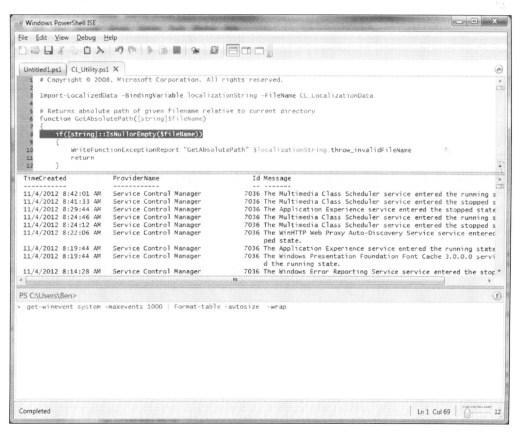

URA PowerShell cmdlets

For URA, PowerShell offers two groups of cmdlets. One group is for the server-side operations and contains about 70 cmdlets, and the other is the client-side stuff. All in all, there are about 80 cmdlets. Some of the cmdlets simply perform an action comparable to what you can do with the console. Why would you want to type in a long command instead of pressing a button, you ask? Well first, typing things up is quite a party, because it makes you feel like you're some kind of programmer! Seriously, though, this can actually save a lot of time if you have a complex environment, or need to deploy many servers. For example, if you need to deploy an 18-member load balanced cluster, you can run the cmdlet `Add-RemoteAccessLoadBalancerNode` in a loop, rather than run through the wizard 18 times (too bad they don't have a cmdlet for golf, huh?). Another advantage of using a script is that automation reduces the risk of human error.

TechNet provides ample and detailed references for all available cmdlets, so we won't list them all here. The server-side cmdlets are documented here:

`http://technet.microsoft.com/en-us/library/hh918399`

The client-side cmdlets are available here:

`http://technet.microsoft.com/en-us/library/hh848426`

Beyond those, another excellent resource on the topic is the following site, which offers a vast collection of tips and code samples for creating your own scripts:

`http://poshtips.com/`

Configuring IPSec policies with advanced options

When you configure URA using the wizard, it creates a Group Policy which contains settings for the IPsec policy that will be used. These settings apply to the Windows Firewall, which establishes the connection on both sides. In some situations, you might want to adjust the settings for IPsec, but that cannot be done from the URA console. To affect these, you'll have to dig deep into Group Policy.

STOP!

Adjusting the IPsec settings is risky business! You could easily render your URA settings invalid, and break the service completely. If you don't keep track of your changes properly, you might have no choice but to reset the entire URA configuration and start it from scratch. Another risk is setting the options in a way that's less secure than the default ones, and thus exposing your network to an attack. Also, not all changes are supported by Microsoft, and if you ever require support, the support engineer might request that you revert your changes to the default ones before focusing on your actual problem. Proceed with caution!

One thing to keep in mind before making these changes is that the IPsec tunnels require both sides to play nice together. Making certain changes on the server policy without changing corresponding settings on the client policy may prevent clients from successfully establishing connections. For example, the key exchange algorithm must match between client and server to allow a successful connection.

Another thing to keep in mind is that the URA server console is designed with certain defaults which you cannot edit directly. This means that if you make changes to the policy via the URA console, they will rewrite the policy, overwriting your settings back to the default. Make sure you keep track of your settings, so you can re-apply them in such a case. You can also backup your GPO settings using the standard GPO backup mechanisms or software.

To edit the IPsec advanced options, you need to edit the Group Policy created by URA. To do so, follow these steps:

1. Open **Group Policy Management**.

2. Right-click on the URA policy for the server or the client and choose **Edit**.

3. The policy will open with the **Group Policy Management** editor

4. **Navigate down** to `Computer configuration/Policies/Windows Settings/Security Settings/Windows Firewall with Advanced Security`.

5. Inside it, you will find a sub-container pertaining to your specific policy. Right-click on it, and choose **Properties**.

6. Go to the **IPsec Settings** tab.

7. Click on **Customize** under **IPsec defaults**.

8. In the **IPsec defaults** page, you can customize the **Key exchange (Main Mode)**, the **Data protection (Quick Mode)**, and **Authentication method**, as shown in the following screenshot:

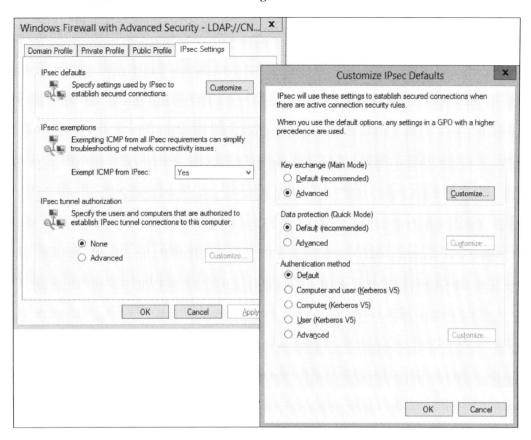

With these, you can add, remove, or edit available security methods, integrity options and encryption options for the key exchange, and other properties. For example, you might want to add the **Diffie-Helman Group 14** or **Diffie-Helman Group 24**, which are more secure than the default **Diffie-Helman Group 2**. This is shown in the following screenshot:

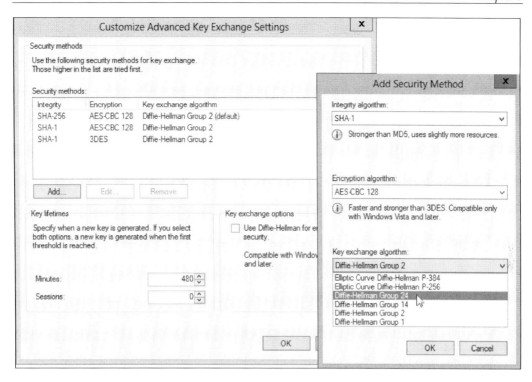

Do you need to make such changes? You certainly don't have to! URA has been designed with security in mind, and the default settings provide an excellent level of security. In fact, it's significantly more secure than the encryption used by most commercial remote-access solutions.

If you do make changes, take into consideration how the interaction goes between the client and server, to make appropriate changes to the client policy. It is located in the same branch, but in the client GPO, of course. Keep in mind that making such changes requires both clients and the URA server (or servers) to re-apply the new policy. Clients that are off-site at the moment will be able to apply the new policy through the URA connection, if they are already connected at the time. If, however, they are not, and the new settings are incompatible with the old ones, these clients will have to come into the office to get the new policy, or use an alternative VPN method.

Fine-tuning SSL and PKI

While most organizations would prefer to deploy URA using the simplest and quickest method (with the Getting Started Wizard), some might prefer to tweak and fine-tune their SSL and PKI infrastructure. One conceivable need would be a tight security policy, and another would be to implement URA in an environment where PKI is already deployed and the two need to coexist.

The IP-HTTPS and NLS certificates are pretty straightforward, and besides issuing them to your URA server(s) and selecting them in the URA interface, there's little to do. The computer authentication certificate, though, has some more properties and options.

When you configure the use of computer certificates (as opposed to the use of the Kerberos proxy feature), you need to select the root CA which issues the certificates. The wizard will then trust certificates received from a client during the connection if they were issued by that CA. If you are using an intermediate CA instead of a root CA, you can also check that option:

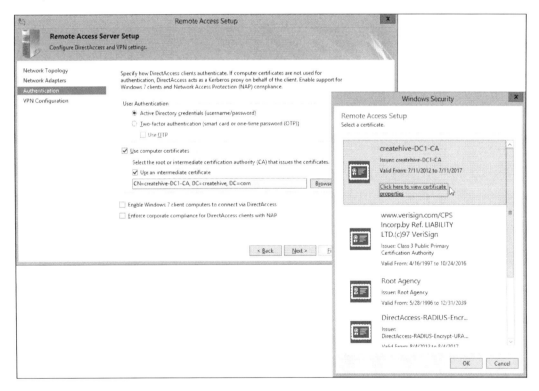

This is about all you can configure with the URA console, but the Group Policy contains additional options which are available in the Group Policy editor. To reach these, follow these steps:

1. Open **Group Policy Management**.

2. Right-click on the URA policy for the server or the client and choose **Edit**.

3. The policy will open with the **Group Policy Management** editor.

4. Navigate down to `Computer configuration/Policies/Windows Settings/Security Settings/Windows Firewall with Advanced Security`

5. Inside it, you will find a sub-container pertaining to your specific policy. Expand it and click on **Connection Security Rules**.

Warning!

Adjusting the policy at this level is not trivial, and could render your URA settings invalid, breaking your configuration completely. We strongly advise to fiddle with this only if you know PKI very well, and can handle the risks involved. Keep in mind that changing the settings may also inadvertently reduce your security and expose your network. Proceed carefully!

Inside **Connection Security Rules**, you will see two items:

- **DirectAccess Policy-DAServerToInfra**
- **DirectAccess Policy-DaServerToCorp**

The first item is, as the name implies, the configuration for the first tunnel. To remind you, this tunnel is used to establish connectivity to the corporate network infrastructure servers. It allows the client to connect to domain controllers so that the client can get a Kerberos ticket from them, and then use that ticket to create the second tunnel. The first tunnel authentication is performed using the computer certificate, and the computer account (using NTLM authentication).

The second item is the configuration for the second tunnel, which is established after the first one is successfully established. The second tunnel is established using the user's Kerberos ticket and the computer certificate, and relies on the first tunnel to pass them to the domain controllers and complete the authentication for the tunnel. Once that tunnel is established, full corporate connectivity is on.

If you find only one item there, this means your URA was configured to not use computer certificates and use the Kerberos Proxy feature instead. This is fine, of course, though in that case, you don't have anything to configure here.

You can edit the policies directly via the Group Policy editor, though most of the settings wouldn't be relevant, and would probably be better left alone. The one place that you might find useful is the **Authentication** tab. In the infra (first tunnel) policy, you would find the first authentication method set to **Computer certificate**, and the second method set to **User (NTLMv2)**, which refers to the computer account. Note that first and second in this context does not refer to the first and second tunnel, but to the two layers of authentication. In the corp tunnel policy (second tunnel), you would find the first authentication mode is set to **Computer certificate**, and the second set to **User (Kerberos V5)**. In the following screenshot, you can see the second tunnel authentication configuration:

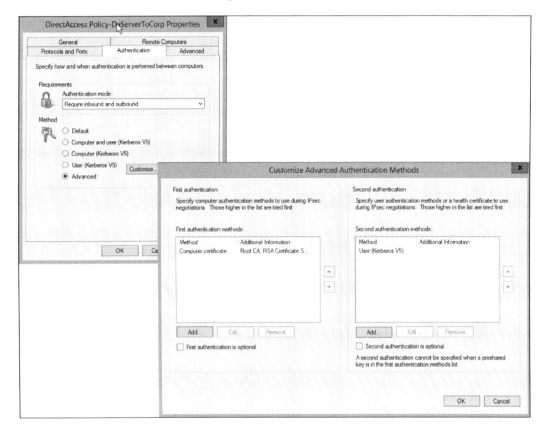

Here, you can edit the properties of the certificate authentication. For example, you could edit the signing algorithm, which is RSA by default. You can also restrict the certificate to use a specific **EKU (Enhanced Key Usage)** or set certificate name restrictions. The possibilities are wide, but do keep in mind that your certificates actually have to meet whatever additional or different requirements you set. Also, remember that some settings could make the connection less secure, so better be sure you know what you're doing and not just random settings that have cool acronyms or threatening-sounding words you see in CNET a lot.

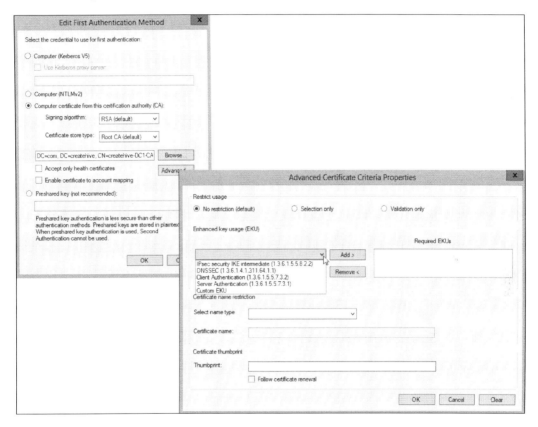

Configuring forced tunneling

With most VPN technologies, once the user establishes the connection, the virtual network takes over everything, and all traffic flows through the tunnel. In such a case, even if the user needs to browse to a website that's on the public Internet, that traffic would still come through the VPN tunnel. This makes sense, because organizations are concerned that if traffic can go directly to or from the Internet, this essentially bridges the networks together without filtering, and this might expose the corporate network to attack. In the networking world, this type of thing is referred to as **Forced Tunneling**, because we force everything through the tunnel.

With URA, on the other hand, the default mode is split tunneling, allowing traffic destined for resources on the public Internet to go out directly, and not through the tunnel. This might seem scary to some administrators, but in fact, it's perfectly safe. The reason for this is that the traffic that goes to the corporate network is specifically handled with end-to-edge IPsec rules, and they would not apply to traffic coming from the public Internet. Even if packets came from the Internet, the IPsec rules would cause them to be dropped. Naturally, it's always a good idea to have the client run security software to protect against malicious websites and software.

If your organization still mandates forced tunneling, then with URA, things are a bit more complicated, because the connection is always on. With other VPN connections, if the user needs to access the public Internet for any reason, they can simply terminate the connection and go about their (shady) business. With URA, they cannot, so this decision should not be taken lightly.

For organizations that prefer it, URA offers the option to enable forced tunneling, and that is configured in step 1 of the configuration, in the **Select Groups** page:

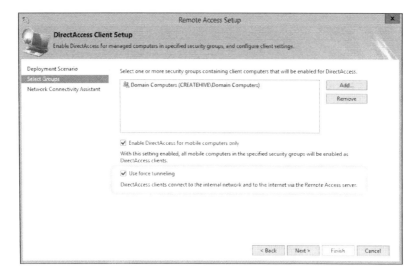

We already discussed some of the challenges and difficulties that using forced tunneling can bring about in *Chapter 2*, *Planning a Unified Remote Access Deployment*, but if you need to do it then you need to do it.

As you may recall, URA has a name resolution policy table (NRPT), and the NRPT controls how traffic and name resolution works. When you enable forced tunneling in step 1, URA automatically adjusts the NRPT accordingly, and the change will look like the following screenshot:

Name Suffix	DNS Server Address
ura.createhive.com	
createhive.com	2002:c00:b:3333::1
NLS	
*	

Name Suffix	DNS Server Address
ura.createhive.com	
<Any Suffix>	2002:c00:b:3333::1
NLS	
*	

As you can see, the change is that instead of specifying that traffic matching your domain suffix uses the URA server as DNS, the name suffix is now **Any Suffix**, so any and all traffic will be handled by the DNS server specified and not just traffic matching the domain suffix.

In addition, the NRPT page offers you additional configuration options for handling local name resolution. This controls how the client handles name resolution on its own local network and is therefore very important for this scenario. For example, if the client is inside some other organizations network, or on a home network. The options are as follows:

- Use local name resolution if the name does not exist in DNS
- Use local name resolution if the name does not exist in DNS or DNS servers are unreachable when the client computer is on a private network
- Use local name resolution for any kind of DNS resolution error

By default, the second option is selected, and we recommend keeping it that way. Another option you need to consider is whether to allow URA clients to use local name resolution. This option is selectable in the **Remote Clients** (step 1) configuration, on the **Network Connectivity Assistant** page. If you enable it, then the client can click on **Disconnect** on the connection:

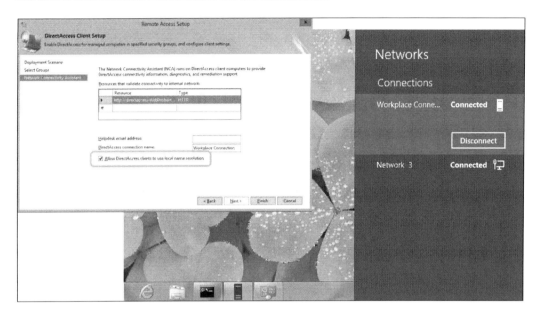

Naturally, the **Disconnect** button will show up only if the connection is actually active. There's another option for forced tunneling which you might want to configure, and that is the routing method. When you enable forced tunneling, the NRPT is configured so that the URA server resolves addresses for anything. This is perfectly fine, of course, but if you have a proxy server in your network, you might prefer that it is used by clients. This would be an advantage if you have a significant amount of users, and thus using a web proxy will optimize traffic both for them, and for your bandwidth. It would also allow you to take advantage of other features your proxy might offer, such as URL filtering.

To configure the use of a web proxy, you need to go into the Group Policy directly. To do so, follow these steps:

1. Open **Group Policy Management**.
2. Right-click on the URA policy for the server or the client and choose **Edit**.
3. The policy will open with the **Group Policy Management** editor.
4. Navigate down to `Computer configuration/Policies/Windows Settings/Name Resolution Policy`.

5. Click on the **DNS Settings for DirectAccess** tab.

6. Enable the **Web Proxy** option, and configure the name of your proxy as shown in the following screenshot:

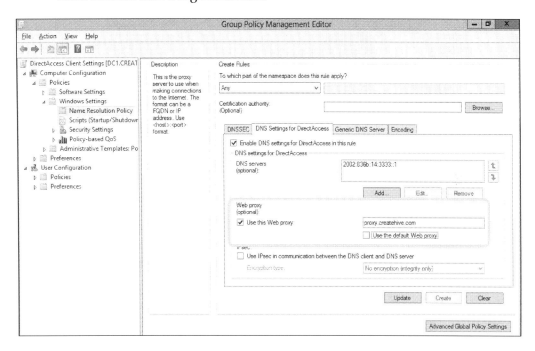

If you prefer to use WPAD to configure your proxy for clients, that's perfectly fine as well, and some organizations prefer this method. But make sure WPAD entries do not have hardcoded IPv4 addresses as you know you can't reach hardcoded IPv4 addresses through DirectAccess. To use WPAD, there's no need to edit the policy, of course. Simply configure your DNS server as described here:

```
http://support.microsoft.com/kb/934864
```

Advanced options with the NCA

As part of the URA configuration console, you can configure the NCA with the connectivity probes, the e-mail of the helpdesk, the name of the connection, and whether to allow users to disconnect the URA connection (by enabling local name resolution) or not. As with other things, Group Policy exposes several additional settings that your specific environment or security policy may suggest.

The client access policy has many settings, of course, and most of them pertain to things we discussed before, such as the IPsec tunneling options and the authentication. Other connection properties are under **Computer Configuration/Administrative Templates**, and the following sub-branches:

- **/Network/DirectAccess Client Experience Settings**
- **/Network/Network Connections**
- **/Network/Network Connectivity Status Indicator**
- **/Network/TCPIP Settings/IPv6 Transition Technologies**
- **/System/Kerberos**
- **Extra Registry Settings**

We won't go into much detail here, because the **Group Policy Management** editor actually provides detailed information about each of the settings on-screen. Here are some settings that you might find particularly interesting. As always, please be advised that editing these settings is risky, and may jeopardize not only the user experience, but cause it to fail for everyone. Make sure any change you make is well documented, in case it has to be reverted.

- **/Network/DirectAccess Client Experience Settings/User Interface**: Setting this option to **Disabled** will set the connection to be completely hidden for the client. This option is there for a situation where you only use URA for remote management, and in that case you might prefer users aren't aware of the connection.

- **/Network/DirectAccess Client Experience Settings/DirectAccess Passive Mode**: This setting configures the NCA to not perform connectivity checks. By default, the NCA (or DCA) connects to the pre-defined internal probes in order to show the user whether the connection is working or not. Normally, this is a good thing to have, but it can sometimes mislead users into thinking that the connection works, when it doesn't, or vice versa. For example, if you defined some internal server as a probe, and that server is down for maintenance, it could lead to a hailstorm of phone calls, even though the connection itself is working fine for everyone.

- **/Network/TCPIP Settings/IPv6 Transition Technologies**: This branch has settings for the three available transition technologies (6to4, Teredo, and IP-HTTPS). By default, all are enabled, but if you need one to be disabled, you can use these settings to do so.

- **/System/Kerberos/Specify KDC proxy servers for Kerberos clients:** When using the Getting Started Wizard, URA sets itself to be the Kerberos proxy for incoming Windows 8 connections. This setting allows you to specify a different resource. Do keep in mind, though, that clients need to be able to access that server, so you can't simply move that role. In some very large environment, controlling that option may be desirable.

Tweaking IPv6 for complex networks

IPv6 has been around for quite a while, but still, most organizations in the United States are still clinging to IPv4 with both hands. This year was particularly significant for IPv6, as some of the major public websites such as Bing, Google, Facebook, and others enabled IPv6 for their services and products (`http://www.worldipv6launch.org/`). This makes IPv6 a whole lot harder to ignore.

If you are deploying URA, IPv6 will become much more important to you, even if it doesn't get you as excited as us. URA was designed to offer full functionality with little knowledge of IPv6 and without any need to deploy it, but if you do want to make the best use of this technology, there might be a thing or two for you to tweak.

ISATAP and you

In case you don't remember, **ISATAP** is a technology which automatically assigns IPv6 addresses to your IPv6-capable hosts on the corporate network. When the URA wizard runs, it checks whether your network has IPv6 running, and if not, it automatically enables the ISATAP router features on itself. However, it doesn't fully enable it, because Active Directory automatically blocks ISATAP using a special DNS entry that URA doesn't touch. All modern Windows computers starting with Windows XP have ISATAP enabled in the form of an ISATAP adapter, and if an ISATAP router is available on the network and not blocked by DNS, that card will get assigned an IP address. If an ISATAP router is not available, the NIC will show as `Media Disconnected`. Linux also has an ISATAP implementation, and so do Cisco devices (starting with IOS release 12.2(14)S).

As you may recall from *Chapter 2*, *Planning a Unified Remote Access Deployment*, URA has the DNS64 and NAT64 features as well, so URA clients can communicate with IPv4-only resources without a hitch, so why do you need ISATAP? Well indeed, many organizations feel they don't need it, and turn it off. The reason it's there to begin with is to support traffic in the other direction, like you would need to perform remote-management of URA clients (a.k.a. manage out). If you need to initiate a connection from a computer on the internal network to a URA client, the internal computer must have an IPv6 address to do this. This is why URA checks if you have IPv6 deployed before enabling the ISATAP router feature.

As a general rule, Microsoft's official position is that ISATAP should be considered as a temporary or limited thing and companies worldwide should deploy full IPv6 on their network, and then do away with ISATAP (this is discussed in the ISATAP deployment guide published by Microsoft on `http://www.microsoft.com/en-us/download/details.aspx?id=18383`). The main argument against ISATAP is that once it's enabled on all computers, it creates one big logical IPv6 subnet for the entire network, which can affect Active Directory replication. In such a situation, it could allow clients to get authenticated by domain controllers in remote sites and thereby causing serious problems. Another problem is that clients would prefer to use the ISATAP interface when communicating with each other, and since ISATAP is a tunneling protocol (IPv6 over IPv4), it adds an overhead to all communications and may degrade performance. Also, with the URA server being the one and only ISATAP router, it has to respond to router-discovery requests by all computers on your network, and generate IPv6 addresses for them all. If your network has thousands of computers, it could be quite a strain on the server.

None of this means that you should be in a hurry to get rid of ISATAP, but you should at least consider moving on to native IPv6 deployment. Another thing some organizations do is to limit the deployment of ISATAP to only specific servers by removing the ISATAP entry from DNS, and putting it in the HOSTS file only on computers that need it (those that are used to remotely-manage URA clients, that is). Another option is to set up a Group Policy to configure the ISATAP router, and adding only specific computers to a domain group that inherits that policy. This procedure is described here: `http://blog.msedge.org.uk/2011/11/limiting-isatap-services-to-uag.html`

If you do want to completely disable ISATAP, you need to issue the following command on your URA server (or servers):

Netsh interface isatap set router state=disabled

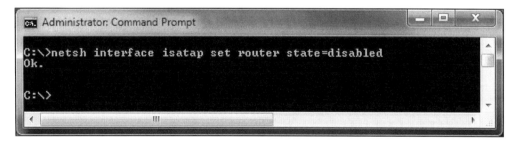

Then, verify that the ISATAP entry in DNS is gone. Following this, once you reboot a host, it will not have the ISATAP address anymore and the NIC will show `Media Disconnected`. You're not expected to reboot all your computers, of course, but within 24 hours, they should all release their addresses on their own.

Moving ISATAP

You might feel that you do need ISATAP, but just prefer it isn't on the same URA server, or to use multiple computers as ISATAP routers. This is relatively simple to do. Just like you disabled the ISATAP router function on the URA server as described earlier, the same command, reversed, enables this feature on any computer on the domain:

```
Netsh interface isatap set router state=enabled
```

Then, add an entry to your DNS server for ISATAP, and point it to the IP of the computer you are setting as your ISATAP router. If you are setting up multiple servers, simply add several A records, each pointing to one of the servers. One more thing you might need to change is the DNS **Global Query Block List** (**GQBL**). The GQBL is a list of host names that DNS will not answer to, even if it has specific entries for them in its database. The GQBL on a Windows DNS server contains two entries by default – ISATAP and WPAD. The reason for this being there is so that if a user accidentally installs a computer with that hostname, it won't be resolvable. If such a computer was installed accidentally and not blocked, it could cause havoc on the network, because all ISATAP-capable computers on the network will try to get it to assign them an ISATAP address. WPAD is also problematic, as that host name would be used for proxy configuration, so a wrongly named computer could also cause serious problems.

When you enable URA with the wizard, it would enable the ISATAP router function on itself. However, it will not add a DNS entry for ISATAP and the block list entry will not be removed either, so you'll have to edit DNS and the GQBL yourself. To add the DNS entry, use the DNS console, and to edit the GQBL run the following command in a CMD prompt on the DNS server:

```
dnscmd /config /globalqueryblocklist wpad
```

No, referring to `wpad` in the previous command is not a typo. Using the `dnscmd` command, one can only add entries to the GQBL, so what we're doing here is telling the server to erase the current GQBL, and then add the `wpad` entry to it. Since we're not including the ISATAP entry explicitly in the command, it won't be added, and won't be blocked. Another way to do this is to edit the registry on the DNS server, and remove the ISATAP directly. To do so, edit the following key:

```
HKLM\SYSTEM\CurrentControlSet\Services\DNS\Parameters\
GlobalQueryBlockList
```

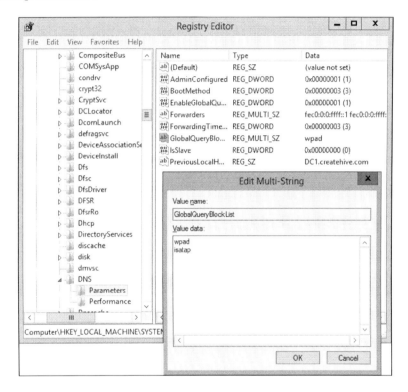

Once you've done that, your computers should receive an ISATAP IP shortly. You could also disable and re-enable a computer's NIC to force it to happen right away.

Summary

In this chapter, we discussed some very advanced things and techniques you can apply to URA, to fine-tune it to your needs, and operate things better and easier. We probably put up enough warnings, but just to be on the safe side, we want to mention once again that many of these settings are risky, and could be a total buzzkill for your URA connection. However, learning how they work and what they can do can really take your deployment to the next level, so we hope this was useful and interesting.

In the next chapter we will discuss two other advanced scenarios – **One Time Password (OTP)** and **Network Access Protection (NAP)**. Both of these are enterprise-level features that could take your URA even further towards a more robust and secure deployment.

9
Deploying NAP and OTP

For the ultrahigh security-focused organization, NAP and OTP are the two magic words that make the information security officer feel all warm and fuzzy (with the occasional nervous breakdown, though, of course). **NAP** stands for **Network Access Protection**, and **OTP** is **one time password**. NAP allows an organization to detect health information about clients and block them from accessing the network if they don't meet specific health criteria such as an antivirus or security updates to the system. OTP allows an organization to implement an extra authentication factor, which generates a new random password for each connection, thus eliminating the risk of an attacker guessing a credential set and getting access to the network. In this chapter, we will see how URA can implement these two technologies to provide a more secure environment. The topics at hand are:

- NAP basic concepts
- NAP and URA
- Enabling NAP on URA
- Introduction to OTP
- How OTP works with URA
- Enabling OTP
- Troubleshooting tips

NAP basic concepts

Network Access Protection (**NAP**) is not new, and can be used independently of URA to provide better network security by ensuring that clients are in good *health*. The well-known cure for computer-sniffles is an antivirus, of course, and organizations throughout the world have always been looking for creative ways to keep their computers safe. NAP was first introduced with Windows Server 2008, and is primarily targeted at protecting the organization's network from computers that move in and out of the network, such as mobile computers. To do its work, NAP has three main components:

- NAP **Health Policy Servers** (**HPS**), which are computers running the **Network Policy Server** (**NPS**) service on a Windows Server.

- **Health Registration Authority** (**HRA**), which can be one computer or more running Windows Server and sometimes hardware Network Switches that have been designed to support NAP.

- **System Health Agent** (**SHA**), which is integrated into Windows clients starting with Windows XP SP3. On a Windows system, the SHA is referred to as **Windows SHA** or **WSHA**, although there are also third-party NAP clients for Mac and Linux computers.

Many organizations elect to use NAP, because it allows them to enforce certain security policies on all their computers, not just those that connect remotely. An organization that has a NAP infrastructure deployed can take advantage of it and configure URA to rely on the same infrastructure to check its own clients when they try to connect.

How does NAP work (generally)?

In order to understand how NAP works, we need to see how the various components work together. The endpoint component of NAP is called the **System Health Agent** (**SHA**), and is included with Windows clients from Windows XP SP3 and onward. The client is running in the background and monitors the status of the system all the time. The client agent periodically generates a **Statement of Health** (**SOH**), which includes information about the client's status and sends it to the **Health Registration Authority** (**HRA**). The HRA sends this to the NAP **Health Policy Server** (**HPS**), which evaluates it and decides if the client is healthy or not, based on the specific **System Health Validator** (**SHV**). This is how the NAP console looks, allowing you to configure a health policy:

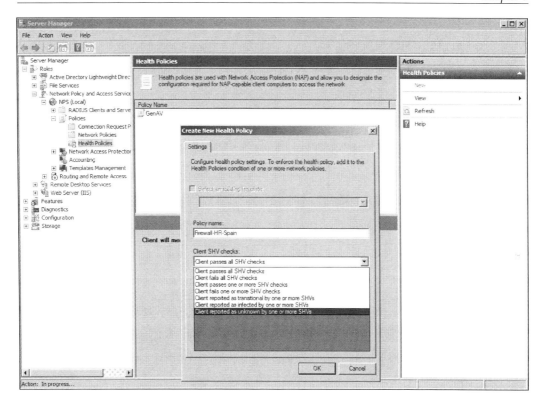

If the client is compliant with the policy (*healthy*), the HPS tells the HRA so by issuing a health certificate for this specific client. The HRA then allows the client access to the network.

If the client is unhealthy, the HPS may issue remediation instructions, if configured to do so, and those are relayed to the client via the HRA. The client can then contact specially designated remediation servers that may offer the organization's antivirus software of choice, or an update to it, and so forth.

At any point, a healthy client may become unhealthy, or vice versa. For example, a user may return with his laptop from a long trip in which he was never online. At that point, his AV software is not updated, so he will be denied access. Within minutes, his software will be updated via the remediation servers, making him healthy. The reverse can occur — a client, while connected, may decide to uninstall or stop his antivirus, turning his computer non-compliant. For this reason, NAP Statement of Health reports have to be resent every time a computer reboots, every four hours while the computer is working, every time a client makes changes to his security settings, and on some other occasions.

A full detail of NAP is beyond the scope of this book, but you can learn more about it and how it works at http://technet.microsoft.com/en-us/network/bb545879.

NAP and URA

With URA, NAP can be used to check the health of connecting clients and block them if they are not healthy. The NAP services and client are separate from URA, and so you need to design and build your NAP infrastructure independently. Unfortunately, you cannot configure the URA server itself to be your NAP server.

Once you enable NAP integration with URA, the URA server will work with your **Health Registration Authority** (**HRA**) and **Health Policy Server** (**HPS**). The NAP agent on your clients will generate a **Statement of Health** (**SOH**) and send it to the URA server. The URA server, before granting full access, will send the SOH to its designated HRA, which will work with the HPS to validate the status. Only if the HPS confirms that the client meets the requirements, will it let the client into the network. If the client doesn't meet the requirements, the HPS will tell URA that this client's a *persona non-grata* right now, and if you have configured it for remediation, will offer information about that. In such a case, you might also configure URA with remediation servers as management servers (which we discussed at the beginning of *Chapter 8, Enhanced Configurations for Infrastructure Servers*) so as to make it easy for the URA client to fix itself up.

Remediation servers could host tools and information about what a user should do to get his computer to meet the security policy. For example, if the computer is missing an antivirus scanner, you could put your corporate antivirus installation binaries on the remediation servers so that the user can install it. This way, the user can fix himself up without having to travel to the office. If the URA client does get healthier, the process will repeat, and once the HRA confirms the client as healthy, URA will let it in.

Like some of the other advanced features, using NAP requires you to use the two-tunnel mode, and cannot use the Kerberos proxy. This also means that you'll have to deploy a full PKI in your network and issue computer certificates to all computers. We discussed the topic of deploying full PKI in the *PKI* section in *Chapter 2, Planning a Unified Remote Access Deployment*, so you might want to go back and review it.

To outline this process with more detail:

1. When the URA client initiates the connection upon detecting that it's on the public Internet, it creates the first tunnel (the Infrastructure tunnel).

2. The NAP agent on the client resolves the HRA, which you designated on your network.

3. The NAP agent sends its current health state information to the HRA.

4. The HRA server sends the health state information to the HPS, which you designated on your network.

5. The HPS checks out the health, and if it's nice and tidy according to the corporate policy, it tells the HRA so, or the opposite.

6. The HRA sends the results to the URA server, which delivers it to the client.

7. If these results are clearing the URA client to go through with the connection, the HRA obtains a health certificate from the CA configured for NAP and gives it to the URA client via the URA server.

8. The URA client proceeds to establish the second tunnel (the Corporate tunnel), using the health certificate as an authentication method.

As you can see, the process that goes on here is pretty complex, and there's a lot that can go wrong. This is not helped by the fact that several chunks of this setup need to be done on totally separate components, and a lot of it manually. Prepare for a shaky ride!

Enabling NAP on URA

Before you enable NAP in the URA configuration console, you first need to install and configure an HRA and NPS. These are roles that you need to install using the regular role wizard. You also need to configure your CA to issue the appropriate certificates, and configure it to automatically issue the certificates and the proper permissions. This is beyond the scope of this book, but if you're new to NAP, the following links contain more information, as well as a lab-guide specifically about NAP and DirectAccess. The guide is for Windows 2008 R2 DA, but the NAP and CA setup portions in it are relevant for URA as well:

- http://technet.microsoft.com/en-us/library/jj649081
- http://technet.microsoft.com/en-US/library/ff528480

The HRA service will be certifying that clients are healthy with the help of digital certificates and so part of installing that role is to provide the name of a certificate authority server. This CA can be the same CA that you installed for deploying computer certificates for your URA clients or another. In fact, the CA role may be enabled on the URA server itself too, if you prefer. Do note, though, that since the NAP certificates are short-lived (4 hours, by default), it would have to generate quite a number of certificates. If you have 3000 clients connected 24x7, we're talking about over half a million certs every month. Better make sure the server can handle it without degradation of other services.

Once all the roles are installed and configured, you can enable NAP integration on the URA server. This is done via step 2 of the Remote Access Server wizard (page 3):

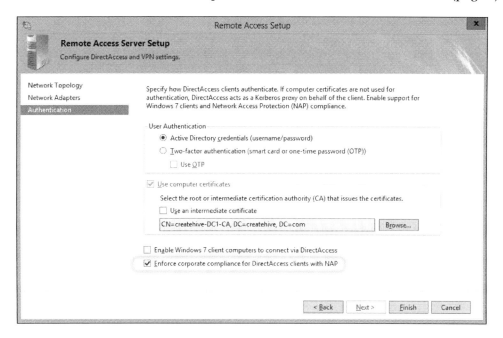

Since computer certificates are required, that option will get automatically checked and grayed-out, and if you haven't selected the root or intermediate CA, you will need to do so to be able to finish the wizard. When you click on **Finish**, you'll need to update Group Policy by clicking on **Finish** on the bottom of the URA console. As usual, once GP has been updated successfully, you'll need to get clients to update their policy, and upon their next connection, NAP enforcement should spring into action.

What the checkbox that's visible in the preceding screenshot actually does is enable an extra setting in the Group Policy for the `DaServerToCorp` policy. As you may recall from *Chapter 8, Enhanced Configurations for Infrastructure Servers* where we looked into the authentication configuration in the policy, the URA Group Policy has two items in the connection security rules—the `DaServerToInfra` item, which governs how the first tunnel is established, and the `DaServerToCorp` item, which governs the second tunnel. With NAP, the first tunnel is identical to a regular two-tunnel configuration, but as you may recall from a few pages ago, the URA clients need to establish its health and get a NAP health certificate to set up the second tunnel. To this end, a checkmark gets added for the **Accept only health certificates** option in the policy:

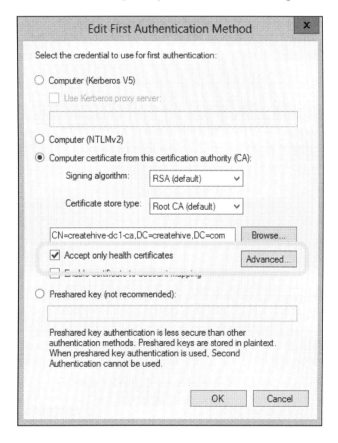

This tells the URA server to allow the URA client to establish the second tunnel only if the certificate it presented was one that is suitable for health validation. Such a certificate would have to have the System Health Authentication **object identifier (OID)** in the **Enhanced Key Usage (EKU)** field, as opposed to a regular computer certificate that doesn't:

When initiating the connection, the client will have to connect to the NAP HRA server via the first tunnel to get his/her certificate, and so the HRA will have to be added to the list of management servers. To do so, open the **Infrastructure Server Setup** (step 3) wizard and go to page 4. Double-click on the blank line and type in an IP address or FQDN name of your HRA. When finished, click on **Finish** to close the wizard, and then click on **Finish** at the bottom of the screen to update Group Policy with the new settings. You should also add any remediation servers that you might have configured as part of NAP, if you want the clients to be able to connect to them and get healthy (unless, of course, those servers are already publicly available on the Internet). In the following screenshot, you can see the add management servers page; that's part of step 3 of the URA configuration:

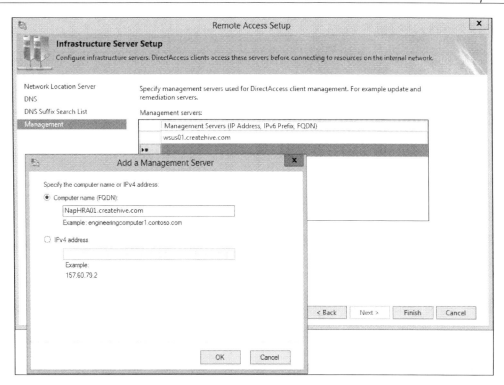

Now, get your URA clients to update their Group Policy. When they initiate the connection, if they are compliant, you would not see any difference in behavior. If, however, they are not, the NAP agent will show a message in your system tray about it:

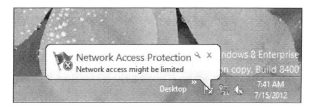

You can also verify if NAP is working well by opening the certificate store on the client and looking for the NAP certificate. It would be a short-lived certificate (with an expiry date set for today) and have the **System Health Authentication** purpose listed on the **Intended Purpose** field, as shown in the screenshot that we showed earlier in this chapter. Yet another method is running the command `napstat` from a command-prompt window. This triggers the NAP status bubble in the system tray. If things aren't working out, refer to the troubleshooting tips at the end of the chapter.

Introduction to OTP

One time password is one of the most common forms of **2 factor authentication (2FA)** in the world, because it provides a level of security that's unmatched by any other technology. With OTP, a unique password is specifically generated for each connection attempt, by special software, and used as part of the login process. Some OTP products generate the unique password automatically every minute and others generate it upon request. The OTP cannot be re-used to connect again, so it cannot be stolen, and there's no use for brute-force guessing, because the OTP will expire before the guess engine can go through more than a few hundred password variations.

The most well-known provider for OTP solutions is RSA (the company, not the algorithm, although the RSA company was named after its founders Ron Rivest, Adi Shamir, and Len Adleman, who also developed the algorithm RSA). RSA's OTP solution uses a piece of software that generates a new PIN every minute. You can run the software on a computer, a smartphone, or as a small key-chain sized device known as a **token**. The token has a small screen that shows the current PIN. Other providers have similar devices and software:

When using OTP, the user carries the token or comparable software solution with him/her, and when he needs to log in to some service, he feeds in his/her username and reads off the current PIN from the token. Some organizations also assign a fixed PIN to every user, which has to be appended to the OTP PIN, while others require a regular password to be provided in addition to the OTP.

How OTP works with URA

With URA, the OTP function is based on the NCA (or DCA 2.0 with Windows 7 clients). When the user starts his/her computer and connects to the Internet, the computer establishes the first URA tunnel and then the NCA shows a prompt for the user to feed in his/her PIN. Assuming the PIN was entered correctly, the computer establishes the second tunnel, and everything is ready to go. Technically, the first tunnel serves as a communication channel to provide access to a designated Certificate Authority server, which provides a special certificate, which is used to establish the second tunnel. These certificates are short-lived, so they expire quickly (normally in one hour). If the user suspends his computer or restarts it, he has to repeat the OTP login process to get a new certificate, as the old one will have expired.

As you can imagine, the use of certificates in this scenario also means that the simplified Kerberos Proxy mechanism cannot be used and you have to deploy a full PKI in your domain.

To use OTP, you will require, of course, an OTP server, such as RSA's Authentication Manager. Installing and configuring Authentication Manager is beyond the scope of this book, but it's well documented by RSA. The administrator's guide and other docs are available at `ftp://ftp.rsa.com/pub/docs/AM7.0/`.

In addition, the URA OTP lab guide is available at `http://technet.microsoft.com/en-us/library/hh831544`. This guide includes detailed setup instructions for the RSA server.

RSA also offers a free evaluation package, which you can use to learn about the product and experience it before you purchase it. It is available at `http://www.emc.com/security/rsa-securid/rsa-authentication-manager.htm`.

If you're using a different OTP solution, it should have its own documentation as well, of course, though some companies do prefer their users to be clairvoyant. If you haven't set up your OTP solution yet, we recommend setting it up and testing it with regular client access first.

Enabling OTP

Before you enable OTP on the URA server, you need to start by setting up your CA for the right type of certificates. This can be the same CA that you are using to issue computer certificates, but you are going to have to prepare two special certificate templates on it. One is the OTP Certificate, and will be used to create the special OTP certificates issued to URA clients. The second one is the OTP request signing certificate, and will be used by the URA server itself to sign requests. These certificates require certain settings that are only available in Windows Server 2008 and onward, so make sure your CA server is running 2008 or later. We will discuss setting up the certificate templates shortly.

OTP and Windows 7 clients

The process wherein the user provides the one time password for the connection is handled by the **Network Connectivity Assistant (NCA)**. The Windows 8 clients have it built into the operating system, but for Windows 7 clients, you have to install it. As you may recall from *Chapter 7, Unified Remote Access Client Access*, the comparable software is called **DirectAccess Connectivity Assistant (DCA)**, and you need to download and install version 2 of it on your Windows 7 clients (do not use the older versions of the DCA that you might have been using with UAG or Windows 2008 R2 DirectAccess).

Creating the OTP certificate template

The OTP certificate template is based on the Smartcard Logon template, so use the CA template console to duplicate it and then edit the duplicate as follows:

1. On the **Compatibility** tab, set the **Certification Authority** list to **Windows Server 2012** and the **Certificate recipient** list to **Windows 8 / Windows Server 2012**.

2. On the **General** tab, give the template a sensible name and set the **Validity Period** to 1 hour and the **Renewal Period** to 0.

3. On the **Security** tab, set the permissions for **Authenticated Users** for **Read** and **Enroll** and for **System** for **Full Control**.

4. On the **Subject Name** tab, in the **Subject name format** list make sure **Fully distinguished name** is selected and that the **User principal name (UPN)** checkbox is checked.

5. On the **Server** tab, check **Do not store certificates and requests in the CA database** and uncheck the **Do not include revocation information in issued certificates** checkbox.

6. On the **Issuance Requirements** tab, check **This number of authorized signatures** and make sure the value is set to **1**. In the **Application policy** list, select your policy (as you named it in step 2):

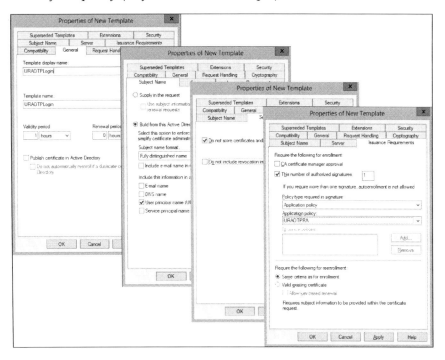

7. On the **Extensions** tab, edit **Application Policies** and remove **Client Authentication** but keep **SmartCardLogon**.

Creating the OTP request signing template

The OTP request signing certificate template is based on the Computer certificate template, so use the CA template console to duplicate the Computer template. Configure the duplicate with the following settings:

1. On the **Compatibility** tab, set the **Certification Authority** list to **Windows Server 2012** and the **Certificate recipient** list to **Windows 8 / Windows Server 2012**.

2. On the **General** tab, give the template a sensible name, and set the **Validity Period** to 2 days and the **Renewal Period** to 1 day.

3. On the **Security** tab, add permissions for your URA server for **Enroll** and **Autoenroll**, and for **System** for **Full Control**:

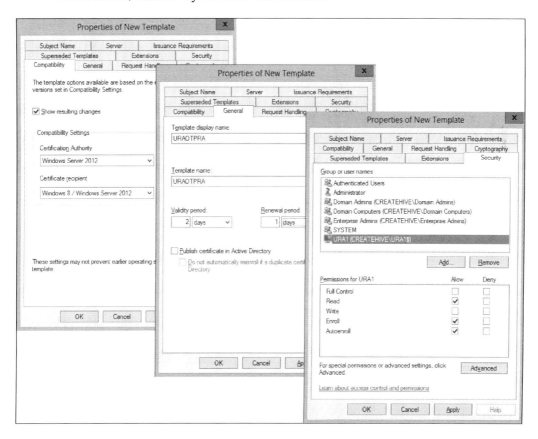

4. On the **Subject Name** tab, in the **Subject name format** list, select **DNS name** and make sure that the **DNS name** checkbox is checked.

5. On the **Extensions** tab, edit the **Application Policies** and remove the existing ones. Click on **Add** to add a new one and click on **New** to create your own policy.

6. Give a name to the new policy and for **Object Identifier**, type 1.3.6.1.4.1.311.81.1.1:

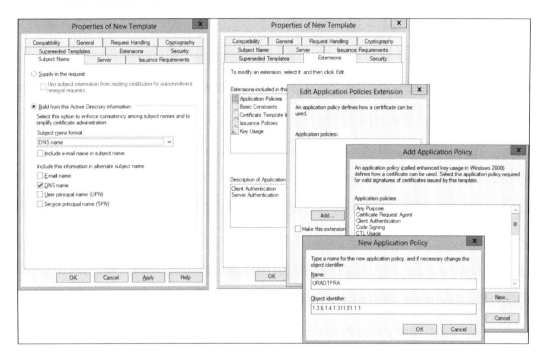

Adding the template to the CA

Now that your two new templates are ready, use the CA console to add them to the list of available options and enable volatile requests. This setting enables non-persistent certificate processing and can help reduce the CA database growth rate and frequency of database management tasks:

1. Open the CA console and right-click on the **Certificate Templates** tab.

2. Choose **New** and select **Certificate template to issue**.

3. Select your new certificates and click on **OK**.

4. Restart the CA service by right-clicking on the server name and choosing **All tasks/Stop** and then **All tasks/Start**.

5. Open an admin command prompt and type `CertUtil.exe -SetReg DBFlags +DBFLAGS_ENABLEVOLATILEREQUESTS`.

Configuring the URA server as an authentication agent

Assuming your RSA or other OTP server is up and running, the next step is to configure the URA server as an authentication agent. This will allow it to represent URA clients to the OTP server, deliver their one time password and generate certificates for them for the connection. This procedure varies among the OTP providers, but essentially, the OTP agent on the URA server talks to the OTP server, using the RADIUS protocol. Naturally, this means that this involves installing some agent on the URA server and configuring it as a "client" or "agent" on the OTP server. The RADIUS protocol uses a unique password known as a node secret or shared secret that you create on the server and then input on the agent (for some solutions you have to choose the password, while others generate it for you automatically). With an RSA server, you would install the RSA SecurID Authentication Agent software on the URA server, create the node secret on the RSA server, create a configuration file, and import it into the SecurID Authentication Agent software on the URA server.

RADIUS stands for **Remote Authentication Dial In User Service**, but it's actually used for far more than dial-in. In fact, it is one of the most versatile protocols out there, and it is used by thousands of systems and products. In the case of OTP, it's used by the OTP providers to communicate with the URA server. For more information about this protocol, read the article available at `http://en.wikipedia.org/wiki/RADIUS`.

Most OTP providers would provide you with more detailed documentation pertaining to their specific solution, as well as some tool to test the configuration and verify that the URA server was successfully set as an agent, and to communicate well with the OTP server. Once that has been confirmed, you can proceed to the next step.

Enabling OTP on URA

The final step is to enable OTP on your URA server, and that is done via step 2 of the Unified Remote Access configuration (**Remote Access Server Setup**), page 3. To enable OTP, check the checkbox next to **Two factor authentication** and **Use OTP**. The wizard should have already been set to use computer certificates for authentication, but if not, it will automatically enable it now. If you haven't configured this until now, you also need to select the root CA for these certificates. As you can see in the following screenshot, the wizard will also show four new pages:

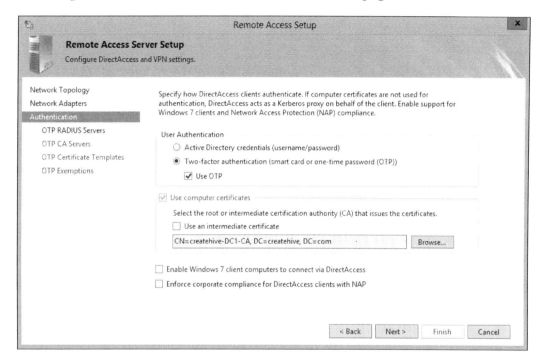

On the **OTP Radius Servers** page, you need to double-click on the list to add your OTP server and set up the shared secret. You can also adjust the TCP port, if it's not using the default RADIUS port of 1812:

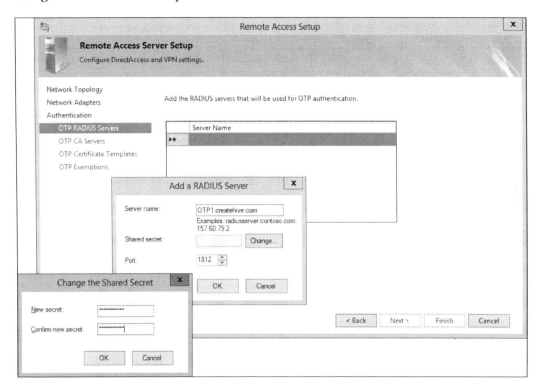

On the next page, you need to select the CA server that will be used to issue the short-lived certificates for OTP. The URA wizard will show a list of CA servers detected on the network and you can add the one that you have set up with the OTP templates earlier. On the next page, you need to select the two templates that you created earlier (the OTP certificate template and the OTP request signing template). Finally, the last page allows you to define certain users as exempt from the OTP requirement. To use this feature, create an active directory security group for it, add users to it, and then select it in this part of the wizard:

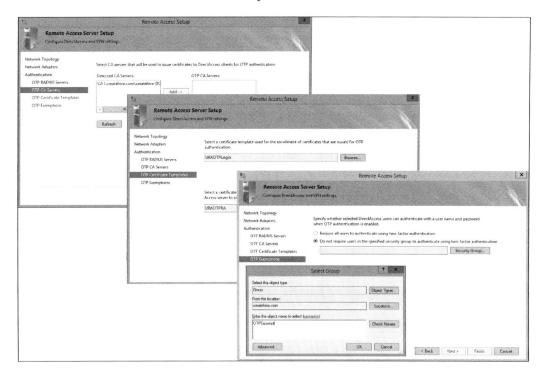

Now that OTP is enabled, you also need to add your CA to the management server list, so that connecting URA clients can connect to it over the first tunnel and obtain the OTP certificate. To do so, go to step 3 of the URA configuration (**Infrastructure Servers**) and go to page 4 (management). Double-click on a blank line and add the CA that you have used for the OTP certificates.

Once you have finished the wizard, you need to apply the new settings by clicking on **Update** at the bottom of the URA console, and once both the URA server (or servers) and clients have updated their Group Policy, everything should be good to go. Now, when clients connect to URA, they will establish the first tunnel, and then show a pop-up for the user to feed in his OTP. Assuming the OTP was correct, the client will be able to complete the process and establish the second tunnel, and full network access would ensue!

Troubleshooting tips

NAP and OTP add significant complications to the URA infrastructure and make troubleshooting a lot more complicated. Unless you're a URA expert (which, if you were, you wouldn't be reading this book...right?), you'd probably want to avoid that for now. We suggest starting by deploying a simple URA connection with the **Getting Started Wizard**, and once that works, proceed to the simple computer certificate deployment. Only when the fundamental configuration works reliably, explore the more advanced scenarios. This way, you will at least know for sure that the building blocks are ok and thus limit your troubleshooting scope.

In *Chapter 10, Monitoring and Troubleshooting Unified Remote Access*, we will discuss troubleshooting Unified Remote Access. We will cover general techniques and methods for solving problems, but we won't be discussing NAP and OTP troubleshooting specifically. Troubleshooting these technologies is done via the event log on the URA server, which should alert you to problems with your configuration. The following articles on TechNet describes some of the problems that you might encounter and how to handle them:

- http://technet.microsoft.com/en-us/library/jj618327
- http://technet.microsoft.com/en-us/library/dd348461

Summary

NAP and OTP are the final building blocks of setting up Unified Remote Access, and having gone through this, you know almost everything to know about this technology. They are also two of the harder things to accomplish, because they depend a lot on the infrastructure, but successfully implementing either or both can boost the security level of your deployment a great deal.

In the next chapter, we will go into the realm of monitoring and troubleshooting, and see how to handle various problems that you might run into with the various scenarios.

10
Monitoring and Troubleshooting Unified Remote Access

Having read through the previous chapters, you now know everything about installing and configuring the various scenarios of Unified Remote Access. However, in the real world, things are rarely perfect and you are going to need to keep an eye on the servers and your users, and occasionally perform some troubleshooting. In this chapter, we will discuss using the URA console and other tools for monitoring things and some troubleshooting techniques.

The topics at hand are:

- Monitoring the URA server (or servers)
- Monitoring URA clients
- Generating reports
- Troubleshooting URA
- Common problems, issues, and mistakes
- Connectivity problems
- Client troubleshooting
- Advanced diagnostics

Monitoring the URA server (or servers)

If your URA server is unhealthy for any reason, this affects everyone, so monitoring the server is the first thing on the priority list. To see the status, the URA console has the **Operations Status** view. The **Operations Status** page shows your URA server, or a list of your servers, if you have more than one, and whether they are operational or not. The status is a no-brainer, really. If there is a problem with the server, it simply shows the status as so, and double-clicking on the server expands the view to show which of the components have a problem. Clicking on that specific item shows more detail about the problem. In the following screenshot, for example, the NLS website has stopped working because the server crashed. The URA server can't always know exactly what happened, but it offers some possible explanations. In our example, shown in the following screenshot, one of the possibilities it suggests is that ICMP traffic is blocked (which means that the server itself may be perfectly fine, but simply not responding to being pinged by the URA monitoring component):

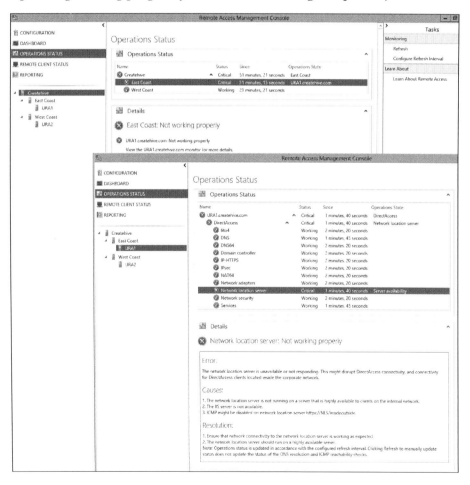

For the most part, if the configuration wizard completes successfully, things rarely go wrong afterwards beyond obvious things such as crashes, certificate expiration, or network problems. We will talk more about actual troubleshooting later in this chapter. One thing to note, though, is that by default, the monitoring console refreshes the status every 5 minutes, so if you're taking action to resolve some issue, make sure you click on **Refresh** on the top-right of the **Tasks** pane. You can also change the refresh rate to faster or slower via **Configure Refresh Interval**.

Monitoring URA clients

The **Remote Client Status** page is where you'll probably be spending a lot of your time. The page shows you a list of currently connected clients, each listing the username, the computer name, the client IP address, the connectivity method, and the duration of the connection. If the client is only partially connected, such as when the first tunnel is established, but the second one is not, you would typically just see the hostname, but not the username.

As is common with views like this, you can click on the column heads to sort the list by any column or reverse the sort order. The view also has a search bar, allowing you to filter the list for specific things. You can also expand the search options and get a list of search criteria (for example, to find which client has accessed a specific internal server). Next to the search bar, you have a pair of buttons to save your search query or load a previously saved one. When you click on a client, the bottom of the console shows some more details, such as the number of bytes that were sent and received by this client via the URA connection, the time when this connection started, the authentication method, and a list of resources that the client accessed via the connection. You can also right-click on any client and ask for more details, which provide even more info such as the connection speed. Note that the view is also for monitoring VPN clients that are not using DirectAccess, and **Disconnect VPN Client** on the **Tasks** pane allows you to disconnect VPN clients, but not DirectAccess clients:

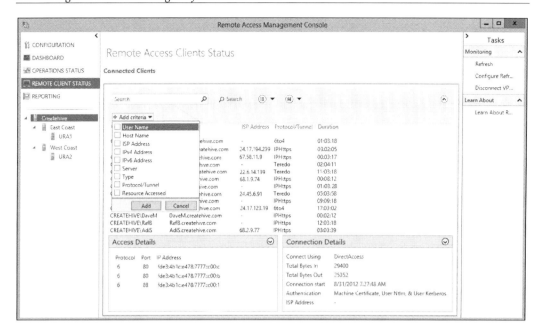

If you do need to disconnect a DirectAccess client, you need to do two things. To actually sever the connection, you need to delete the **Security Associations** (SAs) that the Windows Firewall has established, and disable the computer account of the remote computer. Disabling the computer account prevents the SAs from getting re-established by the client (which it would try to do automatically and instantly). Here are the steps:

1. Open Active Directory Users and Computers.
2. Locate the computer account and disable or delete it.
3. On your URA server, open a PowerShell window.
4. Type the following command to obtain the Security Association ID:

```
Get-NetIPsecQuickModeSA -Name "computer" -CimSession
<RemoteMachineName>
```

5. Type the following command to remove the security association:

```
Remove-NetIPsecMainModeSA -CimSession <RemoteMachineName>
-InputObject <SecurityAssociationID>
```

In addition to the data presented by **Operations Status** and **Remote Client Status**, you also have the **Dashboard** view, which combines the other two and allows you to take a quick glance at things. This is an easy way to keep an eye on things such as how many users are connected. It's particularly useful if you have many servers to keep track-of. It also has an option for tracing, which we will discuss later in this chapter.

Generating reports

Viewing connection data in real time is useful, but you're probably going to need to view data historically as well (if you don't, we're sure some executive will convince you). For this, URA allows you to produce reports for specific periods of time.

To use URA's reporting capabilities, you need to enable accounting; the process of storing connection information somewhere, that is. URA offers two options—one is using a RADIUS server, and the other is using Windows' built-in **WID (Windows Internal Database)** service. WID, also known as SQL Server Embedded Edition, is a service that is included with the operating system (has been there since Windows Server 2008) and several other Microsoft products. When you install the URA role, it automatically adds this service (you can see it in `c:\windows\WID\Binn\sqlserver.exe`) so that it can be used to store data. Note that WID, although based on SQL technology, is not a full SQL server. This means that you cannot access it using tools such as SQL Server Management Studio or write code to interact with it.

By default, neither RADIUS nor WID reporting is enabled, so until you choose to use either or both, no data is collected. To enable reporting, go to the URA console, click on **Reporting**, and then click on **Configure Accounting**. In the **Configure Accounting** page , select which accounting mechanism you want to use (you can use both) and configure the options. If you have an available RADIUS server, configure the server name, port, shared secret, timeout, and initial score. If you're using WID, configure how far back you want to keep your accounting data:

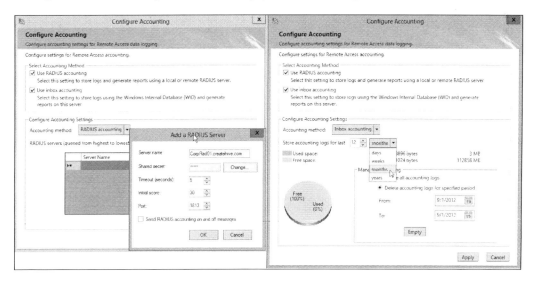

As opposed to RADIUS, WID provides only limited control over the data. Using the URA console, you can monitor the space used by WID, and you can manually clear the collected data, but you cannot move the database to another location nor can you perform a backup or restore of it.

Once you have enabled accounting, URA will start collecting usage information. Essentially, the usage information is identical to what is shown in the monitoring console. URA records the following:

- User Name
- Host Name
- ISP IP Address
- IPv4 Address
- IPv6 Address
- Server (to which the client is connected-to)
- Type (DirectAccess or other VPN)
- Protocol/Tunnel (6to4, Teredo, IP-HTTPS)
- Connection duration
- Accessed resources (protocol, port, IP)
- Total bytes in
- Total bytes out
- Authentication methods

The reporting console allows you to define a specific time period to produce a report for, and to define additional criteria from the preceding list to apply and filter the report. For example, you might need to see which users were accessing your CRM server during Labor-day weekend, and explain to those poor souls that you're not supposed to actually do labor on that weekend:

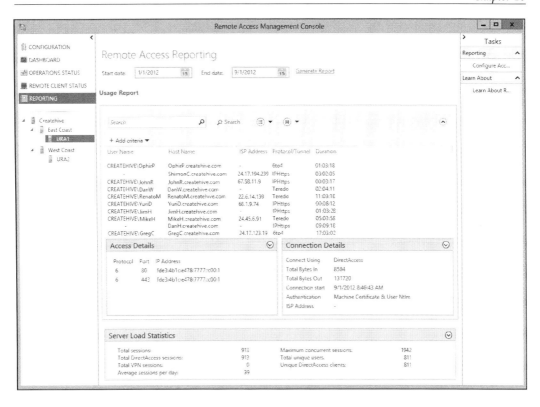

When you produce a report, you cannot save it to disk, but you can select and copy some or all the lines, and then paste them into a text file or an Excel spreadsheet. Another limitation is that you cannot produce a report for a period longer than 3 months. Keep in mind that a busy server can produce a huge amount of information, and this could slow down the report generation process. Naturally, your server won't be all cheers and hugs if you copy a huge amount of lines to the clipboard either. For organizations that have large-scale URA deployments, using a RADIUS server for this is a good idea.

Windows Server includes the IAS role, which makes it a RADIUS server. If you'd like to set up one of your servers for this, the following link provides information about it:

http://technet.microsoft.com/en-us/library/
cc736803(v=WS.10).aspx

Another thing that could make reporting more effective in a large environment is using PowerShell commands to export the stored data. The command is:

```
Get-RemoteAccessConnectionStatistics –Startdatetime <startdate>
  -Enddatetime <enddate>
```

This dumps the output to the PowerShell window itself, but you can also do other things with it. For example, you can dump the output to a CSV file by using the following syntax:

```
Get- RemoteAccessConnectionStatistics -Startdatetime <startdate>
-Enddatetime <enddate> |export-csv
  "report_data_<startdate(yyyymmdd)>_<enddate(yyyymmdd)>.csv
```

You can even export the data to an SQL database, if you're handy enough with PowerShell. There is an article about exporting data to SQL (not specific to URA) at http://blogs.technet.com/b/sqlthoughts/archive/2008/10/03/out-sql-powershell-function-export-pipeline-to-a-new-sql-server-table.aspx.

For more information about the `Get-RemoteAccessConnectionStatistics` command, refer to the TechNet article at http://technet.microsoft.com/en-us/library/hh918379.aspx.

Troubleshooting URA

Unified Remote Access is a complex technology that relies on many moving parts to work correctly. As such, there are plenty of things that can go wrong. As problems go, things are usually divided into server-side problems stemming from a misconfiguration, and client-side problems, which often happen because something went suddenly wrong (you know...those mysterious malfunctions the user reports started right after he/she browsed to `www.doesn'tmatter.com`).

The more complex your configuration is, the more things you have that can possibly go wrong, thus increasing the scope and complexity of troubleshooting, so as a general approach, we suggest the following practices:

* Make sure your server has not been configured with software that could affect this technology. Security software such as antivirus and Firewall software often takes over some aspects of the networking components, and that could cause problems.

* Make sure your server has not been hardened another way, such as by a Group Policy that disabled certain functions or services. For example, if your default Group Policy blocks the Windows Firewall, things will go bad, as you're killing the components that are in charge of setting up the IPsec tunnels.

- Regarding the preceding two practices, it's best to use a blank vanilla server, installed from the official DVD media of Windows Server 2012, rather than a corporate image or a re-use of an already configured server that might have had its innards messed-around with.

- Start with the simplest URA configuration and proceed to add more advanced options only after successfully making the basic ones work.

- Add advanced configuration options incrementally, testing the results well between each.

- Record any changes you make carefully with a notepad and screenshots.

- When making changes, keep in mind that everything is stored in Group Policy. Be sure to perform GPUPDATE not only on your server or servers, but also on your test clients. If you don't, your changes might look good...but turn out to have killed your configuration an hour later when GP finally replicates.

- Use test clients that are also as clean as possible, preferably those installed from official media rather than clients that have been already installed and configured with a collection of software or settings, or built from a corporate image that might conflict with URA.

- Have at least two-three clients to test with, so that if there's a problem, you can see if it affects all clients or just one or some.

- Client connectivity type (6to4, Teredo, or IP-HTTPS) can have a lot of effect on how things work, so it's best to have your test client in various networking environments and see how they behave. For example, if there's a networking problem with your configuration, it might not work for Teredo clients, but work fine for 6to4 clients. Only if you have no 6to4 clients, you might get thrown off-track with your troubleshooting, thinking nothing works.

- Keep in mind that the URA 2-tunnel configuration can give a false positive if just the first tunnel is up. Testing connectivity to a domain controller is not the right way to know if things are well. Also, using ping is not a reliable way to know if things are good, as the ICMP protocol is exempt from the IPsec policy that governs URA traffic. Make sure you contact a real server, using at least one real TCP/IP protocol. For example, a good test would be if you're able to browse to an internal SharePoint server, though just pinging it won't. On a similar note, just being unable to successfully ping a server doesn't mean that URA is broken, as something else could be blocking the ICMP traffic.

- Whether you are deploying a full PKI or not, mark your calendar with the expiration date of your certificates (yes, even self-signed certificates expire) so that you can renew them ahead of time.

Now, let's go into some real troubleshooting.

Common problems, issues, and mistakes

URA's **Getting Started Wizard** was specifically designed to allow an exceptionally simple and straightforward setup of this technology, eliminating almost any possible human error. The more advanced scenarios where you need to configure an NLS site and a certificate infrastructure is where there's a lot more room for error. With the simple setup in mind, the most common issue that you might run into is routing or networking related. The reason for such issues surfacing is typically because most organizations have a complex network, making it difficult to see possible routing conflicts or problems. Also, many organizations have some mix of IPv4 and IPv6 technology, and it could lead to conflicts and other problems. For example, perhaps some servers have been assigned an IPv6 address (with or without your knowledge), or perhaps ISATAP has been enabled on the network already. Some hardware devices, such as routers, have built-in functions related to IPv6, and it's not unusual to find that some have been configured in a way that complicates matters. For example, an external router might be filtering Teredo traffic, making the use of that protocol to communicate with clients impossible for the URA server.

Different software and hardware have different capabilities, and as things are deployed over time, configurations differ. Windows Vista, 7, and 8 clients, for example, all come with the IPv6 stack enabled, but other operating systems may not. So is the case for many hardware devices such as printers. For computers, your organization might have a Group Policy that configures the IPv6 stack to be disabled. The URA servers has the NAT64 and DNS64 components that allow URA clients to interact with IPv4-only hosts, but if certain components or devices are configured in a way that contradicts the defaults for a URA server, it could complicate matters and it's a good idea to get a good understanding how your network runs. Specifically, here are things to look out for:

- Group Policy that disabled the IPv6 stack
- Anything on the network that might be set up as an ISATAP router
- Anything on the network that might assign out IPv6 addresses
- Routing equipment that might specifically block IPv6 traffic, or IPv6 traffic encapsulated in IPv4 (a Stateful Firewall might do this)
- Computers or devices that have been configured with a static IPv6 address in an inconsistent manner with the rest of the network

If there are components or devices that are configured in a way that could cause a problem, it might not be easy to find out. In large organizations, there are often several bodies that deal with the network and security, and it is also possible that some stuff was done before your time. A good way to start is to gather a detailed network map, listing all network devices such as routers, smart switches, gateways, access points, and the likes, and considering whether they can be a complication. A good practice is identifying which devices are supposed to be accessible from a URA client so that you can properly test things. If there are devices which are not under your ownership, or that you have no experience with, you could benefit from organizing a brain-storming session with other engineers and discussing these topics.

ISATAP

ISATAP is a technology that can be very useful for small organizations that are not ready to go full IPv6, but it could also raise problems. ISATAP depends a lot on the ISATAP router computer (which would be your URA server, typically), and this could cause both high network utilization and a single point of failure. As we discussed in *Chapter 8*, *Enhanced Configurations for Infrastructure Servers*, it also configures your entire network as one big site, which could raise problems with Active Directory. Ultimately, ISATAP was not designed to help you avoid getting into IPv6 forever, but rather as an interim and temporary way to ease into it, and as such, its limitations make it far from ideal. The larger and more complex your network is, this becomes more and more problematic. The best thing to do, if possible, is to have your entire network IPv6 capable by upgrading or replacing all relevant computers, devices, and routers. If replacing all the relevant hardware is not possible, it might be possible to re-architect the network around so as to make it as compatible as possible. It is beyond the scope of this book to be a complete IPv6 architecture guide, so if the situation calls for it, it might be best to involve a seasoned network architect in the process.

Group Policy

Because URA settings are assigned using Group Policy, anything wrong with that infrastructure could lead to problems. If you have replication problems that might prevent the policy created by URA from getting to clients (either locally or in other sites), this could jeopardize your deployment. Similarly, existing policies in your domain might interfere if they override settings that are part of the URA policy or disabled components that are critical to it. We mentioned IPv6-related Group Policy earlier, but policy regarding the Windows Firewall could also be a problem. The Windows Firewall is an essential component on both the URA server and client, so if you have a policy that configures it or disables it, you're probably going to have to get rid of it or otherwise make sure it doesn't apply to URA clients and servers while they are outside the corporate network. Similarly, if your organization has a policy that pushes other firewall software to computers (such as Kaspersky, ZoneAlarm, Norton, McAfee, or one of the other common personal firewall solutions out there), it could lead to things breaking up, because such software might conflict with the Windows Firewall.

Another common configuration problem is group matching. By default, URA will configure the URA GPOs to all domain computers, with a WMI filter for Mobile computers when the configuration is deployed using the Getting Started Wizard. It's pretty rare, but the WMI filter might miss, resulting in a non-mobile computer using the URA policy, or a mobile computer that hasn't applied it. A common mistake is to remove the WMI filter without refining the group assignment. Doing this is going to put a major wrinkle in your day (or week), as it will apply the URA policy to all computers in the domain. Keep in mind that if your DCs and other infrastructure servers all start behaving like URA clients, your entire network can come crumbling down, forcing a manual cleanup of all of these critical computers. To prevent this from happening, be careful when configuring the GPO page (Step 1, page 2 in the URA configuration). Later on in this chapter, we will show you how to manually clear the URA configuration from a client, in case that's needed.

DNS resolution

A critical piece of the URA configuration is the **Name Resolution Policy Table** (**NRPT**), which helps the client determine how to resolve names of resources it has to access. Anything misconfigured with the NRPT could cause significant problems. The NRPT itself rarely gets damaged, but misunderstanding how it works can lead to not setting things up right in the URA configuration wizard. The most common mistakes are related to organizations with Split-brains DNS. When using Split-brains, your public DNS setup is the same as your internal one, and that means that unless specifically set as an exception in the NRPT, URA clients will access all resources, matching your domain suffix via the URA tunnels. For example, many organizations have a publicly available Outlook Web Access website to serve as a backup for users who cannot use Outlook Anywhere. In such a situation (public OWA, URA with Split-brains), the OWA URL will not resolve to the public IP, and that may wreak havoc, unless your Exchange is configured to accept connections internally as well. Another common complication is if the URL you set up for the IP-HTTPS site name in URA itself matches the internal domain name. The URA wizard automatically identifies that and adds the exception to the NRPT, but you still need to keep an eye out for that and make sure it was set correctly.

ISP problems

Internet service providers are our friends...or are they?!?! Sometimes, we're not sure. They give us Internet access, sometimes for a reasonable fee, but they have their own problems to worry about. They need to build huge networks across the nation (sometimes the world), and their network needs to handle whatever crazy software all their clients are running. Sometimes, this could lead to ISPs managing traffic in a way that messes with what we need to get done. Earlier in this book, we discussed how some ISPs block certain protocols, such as UDP port 3544 used by Teredo clients or protocol 41 used by 6to4 clients. URA has been specifically designed to handle that kind of blockage by offering IP-HTTPS connectivity that can work in virtually any environment, but when someone else controls the network, it's hard to guess what they might do, so if there are problems, it would be advisable to rule that out as a factor by testing with multiple ISPs. Similar problems could also occur if the client is on a managed network. If, for example, a user visits some company and tries to use URA from the other company network, that network's administrators may block certain traffic. In fact, they might even be blocking outgoing or incoming HTTPS traffic, which could break even IP-HTTPS. In such a situation, you would rarely have any options but to use another ISP or network.

Certificate problems

Certificates are a key to any URA scenarios, and especially for the advanced ones. With the simple scenario, the URA wizard creates self-signed certificates for the IP-HTTPS connection and the NLS website, and these certificates have a long expiration date (5 years), so it's very unlikely to go wrong unless some trigger happy performance tuning freak decides to clean up the certificate store. The advanced scenarios do require you to deploy a full certificate infrastructure, and there are tons of things that can go wrong with that. We discussed some of the challenges and potential problems back in *Chapter 2, Planning a Unified Remote Access Deployment*, and *Chapter 3, Preparing a Group Policy and Certificate Infrastructure*, but let's review them briefly:

- Use the appropriate certificate template based on the Computer template.

- Make sure the CA's root certificate has been replicated to domain computers.

- Make sure the computer certificates and the root CA cert have actually been issued to clients, and that they are ok (cert chain, CDP location , expiration date, and private key exists).

- Make sure the certificate's subject name matches the DNS name of the client.

- Make sure there are no conflicting certificates on the clients (same subject name).

- Keep an eye on certificate expiration. The clients should auto-renew the certificates, but that could fail if a client hasn't connected for a while, or if the CA is not available through the URA connection.

With the advanced scenarios, you need to mind the certificates on the IP-HTTPS site and the NLS site as well. You need to keep a special tab on the IP-HTTPS and NLS certificates, as these don't auto-renew. Make sure you renew them on time (set a reminder on your calendar, as we suggested earlier), and that if the CA itself has changed, it might require other action so that clients can trust the new certificates.

As we discussed back in *Chapter 2, Planning a Unified Remote Access Deployment* the IP-HTTPS certificate requires that its **Certificate Revocation List (CRL)** is available to clients on the public Internet, so be mindful of that, especially if you're using a certificate issued by an internal CA and not a public one. The NLS certificate needs to match the URL that clients use, so if clients use a short name, make sure the subject name on the certificate is for the short name and not the FQDN, and vice versa.

NLS

Network Location Server (NLS) is of particular importance, because if the clients can reach it while connected to the public Internet, they won't even attempt to start the URA connection. If it is unreachable at all, though, that's even worse, because then, the clients will attempt to initiate the URA connection even if they are inside the corporate network. If you have followed our advice to set up a cluster of NLS servers with redundancy, that's terrific, but you need to keep an eye on it either way. A wise thing to do is to set up some kind of monitoring to alert you if it goes down (if you don't, a shower of phone calls from users would be a less-pleasant way of learning of it...). The site itself doesn't need to have any contents, but things could go bad if you use the same server for other purposes.

In such a situation, port conflicts could occur. The NLS site needs to listen on port 443, but if there's another site on the server that uses that port, it could cause the NLS site to stop or fail to start upon reboot. It's also possible for some other software on the server to grab the port before IIS starts and prevent the site from starting. Also, when someone sets up a website in IIS, they usually set it to bind to both port 80 and 443, and not just 443. This is also done by the URA wizard when it sets up the NLS site automatically. If that's the case, if something else grabs either port, it could cause a conflict.

Another type of conflict is host headers. IIS checks the host headers on incoming requests and tries to match them to one of the sites it is running. If it finds none, it would typically return the default website. If someone fiddles with the host-header settings on the bindings, it could cause IIS to match the wrong site, and that could break NLS functionality. Sometimes, a binding conflict could also return a 400 error (Bad Request), which isn't good either, of course. In the following screenshot, you can see the binding setup of a typical and well configured NLS site and a Bad Request error page—if the binding is wrong or conflicting.

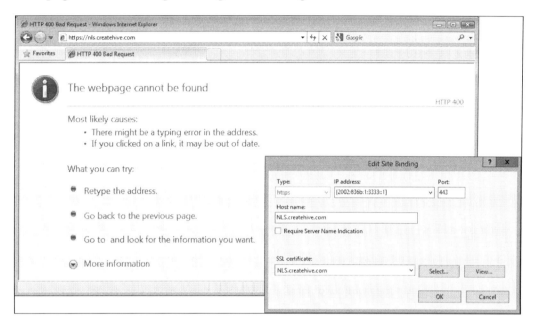

Server troubleshooting

As far as troubleshooting goes, we will assume you know how to install a Windows Server, configure its network, join it to a domain, and add roles to it, and we will start from the basics—running the wizard and configuration console. The first thing that might go wrong is something with the domain. If the computer's domain account is not right, or something is interfering with connectivity to the domain, you'll hit a snag almost immediately. Permission issues are also high on the list here—if you're trying to run the console as a user with restricted permissions, it may not be able to configure anything. After all, creating GPOs in the domain requires privileges, and so do other operations done by the console.

For the most part, the URA console only goes through configuration options, but nothing is applied until you finish the wizard, or if you're adjusting the configuration via the console directly, things start to happen when you click on **Finish** on the bottom-right of the console and then click on **Apply** on the **Summary** page. If there's a problem or some kind of conflict, it will most likely show up during that part. Thankfully, the wizard shows a lot of information about what's going on, and if the wizard shows that it completed with warning, or was not completed successfully, you can click on **More Details**: the information given should point it out, or at least give you some direction to go with. In some situations, it would point out the problem even during the **Summary** page, as shown in the following screenshot. Both errors shown in the following screenshot are related to domain connectivity. The one on the left is about a time difference between the URA server and the domain, and the other one on right is a total lack of connectivity to the domain.

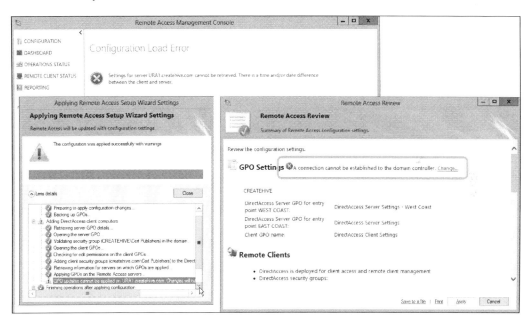

In case of an error, if it's unclear exactly what went wrong, you can also right-click on the **Summary** page and select **Copy Script** to copy the content of the script that configures the server, and then paste it into notepad (or some other text editor of your choice). The result will include the exact PowerShell commands that the wizard attempted to execute and which resulted in the error. Seeing the command or its parameters may shed more light on the problem, and you can also try to launch it yourself inside a PowerShell window to see what the exact results are.

Connectivity problems

If the configuration wizard successfully completes without errors, your next step would be to verify if the GPO replication has completed and check the status of the server in the **Operations Status** page of the URA console. As we've seen earlier in the chapter, it will show you if the server is happy, and if not, what component has gone wrong and why. We can't guarantee that if there's a problem the text will always be 100 percent clear, but it's been carefully designed to be so, and if there's a problem, it will become clear for you how to address it.

If it all checks out, the next step is for you to update your test client's Group Policy. Then, disconnect the test client from the corporate network and connect it to the public Internet. Within a few seconds, you should be able to see the URA connection getting established...or at least trying to. To see it, click on the network icon on the system tray to expand the **View Available Networks** UI, and it should show the URA connection (named by default **Workplace Connection**, unless you renamed it). If it's not there at all, it means either you are not using the right version of Windows 8 (remember that only the Enterprise edition is supported) or that Group Policy has not been applied to the client.

To verify Group Policy, open an Administrator command prompt and type `gpresult /f /h report.html` to generate a report that shows you the applied policies. Keep in mind that the URA policy is a Computer policy, so look for the **DirectAccess Client Settings** policy to show up in the **Applied GPOs** section in the **Computer details** section of the report. If it's not there, you might be having some Group Policy issue, permission issue, group membership issue, or WMI filter issue. All these are in the realm of Group Policy management and troubleshooting, which we discussed in *Chapter 3, Preparing a Group Police and Certificate Infrastructure*.

If the policy was applied correctly, the most common type of problem you will run into is the URA connection showing as **connecting**...and never progressing beyond that.

Hold your horses!

The URA connection establishment is typically pretty fast, and would complete in a few seconds, but before jumping to any conclusions, give the connection at least 2-3 minutes to establish. If the network is slow, or the client has to go through several connectivity methods before finding a good one, it could take a bit of time.

When your clients get stuck on connecting, it is about as confusing as can be, because it doesn't give you any information about what's going on. It could be either a problem with the client itself, a problem with the network or ISP, or a problem with your URA server. In such a situation, the first step is to check out the URA monitoring, but this time, the **Remote Client Status** page. With any luck, you will see something that indicates the client is attempting to connect:

In the preceding screenshot, we see a line pertaining to our client, and we can see the hostname (**URACLIENT1.createhive.com**), but not the username. This means that the client has successfully contacted the URA server and established the first tunnel, but is unable to complete and establish the second tunnel.

If you don't see a line pertaining to your client at all, it means there are more serious connectivity issues at play. It's possible that a firewall or some other network device, is blocking traffic from the client to the URA server. If you do indeed have anything in front of the URA server, your best bet is to inspect it. If it has any kind of monitoring mechanism, it should be able to confirm to you whether the client is reaching it at all or not. If not, it might be something on the network the client is connected to. If the client is on a home network, it's unlikely to interfere, but if it's inside a corporate network or a cellular-based connection, problems like that are not uncommon.

Sometimes, the client will appear in the monitoring console, but the problem would still be client-side network related. It could be some intermittent problems on the network, such as a very slow network or a network that goes in-and-out often. For example, wireless networks are often prone to intermittent disruptions, especially if the user is far from the router, is moving about a lot, or has devices that emit strong electromagnetic radiation or magnetic fields. Naturally, one way to rule that out is to connect the test client directly to the router with a cable. Running a network test off a site such as `http://www.speedtest.net` can also help confirm that the network is behaving well. If the speed test varies significantly from the speed promised by the ISP service, it could indicate a problem with the home network or even a regional issue that might need to be investigated by the ISP support department.

Client logs

If you feel that the network itself runs well and is reliable, the next step in troubleshooting is getting client logs. **Network Connectivity Assistant** (NCA) was designed to collect these for you, so simply open it, and click on **Collect Logs**. The collection should take 10-15 seconds, and then you can click on **View logs** and open the generated HTML file named `DirectAccess Logs`. Note that if you click on **Collect Logs** again, it will overwrite the previous file, so if you want to keep the older log, rename or move it somewhere. Also note that if you haven't specified an e-mail to send the logs to in the URA configuration, the **Collect Logs** button will be grayed out.

The log collection runs a series of scripts and commands, and dumps the output into one large HTML file. Each command's output goes into a frame for easy viewing. The items that are collected are (in the same order as you'd see them in the log file on the client):

- **IP configuration**: This allows you to see if the client has all the appropriate interfaces and their status. For example, if a client is missing the Teredo or IP-HTTPS interfaces, it won't be able to use these technologies as connectivity methods.

- **System information**: This includes the OS version, RAM and CPU configuration, domain membership info, updates installed on the OS, and a few more items. This would allow you to know if the user has an edition of Windows that's compatible with URA, if it hasn't changed domain membership and so forth.

- **6to4 interface configuration**: If the client is expected to use it for the URA connection, you would be able to see its status.

 Clients should have a 6to4 address only if they have a public (as opposed to NAT) IPv4 address.

- **WINHTTP proxy configuration**: If the client is configured with a WINHTTP proxy, it affects how the client communicates with the outside world over HTTP (for example, such a communication would happen as part of CRL checking or Windows Updates), but that setting is invisible to the naked eye (as opposed to the system's proxy configuration).

 If the output is DirectAccess, then in this context, it means that HTTP connections go to the desired resources directly and is not related to the URA's DirectAcces feature we are talking about in this book.

- **Teredo interface configuration**: If the client is expected to use it for the URA connection, you would be able to see its configuration.

- **Teredo interface state (status)**: The preceding point shows the configuration, and this piece shows the status of the interface — whether it was able to establish a connection or not, and a possible reason for a failure if it wasn't successful. The important keywords you should look for in these two are the state of the interface and **ServerName**. The state should be **Qualified**, if it's working correctly, and something else if it is not. **ServerName** should be the public IP or name of your URA server.

 When using the Getting Started Wizard, Teredo is not configured at all, so in that situation, the status is of no consequence.

- **IP-HTTPS interface configuration**: Similar to the Teredo and 6to4 interfaces, this and the next items show the configuration and status of the IP-HTTPS interface.

- **IP-HTTPS interface state (status)**: The configuration and status together allow you to see what's going on with IP-HTTPS. If the Interface Status shows IP-HTTPS interface not installed, this means that Teredo was successful in establishing the connection, and so this is not a problem. If the Last Error Code is not 0x0, then there's probably something wrong with the IP-HTTPS site running on the URA server. For example, the certificate might be bad or its CRL is unreadable. You should also take a look at **ServerURL** and confirm it's the correct one — this should be the URL your URA server is listening on for incoming connections. It is also possible that something else is interrupting traffic to the IP-HTTPS site or otherwise blocking the connection, such as traffic filtering.

- **Root certificate store dump**: This shows which root certificates are trusted by the computer, and could reveal problems with the certificate trust chain.

- **The Name Resolution Policy Table (NRPT) that the client has**: This could show you if the NRPT is correct and matches what you would expect. If it's blank, that means the Group Policies have not been applied correctly.

- **Winsock Catalog**: The catalog shows a list of **Layered Service Providers (LSPs)** installed on the client, and by comparing it to a client that's known to be good, you can potentially find software that is interfering with the connection.

- **Windows Filtering Platform (WFP) events from the system event log**: The WFP logs problems with incoming or outgoing traffic, so any events it generates are crucial to understand the source of a problem. For example, it might be dropping the IPsec traffic that URA is supposed to use. In such a case, you would be able to see the reason. For example:

```
WFP Netevents (netsh wfp show netevents file=-)
              <type>FWPM_NET_EVENT_TYPE_IPSEC_KERNEL_DROP</type>
              <ipsecDrop>
                      <failureStatus>0xC000A010 (STATUS_IPSEC_QUEUE_OVERFLOW)</failureStatus>
                      <direction>FWP_DIRECTION_OUTBOUND</direction>
                      <spi>2654701762</spi>
                      <filterId>9223372036854775898</filterId>
                      <layerId>0</layerId>
              </ipsecDrop>
       </item>
```

The preceding statement means that there's no IPsec policy matching this rule, so that traffic was dropped.

- **IPsec rules configuration from the Windows Firewall**: The IPsec rules determine how the IPsec tunnels are established, what authentication methods are used, and to which type of traffic they apply. You would typically find four rules, and inspecting them could reveal an incorrect configuration. For example, the rule titled **DirectAccess Policy-ClientToInfra** is the rule for creating the Infrastructure tunnel (the first tunnel). In the **RemoteAddress** field, it should show the correct IPv6 address of your URA server. You should also have three Proposal fields, which specify the **MachineCert** authentication method, the **UserNTLM** authentication method, and the various details of the encryption (ESP encapsulation, SHA1 encapsulation hash, AES192 encryption, or other settings that you might have configured manually). In the following screenshot, you can see the **MachineCert** proposal, showing the CA details:

```
IPsec Rules (Show-NetIPsecRule -PolicyStore ActiveStore)

$_ | Get-NetIPsecPhase1AuthSet
    Name                    : {163E1399-479A-47CC-8E60-39291A20DF38}
    DisplayName             : DirectAccess - Phase1 Authentication Set
    Description             : DirectAccess - Phase1 Authentication Set
    DisplayGroup            : DirectAccess
    Goup                   : DirectAccess
    Proposal                : {
                            : 0 : MachineCert
                            :   : Authority: DC=com, DC=createhive, CN=createhiv
                            : e-DC1-CA
                            :   : AuthorityType: Root
                            :   : ExcludeCAName: False
                            :   : AccountMapping: False
                            :   : Signing: RSA
                            : }

    PrimaryStatus           : OK
    Status                  : The rule was parsed successfully from the store. {
                            : 65536}
    EnforcementStatus       :
    PolicyStoreSource       :
    PolicyStoreSourceType   : GroupPolicy
```

- **IPsec Main-Mode security associations**: This allows you to see the details of the three two-way exchanges that are part of the Main-Mode negotiation for establishing the IPsec tunnels.

- **IPsec Quick-Mode security associations**: This shows the IKE phase 2 security association details. If either the **Main-Mode** or **Quick-Mode** box in the report shows no entries, this means the client wasn't able to establish the IPsec tunnels at all.

Troubleshooting the Main-Mode and Quick-Mode key exchanges is a very advanced task that is beyond the scope of this book. For a detailed explanation of this technology and how it works, visit RFC 2409 or TechNet:

http://tools.ietf.org/html/rfc2409

http://technet.microsoft.com/en-us/library/
cc759130(v=WS.10).aspx

- **IP address list for all interfaces**: Hey...we have already got the Network configuration in the first item?!...Well, this view focuses on the IP addresses that the client has, and sorting them by type. This makes it easier to see if there's something wrong with them.

- **The routing table for the computer**: Most people are used to the way the command route print shows the routing table, but this view is different. It lists the IP and subnet in standard CIDR notation (IP address/prefix size), making it easier to read and understand and exposing any wrong routes for easy detection.

- **Information about multisite configuration**: This shows information about the available entry point, if multisite is enabled. If it's not enabled, the box would be blank.

- **DirectAccess additional settings**: This provides generic info about the configuration such as the probe configuration, forced tunneling info, manual entry point options (if multisite is enabled), and a few others.

- **IPv6 prefix policy table**: This is similar to the routing table, but pertains to IPv6 only and lists the address precedence and label in addition to the CIDR.

- **User certificate store dump**: This shows the certificates issued to the user and their status. However, the URA certificates are not stored in the User store, so this serves no purpose.

- **Domain group membership information**: This shows which groups the user is part of, helping you solve Group Policy assignment problems, if they stem from a bad scope of the group.

The client logs package contains a significant amount of information and can be a little hard to digest for people who are new to this technology. Digging through 20 pages of text to find what's wrong takes a level of understanding of this technology that you might still not have, and even seasoned support engineers often spend a lot of time digging through this, and other data, to find the root cause. In other words, if you're looking at the report and have no idea what's up, don't beat yourself up—it takes time and experience.

To help you know what to expect from these logs, we have put up two such logs on the book's page on the publishers website. One file is a "bad" log, where the client is unable to connect, and the other is a "good" log.

Downloading the example code

You can download the example code files for all Packt books you have purchased from your account at http://www.PacktPub.com. If you purchased this book elsewhere, you can visit http://www.PacktPub.com/support and register to have the files e-mailed directly to you.

Manually cleaning up clients

Sometimes, you need to remove URA completely for some reason, such as if you need to move the role to another server, or you need to reset settings that cannot be adjusted after-the-fact (such as the server topology). The challenge here is that if you were using a simple scenario where the URA server also services as the NLS, removing the configuration also removes that site. Then, clients that have already inherited the URA Group Policy won't see it, and think they are on the Internet even if they are on the corporate network. This would usually prevent them from seeing anything else on the network, and so they won't be able to contact the domain controllers to have their URA Group Policy removed.

Ideally, if you do need to remove URA, we would recommend having all URA clients inside the network before removing the role or the server. Then, you would start the process by unlinking the URA client Group Policy from the domain. That will allow the clients to remove the policy via the automatic Group Policy refresh. Once it's been removed from the clients, you can remove the server or role safely.

Unfortunately, if you've removed the URA configuration without considering the things mentioned in the preceding section, then your best option is to set up a dummy NLS server, which would allow the clients to determine they are inside the network. To do so, set up a blank IIS site with the hostname that's configured as the NLS on the clients, and with a certificate that matches that name.

Another option you have is to manually clean up the NRPT from the client. The NRPT is stored in the registry, so to remove it, follow these steps:

1. Open the registry editor on the client.
2. Navigate to `HKLM\SOFTWARE\Policies\Microsoft\Windows NT\DnsClient\DnsPolicyConfig`.
3. Back up the entire key, and then delete every key under it.
4. Exit the registry editor.

In the following screenshot, you can see four keys which were created from the four NRPT rules that were configured for this environment:

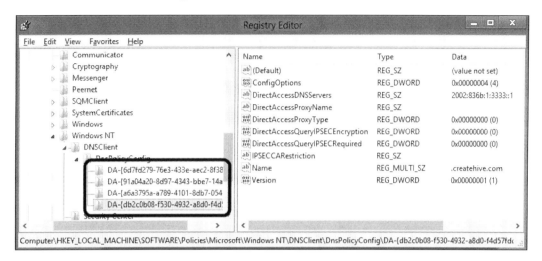

Client troubleshooting

As we described earlier, the first thing to check in case of connectivity problems is the client-side routing and networking. If you can see the client appears in the monitoring console, that usually means that the client-side networking is ok. The first tunnel is "easy" for the client to establish, because it's a simple interaction between the URA client and server. The second tunnel is more complicated, because it requires the client to communicate with a domain controller through the first tunnel.

Establishing the second tunnel could fail for several reasons. First, if something is blocking the traffic from going through to the domain controllers, the Kerberos authentication would not complete. Second, if there's something wrong with the credentials that the client is using, the Kerberos authentication will fail and the tunnel won't be established. The trick is finding out which is it that we're dealing with.

The first step in looking into this is trying to access the domain controller through the first tunnel. You can do this by simply opening a command prompt and pinging the IPv6 address of the domain controller (remember that pinging the IPv4 address will not work over a URA connection). If your corporate network has native v6 or ISATAP, you can ping that address directly. If your network is only IPv4, you have to convert the v4 to v6, using the NAT64 prefix and then ping it. If it doesn't reply, that's a sign of a problem. It could be routing related on either the URA server or the client. If your network has only one domain controller, this is not very likely, but most networks have more, and the more complex the network, the trickier it gets. For example, it's possible that 9 out of your 10 DCs would respond perfectly fine, but the one the client chose to use to perform the authentication is not responding. As part of the URA setup, the wizard discovers your domain controllers and configures the first tunnel to allow access to all of them, but it might have missed one or two, especially if there was a change to the infrastructure since the policy was created or updated. To make sure all your DCs are added to the first tunnel configuration, go to the Remote Access console and select the **configuration** node. On the right pane select the **update management servers** task and apply the configuration and also update the Group Policy on the server and client. This will ensure all current DCs are in the first tunnel config.

A more common situation is that the domain controller is reachable, but authentication itself is failing. Most commonly, this is certificate related, so common problems are as follows:

- The certificate is of the wrong type for this kind of authentication
- The certificate's subject doesn't match the computer name
- The certificate is invalid because it wasn't installed properly or got corrupted
- There are multiple certificates, and the one picked up for this process is the wrong one
- The certificate itself has been revoked or expired

We have discussed the details of the certificate back in *Chapter 3, Preparing a Group Policy and Certificate Infrastructure*, but as a quick reminder, the certificate has to have the intended purpose of Client and Server authentications, so using the Computer certificate template is ideal for this. When you use autoenrollment to issue certificates to computers, the subject name is automatically populated with the computer's fully qualified domain name, and that's how we want it to be. If you are assigning certificates manually, or from a CA server that is not an enterprise CA, the subject name might be wrong. In the following screenshot, you can see an example of a good and bad certificate:

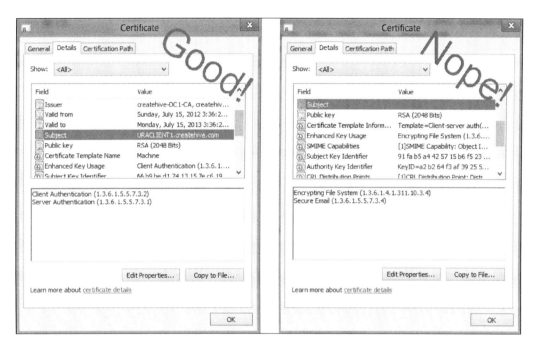

Certificate corruption is not common, because the autoenrollment automation should take care of everything. However, if you are doing things manually, or if someone fiddles with the certificates, they could get corrupted. For example, when you export a certificate, you have the option of exporting its private key with it, but if you don't do so, the certificate will become invalid when you import it somewhere else. This makes sense, because without a private key, the computer cannot perform the encryption it needs to do as part of the secure communication. The easiest way to check if a certificate is good is to simply open it from the certificate management console. If it is bad, the interface will be shown with a red X on it.

The Computer certificate store shows all the certificates it has, so this is also a good way to see if there are certificate conflicts. Normally, the certificate selection process done by URA automatically chooses the appropriate one, but if there are multiple certificates that are similar, it might trip and use one that's invalid. If your test client is a computer that's been around the block, it might have certificates that have accumulated over time, and could cause a problem. This is one of the reasons we recommended using clean and new clients when testing a new URA deployment.

If your certificates all check out, and everything seems OK, but you still cannot connect...time for advanced diagnostics.

Advanced diagnostics

Sometimes, everything appears to be configured perfectly, but clients will still not connect. In this kind of situation, things can get pretty hairy, and troubleshooting this further is not for the timid. The next steps involve tracing, where we can collect extremely detailed info about what's going on.

To perform a trace on the URA server, go to the **Dashboard** view and click on **Start Tracing** on the **Tasks** pane. If you have multiple servers in a cluster or multisite, you need to click on one of them to get the trace task to show up. The trace dialog box allows you to select whether you want to create a new log, append to an existing one, or run in circular mode. Circular mode is very useful for a situation where an issue occurs rarely, requiring you to run a trace over a long period of time. In such a situation, when the trace file reaches a size of 250 MB, it will purge old data from the beginning of the trace file. When whatever issue you're trying to investigate occurs, you stop the trace, and it would cover the past X amount of time, hopefully catching whatever it is you wanted to see. For other situations, you should be fine using the **New Trace** mode.

Another option at your disposal is changing the location of the target trace file and whether you want to capture packet data or not. Capturing packet data is comparable to a Network Monitor capture, allowing you to inspect the traffic with high detail:

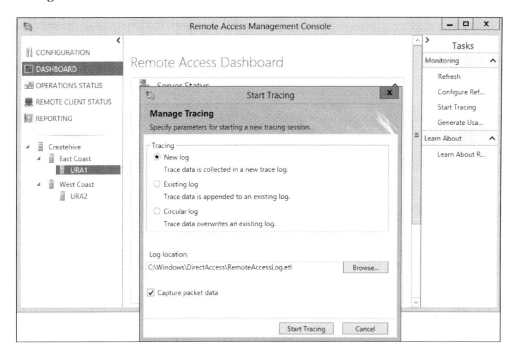

When you stop the tracing, the trace files are flushed to disk, which could take a few seconds, and then you'll find two files in the target folder. One is a CAB file, which contains a few dozen files with information about the computer and its configuration. The information files have data such as the network adapter configuration, the Winsock catalog, the Windows Firewall configuration and log, and system information. In other words, it is very similar to what the client-side NCA log collection does. The second file is an **ETL (Event Trace Log)** file, which can be opened using Network Monitor, Microsoft's utility for network diagnostics. You can download the current version 3.4 at `http://www.microsoft.com/en-us/download/details.aspx?id=4865`.

Usually, you would want to collect a trace file on the client, and not just the server. On the client, there's no shortcut for this, so this can be done using the NETSH command. This is built-in to the operating system, and to run it, open an administrative command prompt, and type the following command to start a trace:

```
netsh trace start scenario=directaccess capture=yes report=yes
```

When ready to stop, type `netsh trace stop`. Like on the server, it would take the command a bit to compile the collected data, and then it will inform you where the resulting file is and its name. Typically, that would be in the user's `AppData` folder.

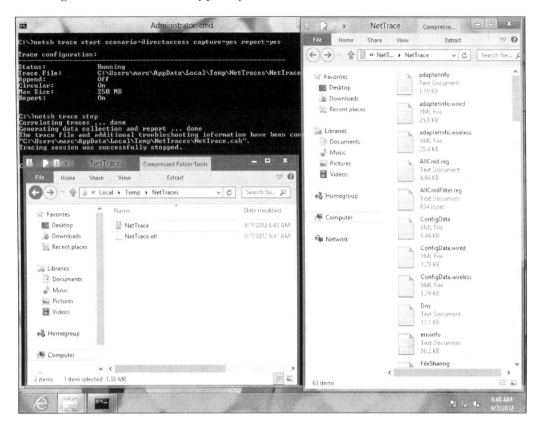

If the purpose of your tracing is to understand why clients or a particular client cannot connect, the procedure you should follow would be as follows:

1. Verify the client has been updated with the URA Group Policy.

2. Disconnect the client from the Internet (by pulling the cable or simply disabling the network interface temporarily).

3. Close any non-essential software on it, so as to collect as little background noise as possible.

4. Flush the clients caching by running the following commands:

   ○ `Ipconfig /flushdns`

   ○ `Arp -d *`

   ○ `Klist purge`

5. Start the tracing on both the client and server.

6. Connect the client back to the Internet.

7. Give it at least 3-4 minutes to connect.

8. Stop the tracing and analyze it.

The first analysis steps would be opening the CAB files and examining the configuration. We assume you already did this earlier with the regular client log, so do the same with the server. Of particular interest are the following files:

- `Dns.txt`: Contains a list of DNS records related to URA

- `Envinfo.txt`: Contains your network card configuration, route table, and certificate info

- `Report.etl`: This is identical to the other ETL file generated

- `Report.html`: This is a vast collection of info about the system and other components

- `Windowsfirewall logs`: These are 10 files containing the firewall logs and connection security logs

- `Winsockcatalog.txt`: Shows a list of **Layered Service Providers (LSPs)** installed on the server, allowing you to find software that is interfering with the connection

- `Wcninfo.txt`: Gives you the IP information of the server

Having gone through these, the next step is to open the ETL with Network Monitor. The filetype is not normally associated with Network Monitor, but you can simply open the application and drag the file into it. By default, Network Monitor cannot fully parse this data, so you need to set the active parser profile to the Windows parsers. To do so, follow these steps:

1. Open Network Monitor.

2. Click on **Tools** and **Options**.

3. Go to the **Parser Profiles** tab.

4. Right-click on **Windows** and select **Set As Active**.

5. Click on **OK**.

Now, Network Monitor will reparse the file and show you a plethora of info. If your server is busy, it could easily capture thousands of lines every second, so a 3-minute trace could be an eyeful. Naturally, we cannot cover every possible scenario, error, or message here, but with careful observation and time, you will gain enough experience to identify successful and failed scenarios. One thing to help you is Network Monitor's powerful filtering abilities. For example, if you are looking for problems, type the following expression into the **Display Filter** box:

```
Property.Description.Contains("fail")
```

In the following screenshot, for example, we can see that communications to the domain controller is failing with error 51:

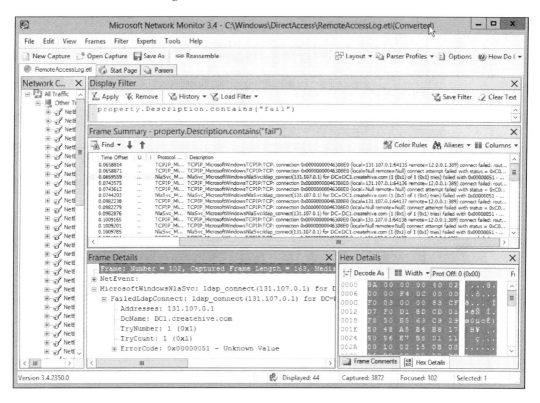

You can use other keywords to look for other things. For example, beyond the obvious **error** and **fail**, you can use **nls** to troubleshoot issues with your Network Location Server, **dns** to inspect name resolution problems or even type in a specific IP, server name, or user name. You can even use Boolean logic to combine keywords and narrow things down even further.

If the size of the capture file is very large, using the Network Monitor to view the file can be CPU intensive. In such a situation, you can convert the ETL file to a text file by running the following command:

```
netsh trace convert <ETL file name>
```

Make sure you perform this conversion on the same computer where you captured the file. The converted text file is easier to work with using one of the many available text editors and analyzers. We recommend *TextAnalysisTool* by *David Anson*. An article about it is available at http://blogs.msdn.com/b/delay/archive/2007/06/21/powerful-log-file-analysis-for-everyone-releasing-textanalysistool-net.aspx.

Windows Firewall tracing

Sometimes, tracing DirectAccess is not enough, because whatever issue you're having might be related to the Windows Firewall. URA and the Firewall are strongly tied, but they have separate tracing. To turn on Windows Firewall tracing, you can use the NETSH command, using the following syntax from an administrator command window:

```
netsh wfp capture start cab=off
```

After reproducing the error, type `netsh wfp capture stop` to stop the capture. The trace generates a set of files in the folder from which you ran the command. XML can be viewed with Internet Explorer, or any other XML viewer, and in it, you could look around for common keywords like `error` and `fail`. The ETL file can be opened by Network Monitor, but as opposed to the other ETL we discussed, it won't actually show you anything useful. The ETL file requires special processing and might come in handy if you need to work with Microsoft Technical Support to resolve your issue.

IP Helper Service tracing

Sometimes tracing the **IP Helper Service (Iphlpsvc)** is useful in determining whether the IP-HTTPS or Teredo interfaces have encountered any problems. To enable this tracing, you need to make changes to the registry, and then update the service. To do so, follow these steps:

1. Open the registry editor.
2. Navigate to HKLM\SOFTWARE\Microsoft\Tracing\iphlpsvc.
3. Set EnableFileTracing to 1.
4. Set FileTracingMask to ffffffff (that's 8 f's!).
5. Set the MaxFileSize to 1000000 (1 million, instead of the default, which is 100,000 only).
6. Exit the registry editor.
7. Run the following command:

   ```
   sc control iphlpsvc paramchange
   ```

8. Reproduce the error.
9. Open the registry editor and set the EnableFileTracing key back to 0.
10. Run the command `sc control iphlpsvc paramchange` again.
11. The trace will generate the files IpHlpSvc.LOG and IpHlpSvc.OLD in the C:\Windows\tracing folder.

Final thoughts on troubleshooting

Unified Remote Access is by all means a complex piece of technology. For everything to work well, especially the advanced enterprise scenarios, you need a lot of components to be configured correctly. We have attempted to give you not only ideas on what to look for, but also the tools to dig deeper and look at the innards of this technology, but ultimately, a time may come where you simply cannot get things to go the way you want them. In such a situation, keep in mind that Microsoft offers multiple ways for you to get help. At your disposal are many blogs, as well as Microsoft's public support forums at `http://social.technet.microsoft.com/Forums/`. The blogs and forums are written by people from within Microsoft, and out; consultants, field engineers, support professionals, and even people from the product groups themselves. If you need closer help, Microsoft also offers commercial technical support via `http://support.microsoft.com`, where you can open a support case and have a dedicated engineer work with you. Commercial support is available for everyone, whether you are an individual developer or a senior administrator at a multinational corporation. For customer participating in Microsoft's premier customer offerings, you can also request that a consultant from **Microsoft Consulting Services** (**MCS**) or an expert from **Microsoft Premier Field Engineering group** (**PFE**) be sent over to your offices and help with whatever tasks you need to do (to do so, contact your Microsoft account manager). For other organizations, Microsoft has hundreds of partners, some of which are individual consultants and others are large consulting companies. You can easily find a partner in your region by visiting `http://www.partnerpoint.com`.

Here are some blogs that deal particularly with Unified Remote Access, windows 2008 R2 DirectAccess and UAG DirectAccess:

- **Additional support forums**:

    `http://forums.isaserver.org/DirectAccess/forumid_8042/tt.htm`

- **Blogs and resources**:
    - `http://blogs.technet.com/b/ben/`
    - `http://directaccess.richardhicks.com/`
    - `http://blogs.technet.com/b/tomshinder/`
    - `http://blogs.technet.com/b/edgeaccessblog/`
    - `http://blogs.technet.com/b/yuridiogenes/`
    - `http://blog.gocloud-security.ch/`
    - `http://blog.msfirewall.org.uk/`
    - `http://blog.msedge.org.uk/`
    - `http://www.nappliance.com/blogs/inder`

- ○ http://blog.concurrency.com/
- ○ http://blogs.technet.com/b/rhalbheer/
- ○ http://blogs.isaserver.org/shinder/
- ○ http://www.ivonetworks.com/news/
- ○ http://channel9.msdn.com/Events/TechEd/Europe/2012
- ○ http://technet.microsoft.com/library/jj204618
- ○ http://technet.microsoft.com/en-us/library/hh831416.aspx
- ○ http://danstoncloud.com/blogs/simplebydesign/
- ○ http://danstoncloud.com/blogs/simplebydesign/
- ○ http://blog.idam.ch

- **Non-English blogs:**
  - ○ http://security.sakuranohana.fr/
  - ○ http://svenskaforefront.wordpress.com/
  - ○ Http://www.it-training-Grote.de/blog

- **Books**:
  - ○ *Windows Server 2012 Unleashed* by *Rand Morimoto, Michael Noel, Guy Yardeni, Omar Droubi, Andrew Abbate,* and *Chris Amaris, Sams Publishing, ISBN 978-0672336225*
  - ○ *Introducing Windows Server 2012* by *Mitch Tulloch, Microsoft Press, ISBN 978-0735675353*
  - ○ *Windows Server 2012 Pocket Consultant* by *William R. Stanek, Microsoft Press, ISBN 978-0735666337*

Summary

At the time of writing, Unified Remote Access was just a baby. It came out into the world merely days ago, valiantly attempting to improve upon its famous predecessor UAG. With this book, we attempted to provide unprecedented information about this technology...not only how to deploy it, but also how it works under the hood and how it interacts with other technology. We hope you have found this not only useful as a reference, but also as an eye opening experience and a fun read. Have fun with Unified Remote Access, and a successful deployment!

Index

datalink layer routing 143
DCDIAG 95
Dead Peer Detection (DPD) 182
dedicated IP address (DIP) 66
default gateway (DG) 158
demand-dial connection 188
demand-dial interface
  configuring 190-195
DHCP 22, 157
DHCP scopes 23
DigiCert 102
digital certificate 100
DIPs 143
DIR command 222
DirectAccess
  about 181, 182, 201
  entry-point, in cloud 185, 186
DirectAccess Connectivity Assistant (DCA)
  about 64, 202, 253
  URL 209
DirectAccess-corpConnectivityhost 167
directaccess-WebProbeHost 167
disaster recovery 161
DMZ 118
DNS
  about 118, 160
  considerations 160
  overview 25, 26
DNS64 service 25, 30, 139
dnscmd command 240
DNS name resolution 160
DNS resolution 275
DNS scavenging 167
DNS Six-to-four. *See* DNS64 service
Dns.txt 294
domain controller 82
domain replication 83
dual stack 26
dynamic cloud
  accessing, with URA 181-183
  migration to 180
Dynamic Host Configuration Protocol. *See*
  DHCP

E

encryption 98

end-to-edge 132
Enhanced Key Usage (EKU) 106, 231, 250
Enterprise CA
  about 112, 163
  advantages 112
  versus Standalone CA 112
Entrust 100
entry point
  about 154
  adding 172-176
Envinfo.txt 294
ETL (Event Trace Log) 292

F

F5 Networks 161
Facebook 237
FileSystemObject (FSO) 220
filtering 80
forced tunneling
  about 72-74, 129
  configuring 232-235
full-cone NAT 34

G

Geotrust 38
Get-DaServer cmdlet 222
Get-RemoteAccessConnectionStatistics
    command 270
Getting Started Wizard 272
Global Load Balancing (GLB) 142, 155,
    161, 168
global load balancing solution 161
Global Query Block List (GQBL) 239
Google 237
GPO
  client specific issues 96-98
  deploying, in organization 78
  editing 124
  issues 91, 93
  managing, on URA clients 89
  managing, on URA servers 89
  troubleshooting 91, 93
GPO management authorities 87
GPO management policies 87
GPOs 159

PowerShell scripts
  writing 222, 223
PPTP 118
practical considerations, IPv4 36, 37
practical considerations, IPv6 36, 37
Pre Shared Key (PSK) 186
private certificates
  versus public certificate 110, 111
private key 99
probes 167
Protocol 41 42
protocol transition technologies
  6to4 31, 32
  about 28
  DNS64 30
  IP-HTTPS 34, 35
  ISATAP 28-30
  NAT64 31
  Teredo 32-34
public certificate
  versus private certificates 110, 111
public hostname 163
public key 99
Public Key Infrastructure. *See* PKI

Q

Quad-A records 24

R

RADIUS 64, 257, 268
Radware 161
Receive Side Scaling (RSS) 44
re-convergence 143
registry 81
remote access
  challenges, evolving 180
Remote Access Dial-In User Service. *See*
        RADIUS
remote access server
  about 126
  options 126, 129
remote access server, options
  about 129
  certificate selection, for IP-HTTPS
        interface 130
  computer certificate usage, configuring 130

computer certificate usage, enabling 130
NAP, enabling 131
public URL 130
topology 130
Remote Authentication Dial In User
        Service. *See* RADIUS
remote clients
  about 125
  options 125, 129
remote clients, options
  about 129
  force tunneling 129
  Full DirectAccess 129
  helpdesk e-mail address 129
  remote management 129
Remote Client Status page 265
remote-management 149
replication 96
Report.etl 294
Report.html 294
reporting capabilities, URA 267-270
reports
  generating 267-270
root CA 113
root certificate store dump 283
roots 101, 102
routes 157, 158
routing 157
Routing and Remote Access Server (RRAS)
  about 182
  enabling, steps 187-189
RSA 252, 253

S

SAN certificates 108
scheduled task 84
SecureDirect 202
Secure Socket Tunneling Protocol. *See* SSTP
Security Associations (SAs) 266
security group 159
self-signed certificate 118, 131, 163, 165
server requisites, URA deployment 42
  considerations 46
Session Initiation Protocol. *See* SIP
Single Root I/O Virtualization (SR-IOV) 43
SIP 36

Thank you for buying
Windows Server 2012 Unified Remote Access
Planning and Deployment

About Packt Publishing

Packt, pronounced 'packed', published its first book "Mastering phpMyAdmin for Effective MySQL Management" in April 2004 and subsequently continued to specialize in publishing highly focused books on specific technologies and solutions.

Our books and publications share the experiences of your fellow IT professionals in adapting and customizing today's systems, applications, and frameworks. Our solution based books give you the knowledge and power to customize the software and technologies you're using to get the job done. Packt books are more specific and less general than the IT books you have seen in the past. Our unique business model allows us to bring you more focused information, giving you more of what you need to know, and less of what you don't.

Packt is a modern, yet unique publishing company, which focuses on producing quality, cutting-edge books for communities of developers, administrators, and newbies alike. For more information, please visit our website: www.packtpub.com.

About Packt Enterprise

In 2010, Packt launched two new brands, Packt Enterprise and Packt Open Source, in order to continue its focus on specialization. This book is part of the Packt Enterprise brand, home to books published on enterprise software – software created by major vendors, including (but not limited to) IBM, Microsoft and Oracle, often for use in other corporations. Its titles will offer information relevant to a range of users of this software, including administrators, developers, architects, and end users.

Writing for Packt

We welcome all inquiries from people who are interested in authoring. Book proposals should be sent to author@packtpub.com. If your book idea is still at an early stage and you would like to discuss it first before writing a formal book proposal, contact us; one of our commissioning editors will get in touch with you.

We're not just looking for published authors; if you have strong technical skills but no writing experience, our experienced editors can help you develop a writing career, or simply get some additional reward for your expertise.

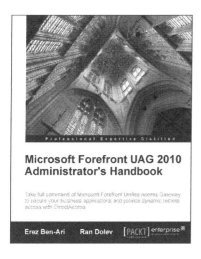

Microsoft Forefront UAG 2010 Administrator's Handbook

ISBN: 978-1-84968-162-9   Paperback: 484 pages

Take full command of Microsoft Forefront Unified Access Gateway to secure your business applications and provide dynamic remote access with DirectAccess

1. Maximize your business results by fully understanding how to plan your UAG integration

2. Consistently be ahead of the game by taking control of your server with backup and advanced monitoring

3. An essential tutorial for new users and a great resource for veterans

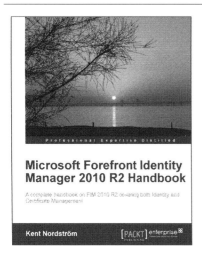

Microsoft Forefront Identity Manager 2010 R2 Handbook

ISBN: 978-1-84968-536-8   Paperback: 446 pages

A complete handbook on FIM 2010 R2 covering both Identity and Certificate Management

1. A comprehensive handbook that takes you through how to implement and manage FIM 2010 R2

2. Includes how to implement a complete FIM 2010 R2 infrastructure

3. Covers codeless identity management using FIM 2010 R2

Please check **www.PacktPub.com** for information on our titles

[PACKT] enterprise
PUBLISHING
professional expertise distilled

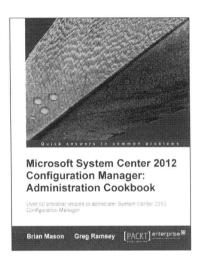

Microsoft System Center 2012
Configuration Manager:
Administration Cookbook

Over 50 practical recipes to administer System Center 2012
Configuration Manager

Brian Mason   Greg Ramsey   [PACKT] enterprise

Microsoft System Center 2012 Configuration Manager: Administration Cookbook

ISBN: 978-1-84968-494-1   Paperback: 224 pages

Over 50 practical recipes to administer System Center 2012 Configuration Manager

1. Administer System Center 2012 Configuration Manager

2. Provides fast answers to questions commonly asked by new administrators

3. Skip the why's and go straight to the how-to's

4. Gain administration tips from System Center 2012 Configuration Manager MVPs with years of experience in large corporations

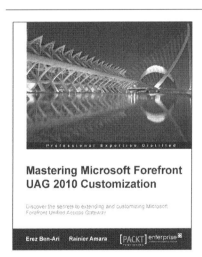

Mastering Microsoft Forefront
UAG 2010 Customization

Discover the secrets to extending and customizing Microsoft
Forefront Unified Access Gateway

Erez Ben-Ari   Rainier Amara   [PACKT] enterprise

Mastering Microsoft Forefront UAG 2010 Customization

ISBN: 978-1-84968-538-2   Paperback: 186 pages

Discover the secrets to extending and customizing Microsoft Forefront Unified Access Gateway

1. Perform UAG extension magic with high level tips and tricks only few have had knowledge of – until now!

2. Get to grips with UAG customization for endpoint detection, client components, look and feel, and much more in this book and e-book

3. An advanced, hands on guide with customization tips and code samples for extending UAG

Please check **www.PacktPub.com** for information on our titles